HOW TO BE AN EVEN
BETTER
MANAGER

A COMPLETE A–Z OF PROVEN TECHNIQUES AND ESSENTIAL SKILLS

FIFTH EDITION

Michael Armstrong

KOGAN
PAGE

Note: Masculine pronouns have been used in this book. This stems from a desire to avoid ugly and cumbersome language, and no discrimination, prejudice or bias is intended.

First published in Great Britain in 1983, entitled *How to be a Better Manager*
Second edition, 1988, *How to be an Even Better Manager*
Third edition 1990
Fourth edition 1994
Reprinted 1994, 1995, 1997, 1998 (twice)
Fifth edition 1999
Reprinted 2000, 2001, 2002, 2003

Kogan Page Limited
120 Pentonville Road
London
N1 9JN
UK

Kogan Page US
22883 Quicksilver Drive
Sterling VA 20166-2012
USA

www.kogan-page.co.uk

© Michael Armstrong 1983, 1988, 1990, 1994, 1999

British Library Cataloguing in Publication Data

A CIP record for this book is available from the British Library.

ISBN 0–7494–2970–4

Typeset by Jean Cussons Typesetting, Diss, Norfolk
Printed and bound by Clays Ltd, St Ives plc

Contents

v

Foreword to the Fifth Edition

This fifth edition of *How to be an Even Better Manager* covers 50 key aspects of management and has been extensively revised in the light of new thinking on management since the fourth edition was published in 1994. Eleven new chapters have been included, dealing with how to enhance commitment, customer care, handling negative behaviour, managing morale, managing the psychological contract, managing under-performers, project management, providing feedback, risk management, self-development, and valuing people.

The book therefore covers a wide range of the skills and approaches used by effective managers – what they need to understand and be able to do to be fully competent in their roles. It will be an invaluable handbook for existing and aspiring managers and will be particularly useful fo those seeking to obtain Management Charter Institute (MCI) qualifications or those studying for the core management qualification (Institute of Personnel and Development).

Preface

HOW TO USE THIS BOOK

This book is for those who want to develop their managerial skills and competences. It covers all the key skills that managers use and refers to the main aspects of managing people, activities and themselves with which they need to be familiar.

You can dip into this book at any point – each chapter is self-contained. But it would be useful to read the introduction first. This defines the overall concept of management and the areas in which managers need to be competent, thus providing a framework for the succeeding 50 chapters. These cover the following areas:

● *Managing people* – coaching, commitment, communicating, conflict management, counselling, delegating, developing people, empowering people, handling negative behaviour, leadership, managing morale, managing the psychological contract, managing under-performers, managing your boss, motivating people, objective setting, performance management, power and politics, providing feedback, selection interviewing, team management and valuing people.

- *Managing activities* – change management, continuous improvement, controlling, co-ordinating, crisis management, culture management, customer care, how things go wrong and how to put them right, improving business performance, meetings, organizing, planning, project management, strategic management and risk management.
- *Managing and developing yourself (enhancing personal skills)* – achieving results, assertiveness, clear thinking, communicating, effective speaking, getting on, influencing, negotiating, problem-solving and decision-making, report writing, self-development and time management.

Introduction: on being a better manager

Better managers recognize that the art of management is something they need to learn. No one becomes a fully competent manager overnight. There are, of course, many ways of learning how to be a competent manager. There is no doubt that experience is the best teacher – the time you have spent as a manager or team leader and your analysis of how good managers you come across operate effectively. You can learn from your own boss and from other bosses. This means accepting what you recognize as effective behaviour and rejecting inappropriate behaviour – that is, behaviour that fails to provide the leadership and motivation required from good managers and which does not deliver results.

There is an old saying – 'People learn to manage by managing under the guidance of a good manager'. This is just as true today, but to make the best use of experience it is helpful to place it in a framework which defines your understanding of what management is about, and helps you to reflect on and analyse your own experience and the behaviour of others. There is also a wealth of knowledge about the skills that managers need to use and the aspects of managing people, activities and themselves that they need to understand. None of these skills provide a quick fix which is universally applicable. It is useful to know about them but it is also necessary to develop an understanding of how they are best applied and modified to meet the particular demands of the situation in which you find yourself. This is not a prescriptive book – 'Do this and all will be well' – rather, its aim is to present approaches which have been proved to be generally effective. But they have to be adapted to suit your own style of managing and the circumstances where their application is required.

To become a better manager it is necessary to develop each of the 50 areas of skills and knowledge covered by this handbook. But you will be better prepared to do this if you have a general understanding of the process of management. This will provide a framework into which you can fit the various approaches and techniques described in each chapter. The aim of this introduction is to provide such a framework under the following headings:

- What management is about
- The aims of management
- The processes of management
- Managerial roles
- The fragmentary nature of managerial work
- What managers actually do
- What managers can do about it
- Managerial qualities
- Managerial effectiveness
- Developing managerial effectiveness.

WHAT MANAGEMENT IS ABOUT

Essentially, management is about deciding what to do and then getting it done through people. This definition emphasizes that people are the most important resource available to managers. It is through this resource that all other resources – knowledge, finance, materials, plant, equipment, etc – will be managed.

However, managers are there to achieve results. To do this they have to deal with events and eventualities. They may do this primarily through people, but an over-emphasis on the people content of management diverts attention from the fact that in

2

managing events managers have to be personally involved. They manage themselves as well as other people. They cannot delegate everything. They frequently have to rely on their own resources to get things done. These resources consist of experience, know-how, skill, competences and time, all of which have to be deployed, not only in directing and motivating people, but also in understanding situations and issues, problem analysis and definition, decision-making and taking direct action themselves as well as through other people. They will get support, advice and assistance from their staff, but in the last analysis they are on their own. They have to make the decisions and they have to initiate and sometimes take the action. A chairman fighting a take-over bid will get lots of advice, but he or she will personally manage the crisis, talking directly to the financial institutions, merchant banks, financial analysts, City editors and the mass of shareholders.

The basic definition of management should therefore be extended to read 'deciding what to do and then getting it done through the effective use of resources'. The most important part of management will indeed be getting things done through people, but managers will be concerned directly or indirectly with all other resources, including their own.

THE AIMS OF MANAGEMENT

Management is a process which exists to get results by making the best use of the human, financial and material resources available to the organization and to individual managers. It is very much concerned with adding value to these resources, and this added value depends on the expertise and commitment of the people who are responsible for managing the business.

THE PROCESSES OF MANAGEMENT

The overall process of management is subdivided into a number of individual processes which are methods of operation specially designed to assist in the achievement of objectives. Their purpose is to bring as much system, order, predictability, logic and consistency to the task of management as possible in the ever-changing, varied and turbulent environment in which managers work. The main

3

processes of management were defined by the classical theorists of management as:

1. *Planning* – deciding on a course of action to achieve a desired result.
2. *Organizing* – setting up and staffing the most appropriate organization to achieve the aim.
3. *Motivating* – exercising leadership to motivate people to work together smoothly and to the best of their ability as part of a team.
4. *Controlling* – measuring and monitoring the progress of work in relation to the plan and taking corrective action when required.

But this classical view has been challenged by the empiricists, such as Rosemary Stewart (59) and Henry Mintzberg (40), who studied how managers actually spend their time. They observed that the work of managers is fragmented, varied and subjected to continual adjustment. It is governed to a large degree by events over which managers have little control and by a dynamic network of interrelationships with other people. Managers attempt to control their environment but sometimes it controls them. They may consciously or unconsciously seek to plan, organize, direct and control, but their days almost inevitably become a jumbled sequence of events.

To the empiricists, management is a process involving a mix of rational, logical, problem-solving, decision-making activities, and intuitive, judgemental activities. It is therefore both science and art.

Managers carry out their work on a day-to-day basis in conditions of variety, turbulence and unpredictability. A single word to describe all these features would be chaos. Tom Peters (50), however, has suggested that it is possible for managers to thrive on chaos.

Managers also have to be specialists in ambiguity, with the ability to cope with conflicting and unclear requirements, as Rosabeth Moss Kanter (32) has demonstrated.

MANAGERIAL ROLES

During the course of a typical day a chief executive may well meet the marketing director to discuss the programme for launching a new product, the HR director to decide how best to reorganize the distribution department, the production director to ask him why costs per unit of output are going up and what he is going to do about it, and the finance director to review the latest set of management accounts before the next board meeting. He may have had to meet a journalist to be interviewed about how the company is going to deliver better results next year. Lunch may have been taken with a major customer, and the evening spent at a business dinner. Some of these activities could be categorized under the headings of planning, organizing, directing and controlling, but the chief executive would not have attached these labels when deciding how to spend his time (in so far as there was any choice). The fact that these processes took place was imposed by the situation and the need to take on one or more of the roles inherent in the manager's job. These roles are fundamentally concerned with:

- getting things done – maintaining momentum and making things happen
- finding out what is going on
- reacting to new situations and problems
- responding to demands and requests.

They involve a great deal of interpersonal relations, communicating, information processing and decision-making.

THE FRAGMENTARY NATURE OF MANAGERIAL WORK

Because of the open-ended nature of their work, managers feel compelled to perform a great variety of tasks at an unrelenting pace. Research into how managers spend their time confirms that their activities are characterized by fragmentation, brevity and variety. This arises for the following six reasons:

1. Managers are largely concerned with dealing with people – their staff and their internal and external customers. But people's behaviour is often unpredictable; their demands and responses are conditioned by the constantly changing circumstances in which they exist, the pressures to which *they* have to respond and their individual wants and needs. Conflicts arise and have to be dealt with on the spot.
2. Managers are not always in a position to control the events that affect their work. Sudden demands are imposed upon them

from other people within the organization or from outside. Crises can occur which they are unable to predict.

3. Managers are expected to be decisive and deal with situations as they arise. Their best-laid plans are therefore often disrupted; their established priorities have to be abandoned.

4. Managers are subject to the beck and call of their superiors, who also have to respond instantly to new demands and crises.

5. Managers often work in conditions of turbulence and ambiguity. They are not clear about what is expected of them when new situations arise. They therefore tend to be reactive rather than proactive, dealing with immediate problems rather than trying to anticipate them.

6. For all the reasons given above, managers are subject to constant interruptions. They have little chance to settle down and think about their plans and priorities or to spend enough time in studying control information to assist in maintaining a 'steady state' as far as their own activities go.

WHAT MANAGERS ACTUALLY DO

What managers do will be dependent on their function, level, organization (type, structure, culture, size) and their working environment generally (the extent to which it is turbulent, predictable, settled, pressurized, steady). Individual managers will adapt to these circumstances in different ways and will operate more or less successfully in accordance with their own perceptions of the behaviour expected of them, their experience of what has or has not worked in the past, and their own personal characteristics.

There are, however, the following typical characteristics of managerial work:

Reaction and non-reflection

Much of what managers do is, of necessity, an unreflecting response to circumstances. Managers are usually not so much slow and methodical decision-makers as doers who have to react rapidly to problems as they arise and think on their feet. Much time is spent in day-to-day trouble shooting.

Choice

Managers can often exercise choice about their work. They informally negotiate widely different interpretations of the boundaries and dimensions of ostensibly identical jobs, with particular emphasis upon the development of 'personal domain' (ie establishing their own territory and the rules that apply within it).

Communication

Much managerial activity consists of asking or persuading others to do things, which involves managers in face-to-face verbal communication of limited duration. Communication is not simply what managers spend a great deal of time doing but the medium through which managerial work is constituted.

Identification of tasks

The typical work of a junior manager is the 'organizational work' of drawing upon an evolving stock of knowledge about 'normal' procedures and routines in order to identify and negotiate the accomplishment of problems and tasks.

Character of the work

The character of work varies by duration, time span, recurrence, unexpectedness and source. Little time is spent on any one activity and in particular on the conscious, systematic formulation of plans. Planning and decision-making tend to take place in the course of other activities. Managerial activities are riven by contradictions, cross-pressures, and the need to cope with and reconcile conflict. A lot of time is spent by managers accounting for and explaining what they do, in informal relationships and in 'participating'.

WHAT MANAGERS CAN DO ABOUT IT

To a degree, managers have simply to put up with the circumstances in which they work as described above – they have to manage in conditions of turbulence, uncertainty and ambiguity. That is why one of the characteristics of effective managers is their resilience – they have to be able to cope with these inevitable pressures. But there are competencies as described below and skills as discussed in the rest of this book which can help them to manage in these circumstances. To a considerable extent it is up to managers to be aware of these requirements, the behaviours expected of them and the skills they can use to help in carrying out their often demanding responsibilities. They must treat these as guidelines for personal development plans. Managers can learn from the example of their bosses, by guidance from those bosses and from mentors, and through formal training courses, but self-managed learning is all-important. The starting point is an understanding of the key managerial qualities and the criteria for measuring managerial effectiveness as described in the next two sections.

MANAGERIAL QUALITIES

Pedler *et al* (47) suggest, on the basis of their extensive research, that there are 11 qualities or attributes that are possessed by successful managers:

1. Command of basic facts.
2. Relevant professional knowledge.
3. Continuing sensitivity to events.
4. Analytical, problem-solving and decision/judgement-making skills.
5. Social skills and abilities.
6. Emotional resilience.
7. Proactivity.
8. Creativity.
9. Mental agility.
10. Balanced learning habits and skills.
11. Self-knowledge.

Studies carried out on the qualities displayed by successful top managers as quoted by Rosemary Stewart (59) show a number of common characteristics, such as:

● Willingness to work hard.
● Perseverance and determination.
● Willingness to take risks.
● Ability to inspire enthusiasm.
● Toughness.

MANAGERIAL EFFECTIVENESS

Managerial effectiveness is assessed by reference to the extent to which what managers *actually* do matches what they are *supposed* to do. It is about performance, which refers both to what people do (their achievements) and to how people do it (their behaviour). To measure effectiveness it is necessary to understand and define both sides of the equation; that is, inputs (skills and behaviour) and outputs (results). The measurement of effectiveness and performance therefore compares expectations about achievements and behaviour with actual results and behaviour.

When assessing managerial effectiveness in terms of behaviour, most organizations now use competencies as the criteria. Competencies are those aspects of management behaviour which lead to effective performance. They refer to the personal characteristics that people bring to their work roles in such areas as team working, achievement orientation, leadership and strategic perspective.

Competency magazine in 1996 reported that the 10 most common managerial behaviours sought by the 126 organizations they surveyed were:

1. communication;
2. achievement/results orientation;
3. customer focus;
4. teamwork;
5. leadership;
6. planning and organizing;
7. commercial/business awareness;
8. flexibility/adaptability;
9. developing others;
10. problem-solving.

The MCI list of personal competencies

The Management Charter Institute has produced the following list of personal competencies which provide a useful guide to areas for personal development.

Building teams

- Keep others informed about plans and progress.
- Clearly identify what is required of others.
- Invite others to contribute to planning and organizing work.

Communicating

- Identify the information needs of listeners.
- Adopt communication styles appropriate to listeners and situations, including selecting an appropriate time and place.
- Use a variety of media and communication aids to reinforce points and maintain interest.

Focusing on results

- Maintain a focus on objectives.
- Tackle problems and take advantage of opportunities as they arise.
- Actively seek to do things better.
- Use change as an opportunity for improvement.
- Monitor quality of work and progress against plans.

Thinking and taking decisions

- Break processes down into tasks and activities.
- Identify a range of elements in and perspectives on a situation.
- Identify implications, consequences or causal relationships in a situation.
- Take decisions which are realistic for the situation.

DEVELOPING MANAGERIAL EFFECTIVENESS

The development of managerial effectiveness should be focused on the qualities and competencies listed above. The fundamental question which is addressed by this book is: 'How can I learn to be a manager?'

A familiar answer to this question is to say that 'managers learn to manage by managing under the guidance of a good manager'. But can experience alone be the best teacher? Several writers have expressed their doubts on this score. Tennyson called it a 'dirty nurse'. Oscar Wilde noted that 'experience is the name everyone gives to their mistakes'. And the historian Froude wrote that 'experience teaches slowly and at the cost of mistakes'.

Experience is an essential way of learning to improve but it is an imperfect instrument. We also need guidance from a good manager and from other sources such as this book which will help us to interpret our experience, learn from our mistakes and make better use of our experience in the future.

What you can do

Perhaps Francis Bacon provided the best answer to this question when he wrote: 'Studies perfect nature and are perfected by experience.' The art of management, and it is an art, is important enough to be studied. The aim of such studies should be to help us to make better use of our natural attributes – our personality and intelligence – and to ensure that past experience is better interpreted and more fully used, and that future experience is more quickly and purposefully absorbed. And the rest of this book provides practical guidance on what you need to know and be able to do to become a better manager.

1

Achieving results

Achieving results, getting things done, making things happen. This is what management is all about.

It can be said that there are three sorts of managers: those who make things happen, those who watch things happening, and those who don't know what is happening. Before finding out how to get into the first category, there are three questions to answer:

- Is getting things done simply a matter of personality – characteristics like drive, decisiveness, leadership, ambition – which some people have and others haven't?
- And if you haven't got the drive, decisiveness and so forth which it takes, is there anything you can do about it?
- To what extent is an ability to make things happen a matter of using techniques which can be learnt and developed?

Personality is important. Unless you have willpower and drive nothing will get done. But remember that your personality is a function of both nature and nurture. You are born with certain characteristics. Upbringing, education, training and, above all, experience, develop you into the person you are.

We may not be able to change our personality which, according to Freud, is formed in the first few years of life. But we can develop and adapt it by consciously learning from our own experience and by observing and analysing other people's behaviour.

Techniques for achieving results, such as planning, organizing, delegating, communicating, motivating and controlling, can be learnt. These are dealt with later in this book. But these techniques are only as effective as the person who uses them. They must be applied in the right way and in the right circumstances. And you still have to use your experience to select the right technique and your personality to make it work.

To become a person who makes things happen you therefore have to develop skills and capacities by a process of understanding, observation, analysis and learning. The four actions you should take are:

1. Understand what makes achievers tick – the personality characteristics they display in getting things done.
2. Observe what achievers do – how they operate, what techniques they use.
3. Analyse your own behaviour (*behaviour*, not personality), compare it with that of high achievers, and think how to improve your effectiveness.
4. Learn as much as you can about the management techniques available.

WHAT MAKES ACHIEVERS TICK?

David McClelland (38) of Harvard University carried out extensive research into what motivates managers. He interviewed, observed and analysed numbers of managers at their place of work and recorded findings before producing his theory. And before you dismiss anything which comes under the heading of theory, remember what Douglas McGregor (39) of the Massachusetts Institute of Technology said: 'There is nothing as practical as a good theory.'

McClelland identified three needs which he believes are key factors in motivating managers. These are:

●   The need for achievement.

- The need for power (having control and influence over people).
- The need for affiliation (to be accepted by others).

All effective managers have these needs to a certain degree, but by far the most important one is achievement.

Achievement is what counts and achievers, according to McClelland, have these characteristics:

- They set themselves realistic but achievable goals with some 'stretch' built in.
- They prefer situations which they themselves can influence rather than those on which chance has a large influence.
- They are more concerned with knowing they have done well than with the rewards that success brings.
- They get their rewards from their accomplishment rather than from money or praise. This does not mean that high achievers reject money, which does in fact motivate them as long as it is seen as a realistic measure of performance.
- High achievers are most effective in situations where they are allowed to get ahead by their own efforts.

WHAT DO ACHIEVERS DO?

High achievers do some, if not all, of the following:

- They define to themselves precisely what they want to do.
- They set demanding but not unattainable time-scales in which to do it.
- They convey clearly what they want done and by when.
- They are prepared to discuss how things should be done and will listen to and take advice. But once the course of action has been agreed they stick to it unless events dictate a change of direction.
- They are single-minded about getting where they want to go, showing perseverance and determination in the face of adversity.
- They demand high performance from themselves and are somewhat callous in expecting equally high performance from everyone else.
- They work hard and work well under pressure; in fact, it brings out the best in them.

- They tend to be dissatisfied with the status quo.
- They are never completely satisfied with their own performance and continually question themselves.
- They will take calculated risks.
- They snap out of setbacks without being personally shattered and quickly regroup their forces and their ideas.
- They are enthusiastic about the task and convey their enthusiasm to others.
- They are decisive in the sense that they are able quickly to sum up situations, define alternative courses of action, determine the preferred course, and convey to their subordinates what needs to be done.
- They continually monitor their own and their subordinates' performance so that any deviation can be corrected in good time.

HOW TO ANALYSE YOUR OWN BEHAVIOUR

It is no good trying to analyse your own behaviour unless you have criteria against which you can measure your performance. You have to set standards for yourself, and if you don't meet them, ask yourself why. The answer should tell you what to do next time.

The basic questions you should ask yourself are:

- What did I set out to do?
- Did I get it done?
- If I did, why and how did I succeed?
- If not, why not?

The aim is to make effective use of your experience.

Use the list of what high achievers do to check your own behaviour and actions. If your performance has not been up to scratch under any of these headings, ask yourself specifically what went wrong and decide how you are going to overcome this difficulty next time. This is not always easy. It is hard to admit to yourself, for example, that you have not been sufficiently enthusiastic. It may be even harder to decide what to do about it. You don't want to enthuse all over the place, indiscriminately. But you can consider whether there are better ways of displaying and conveying your enthusiasm to others in order to carry them with you.

LEARNING

There are a number of management skills and techniques that you need to know about. These techniques are discussed in subsequent chapters in this book. The ones you should be particularly interested in are:

- communicating;
- controlling;
- co-ordinating;
- decision-making;
- delegating;
- leadership;
- motivating;
- objective setting;
- planning and prioritizing;
- project management.

CONCLUSION

This process of observation, analysis and learning will help you to become an achiever. But remember, achieving results is ultimately about making promises – to others and to yourself – and keeping them. Robert Townsend (62), in his book *Up the Organization*, has some excellent advice: 'Promises: keep. If asked when you can deliver something ask for time to think. Build in a margin of safety. Name a date. Then deliver it earlier than you promised.'

2

Assertiveness

ASSERTION AND AGGRESSION

Assertiveness, as defined by Ken and Kate Back (3) in *Assertiveness at Work*, is:

- Standing up for your own rights in such a way that you do not violate another person's rights.
- Expressing your needs, wants, opinions, feelings and beliefs in direct, honest and appropriate ways.

When you are being assertive you are not, therefore, being aggressive, which means violating or ignoring other people's rights in order to get your own way or dominate a situation. Aggressive behaviour causes two counter-productive reactions: fight or flight. In other words, aggression either breeds aggression, which gets you nowhere, or it forces people to retreat in a demoralized or dissatisfied way. Including this sort of behaviour will not help to achieve your aim of getting them to go along with you.

ASSERTIVE BEHAVIOUR

Behaving assertively puts you into the position of being able to influence people properly and react to them positively. Assertive statements:

- are brief and to the point;
- indicate clearly that you are not hiding behind something or someone and are speaking for yourself by using words such as: 'I think that ...', 'I believe that ...', 'I feel that ...', – your beliefs and views are important;
- are not overweighted with advice;
- use questions to find out the views of others and to test their reactions to your behaviour;
- distinguish between fact and opinion;
- are expressed positively but not dogmatically;
- indicate that you are aware that the other people have different points of view;
- express, when necessary, negative feelings about the effects of other people's behaviour on you – pointing out in dispassionate and factual terms the feelings aroused in you by that behaviour, and suggesting the behaviour you would prefer;
- point out to people politely but firmly the consequences of their behaviour.

HANDLING AGGRESSION

If you are faced by aggression, take a breath, count up to 10 and then:

- Ask calmly for information about what is bugging the aggressors.
- State clearly, and again calmly, the position as you see it.
- Empathize with the aggressors by making it plain that you can see it from their point of view, but at the same time explaining in a matter-of-fact way how you see the discrepancy between what they believe and what you feel is actually happening.
- Indicate, if the aggressive behaviour persists, your different beliefs or feelings, but do not cut aggressors short – people often talk, or even shout, themselves out of being aggressive

when they realize that you are not reacting aggressively and that their behaviour is not getting them anywhere.

● Suggest, if all else fails, that you leave it for the time being and talk about it again after a cooling-off period.

INFLUENCING STYLES

Assertiveness is about fighting your own corner. You have to believe in yourself and what you are doing and express these beliefs confidently and without hesitation. It is about using influencing skills.

There are four influencing styles you can use:

1. *Asserting* – making your views clear.
2. *Persuading* – using facts, logic and reason to present your own case, emphasizing its strong points (benefits to the organization or the individual(s) you are dealing with), anticipating objections to any apparent weaknesses and appealing to reason.
3. *Bridging* – drawing out other people's points of view, demonstrating that you understand what they are getting at, giving credit and praise in response to their good ideas and suggestions, joining your views with theirs.
4. *Attracting* – conveying your enthusiasm for your ideas, making people feel that they are all part of an exciting project.

There is more about influencing people in Chapter 26.

3

Change management

Change is the only constant process which exists in organizations. An effective organization is one that takes deliberate steps to manage change smoothly. It will not always succeed – change can be a traumatic process – but at least it will try, and attempts to manage change can have the minimum objective of mitigating its effects on the organization and its employees.

The approach to the management of change will recognize that the key to success lies not only in a transformational leader, supported by powerful change mechanisms, but also by understanding that change is implemented by people and that it is their behaviour and support that count. The most important aim of change management is to achieve commitment to change.

Successful change management requires an understanding of:

● the main types of change;
● how change affects individuals;
● the process of change;
● how to build commitment to change.

TYPES OF CHANGE

There are two main types of change: strategic and operational.

Strategic change

Strategic change is concerned with broad, long-term and organiza-
tion-wide issues. It is about moving to a future state which has been
defined generally in terms of strategic vision and scope. It will
cover the purpose and mission of the organization, its corporate
philosophy on such matters as growth, quality, innovation and
values concerning people, the customer needs served and the technologies employed. This overall definition leads to specifications of
competitive positioning and strategic goals for achieving and maintaining competitive advantage and for product market development. These goals are supported by policies concerning marketing,
sales, manufacturing, product and process development, finance
and human resource management.

Strategic change takes place within the context of the external
competitive, economic and social environment, and the organization's internal resources, capabilities, culture, structure and
systems. Its successful implementation requires thorough analysis
and understanding of these factors in the formulation and planning
stages.

Operational change

Operational change relates to new systems, procedures, structures
or technology which will have an immediate effect on working
arrangements within a part of the organization. But the impact of
such changes on people can be more significant than broader
strategic change and they have to be handled just as carefully.

HOW PEOPLE CHANGE

The ways in which people change are best explained by reference to
the following assumptions developed by Bandura (4):

● People make conscious choices about their behaviour.
● The information people use to make their choices comes from
  their environment.

● Their choices are based upon:

 − the things that are important to them;
 − the views they have about their own abilities to behave in certain ways;
 − the consequences they think will accrue to whatever behaviour they decide to engage in.

For those concerned in change management, the implications of this theory are that:

● The tighter the link between a particular behaviour and a particular outcome, the more likely it is that we will engage in that behaviour.
● The more desirable the outcome, the more likely it is that we will engage in behaviour that we believe will lead to it.
● The more confident we are that we can actually assume a new behaviour, the more likely we are to try it.

To change people's behaviour, therefore, we have first to change the environment within which they work; second, convince them that the new behaviour is something they can accomplish (training is important); and third, persuade them that it will lead to an outcome that they will value. None of these steps is easy. To achieve them, it helps to know more about the process of change.

THE PROCESS OF CHANGE

Change, as Rosabeth Moss Kanter (32) puts it, is the process of analysing 'the past to elicit the present actions required for the future'. It involves moving from a present state, through a transitional state, to a future desired state.

The process starts with an awareness of the need for change. An analysis of this state and the factors that have created it leads to a diagnosis of the distinctive characteristics of the situation and an indication of the direction in which action needs to be taken. Possible courses of action can then be identified and evaluated and a choice made of the preferred action.

It is then necessary to decide how to get from here to there. Managing the change process in this transitional state is a critical phase in the change process. It is here that the problems of introducing change emerge and have to be managed. These problems can include resistance to change, low stability, high levels of stress, misdirected energy, conflict and losing momentum. Hence the need to do everything possible to anticipate reactions and likely impediments to the introduction of change.

The installation stage can also be painful. When planning change there is a tendency for people to think that it will be an entirely logical and linear process of going from A to B. It is not like that at all. As described by Pettigrew and Whipp (51), the implementation of change is an 'iterative, cumulative and reformulation-in-use process'.

THE APPROACH TO CHANGE MANAGEMENT

Michael Beer and his colleagues suggested in a seminal *Harvard Business Review* article, 'Why change programs don't produce change' (7), that most such programmes are guided by a theory of change which is fundamentally flawed. This theory states that changes in attitude lead to changes in behaviour. 'According to this model, change is like a conversion experience. Once people "get religion", changes in their behaviour will surely follow.'

They believe that this theory gets the change process exactly backwards:

In fact, individual behaviour is powerfully shaped by the organizational roles people play. The most effective way to change behaviour, therefore, is to put people into a new organizational context, which imposes new roles, responsibilities and relationships on them. This creates a situation that in a sense 'forces' new attitudes and behaviour on people.

They prescribe six steps to effective change which concentrate on what they call 'task alignment' – reorganizing employees' roles, responsibilities and relationships to solve specific business problems in small units where goals and tasks can be clearly defined. The aim of following the overlapping steps is to build a self-reinforcing cycle of commitment, co-ordination and competence. The steps are:

1. Mobilize commitment to change through the joint analysis of problems.
2. Develop a shared vision of how to organize and manage to achieve goals such as competitiveness.

3. Foster consensus for the new vision, competence to enact it, and cohesion to move it along.
4. Spread revitalization to all departments without pushing it from the top – don't force the issue, let each department find its own way to the new organization.
5. Institutionalize revitalization through formal policies, systems and structures.
6. Monitor and adjust strategies in response to problems in the revitalization process.

The approach suggested by Michael Beer and his colleagues is fundamental to the effective management of change. It can, however, be associated with a number of other guidelines as set out below.

GUIDELINES FOR CHANGE MANAGEMENT

- The achievement of sustainable change requires strong commitment and visionary leadership from the top.
- Understanding is necessary of the culture of the organization and the levers for change most likely to be effective therein.
- Those concerned with managing change at all levels should have the temperament and leadership skills appropriate to the circumstances of the organization and its change strategies.
- It is important to build a working environment which is conducive to change. This means developing the firm as a 'learning organization'.
- Although there may be an overall strategy for change, it is best tackled incrementally (except in crisis conditions). The change programme should be broken down into actionable segments for which people can be held accountable.
- The reward system should encourage innovation and recognize success in achieving change.
- Change implies streams of activity across time and 'may require the enduring of abortive efforts or the build up of slow incremental phases of adjustment which then allow short bursts of incremental action to take place' – Pettigrew and Whipp.
- Change will always involve failure as well as success. The failures must be expected and learned from.

- Hard evidence and data on the need for change are the most powerful tools for its achievement, but establishing the need for change is easier than deciding how to satisfy it.
- It is easier to change behaviour by changing processes, structures and systems than to change attitudes or the corporate culture.
- There are always people in organizations who welcome the challenges and opportunities that change can provide. They are the ones to be chosen as change agents.
- Resistance to change is inevitable if the individuals concerned feel that they are going to be worse off – implicitly or explicitly. The inept management of change will produce that reaction.
- In an age of global competition, technological innovation, turbulence, discontinuity, even chaos, change is inevitable and necessary. The organization must do all it can to explain why change is essential and how it will affect everyone. Moreover, every effort must be made to protect the interests of those affected by change.

See also Chapter 15 on how to manage culture change in organizations.

GAINING COMMITMENT TO CHANGE

These guidelines point in one direction: having decided why changes are necessary, what the goals are and how they are to be achieved, the most important task is to gain the commitment of all concerned to the proposed change.

A strategy for gaining commitment to change should cover the following phases:

1. *Preparation.* In this phase, the person or persons likely to be affected by the proposed change are contacted in order to be made aware of it.
2. *Acceptance.* In the second phase, information is provided on the purpose of the change, how it is proposed to implement it and what effect it will have on those concerned. The aim is to achieve understanding of what the change means and to obtain a positive reaction. This is more likely if:

- the change is perceived to be consistent with the mission and values of the organization;
- the change is not thought to be threatening;
- the change seems likely to meet the needs of those concerned;
- there is a compelling and fully understood reason for change;
- those concerned are involved in planning and implementing the change programme on the principle that people support what they help to create;
- it is understood that steps will be taken to mitigate any detrimental effects of the change.

It may be difficult, even impossible to meet these requirements. That is why the problems of gaining commitment to change should not be underestimated.

During this phase, the extent to which reactions are positive or negative can be noted and action taken accordingly.

It is at this stage that original plans may have to be modified to cater for legitimate reservations or second thoughts.

3. *Commitment.* During the third phase, the change is implemented and becomes operational. The change process and people's reaction to it need to be monitored. There will inevitably be delays, setbacks, unforeseen problems and negative reactions from those faced with the reality of change. A response to these reactions is essential so that valid criticisms can be acted upon or reasons given why the change should proceed as planned.

Following implementation, the aim is to have the change adopted as, with use, its worth becomes evident. The decision is made at this stage whether to continue with the change or to modify or even abort it. Account should again be taken of the views of those involved.

Finally, and after further modifications as required, the change is institutionalized and becomes an inherent part of the organization's culture and operations.

4

Clear thinking

Clear thinking is logical thinking. It is a process of reasoning by which one judgement is derived from another and correct conclusions are drawn from the evidence. Clear thinking is analytical: sifting information, selecting what is relevant, establishing and proving relationships.

If you say people are logical, you mean that they draw reasonable inferences – their conclusions can be proved by reference to the facts used to support them. They avoid ill-founded and tendentious arguments, generalizations and irrelevancies. Their chain of reasoning is clear, unemotional and based on relevant facts.

Clear thinking – a logical approach to problem-solving, decision-making and case presentation – is an essential attribute of an effective manager. This does not mean that it is the only way to think. Edward de Bono has made out an incontrovertible case for lateral, ie creative, thinking as a necessary process for innovative managers to use alongside the more traditional vertical or logical thinking pattern. But a logical approach is still an essential requirement.

A further attribute of a good manager is the ability to argue persuasively and to detect the flaws in other people's arguments. To think clearly and to argue well, you need to understand: first, how to develop a proposition or a case from basic principles; second, how to test your proposition; and third, how to avoid using fallacious arguments and how to expose the fallacies used by others.

DEVELOPING A PROPOSITION

The first rule is to 'get the facts'. It is the starting point for clear thinking. The facts must be relevant to the issue under consideration. If comparisons are being made, like must be compared with like. Trends must be related to an appropriate base date and, if trends are being compared, the same base should be used. Treat opinions with caution until they are supported by evidence. Avoid a superficial analysis of surface data. Dig deep. Take nothing for granted. Sift the evidence and discard what is irrelevant.

Your inferences should be derived *directly* from the facts. Where possible, the connection between the facts and the conclusion should be shown to be justified on the basis of verifiable and relevant experience or information on similar relationships occurring elsewhere.

If, as is likely, more than one inference can be deduced from the facts, you should test each inference to establish which one most clearly derives from the evidence as supported by experience. But it is no good saying 'it stands to reason' or 'it's common sense'. You have to produce the evidence which proves that the inference is reasonable and you have to pin down the vague concept of common sense to the data and experience upon which it is based. It was Descartes who wrote: 'Common sense is the best distributed commodity in the world, for every man is convinced that he is well supplied with it.'

TESTING PROPOSITIONS

Susan Stebbing (57) in *Thinking to Some Purpose* wrote: 'We are content to accept without testing any belief that fits in with our prejudices and whose truth is necessary for the satisfaction of our desires.' Clear thinking must try to avoid this trap.

When we form a proposition or belief we generalize from what is observed – our own analysis or experience – and thence infer to what is not observed. We also refer to testimony – other people's observations and experience.

If your proposition or belief is derived from a generalization based upon particular instances you should test it by answering the following questions:

- Was the scope of the investigation sufficiently comprehensive?
- Are the instances representative or are they selected to support a point of view?
- Are there contradictory instances that have not been looked for?
- Does the proposition or belief in question conflict with other beliefs for which we have equally good grounds?
- If there are any conflicting beliefs or contradictory items of evidence, have they been put to the test against the original proposition?
- Could the evidence or testimony lead to other equally valid conclusions?
- Are there any other factors which have not been taken into account which may have influenced the evidence and, therefore, the conclusion?

If your belief is based on testimony, you should test the reliability of the testimony, its relevance to the point, and whether or not your belief follows logically from the evidence, ie can reasonably be inferred from the facts.

FALLACIOUS AND MISLEADING ARGUMENTS

A fallacy is an unsound form of argument leading to a mistake in reasoning or a misleading impression. The main fallacies to avoid or to spot in other people's arguments are:

- sweeping statements;
- potted thinking;
- special pleading;
- over-simplification;
- reaching false conclusions;
- begging the question;

- false analogy;
- using words ambiguously;
- chop logic.

These are discussed briefly below.

Sweeping statements

In our desire for certainty and to carry the point we often indulge in sweeping statements. We sometimes then repeat them more and more loudly and angrily in order to convince our opponent. If we do it often enough and forcibly enough we can even deceive ourselves.

It has been said that 'it's never fair, it's never wise, it's never safe to generalize'. But that is a generalization in itself. Scientific method is based on generalizations. They can be valid if they are inferred properly from adequate, relevant and reliable evidence.

Generalizations are invalid when they have been produced by over-simplifying the facts or by selecting instances favourable to a contention while ignoring those that conflict with it. The classic form of a fallacious generalization is the contention that if some A is B then all A must be B. What frequently happens is that people say A is B when all they know is that *some* A is B or, at most, A *tends* to be B. The argument is misleading unless the word 'some' or 'tends' is admitted.

Many of the fallacies considered below are special cases of unsafe generalization, the most common symptom of unsound reasoning.

Potted thinking

Potted thinking happens when we argue using slogans and catch phrases, when we extend an assertion in an unwarrantable fashion.

It is natural to form confident beliefs about complicated matters when we are proposing or taking action. And it is equally natural to compress these beliefs into a single phrase or thought. But it is dangerous to accept compressed statements that save us the trouble of thinking. They are only acceptable if fresh thinking has preceded them.

Special pleading

If anyone says to you: 'everyone knows that', 'it's obvious that' or 'it's indisputably true that', you can be certain that he has taken for granted what he is about to assert.

We indulge in special pleading when we stress our own case and fail to see that there may be other points of view, other ways of looking at the question. Special pleading happens when we cannot detach ourselves from our own circumstances. We often blunder because we forget that what is true of one of us is also true of the other in the same situation.

A safeguard against this mistake is to change *you* into *I*. Thus, *I* feel that you can't see what is straight in front of your nose; *you* feel that I can't see what is on the other side of my blinkers. A rule that appears to be sound when I apply it to you may seem to be unsatisfactory when you ask me to apply it to myself.

Of course, thinking for too long about other points of view is a recipe for indecision. There are not necessarily two sides to every question and even if there are, you eventually – and often quickly – have to come down firmly on one side. But before you do this, check in case the other points of view or the alternative approaches are valid, and take them into account.

Over-simplification

Over-simplification is a special form of potted thinking or special pleading. It often arises in the form of what Susan Stebbing terms 'the fallacy of either black or white', the mistake of demanding that a sharp line should be drawn, when in fact no sharp line can be drawn. For example, we cannot ask for a clear distinction to be drawn between the sane and the insane, or between the intelligent and the unintelligent. Our readiness to make this mistake may be taken advantage of by a dishonest opponent, who insists that we define precisely that which does not permit such definition.

Reaching false conclusions

One of the most prevalent fallacies is that of forming the view that because *some* are or may be, *all* are. An assertion about several cases is twisted into an assertion about all cases. The conclusion does not follow the premise.

The most common form of this fallacy is what logicians call the 'undistributed middle', which refers to the traditional syllogism consisting of a premise, a middle term and a conclusion. A valid syllogism takes the following form:

Premise   : All cows are quadrupeds.
Middle term : All quadrupeds are vertebrates.
Conclusion : Therefore, all cows are vertebrates.

This may be represented as:

Premise   : All A is B.
Middle term : All B is C.
Conclusion : Therefore, all A is C.

This is logical. The middle term is fully distributed. Everything that applies to A also applies to B, everything that applies to B also applies to C, therefore, everything that applies to A must apply to C.

An invalid syllogism would take the following form:

All cows are quadrupeds.
All mules are quadrupeds.
Therefore, all cows are mules.

This may be represented as:

All A is B.
All C is B.
Therefore, all A is C.

This is false because, although everything that applies to A and C also applies to B, there is nothing in their relationship to B which connects A and C together.

The difference between the true and false syllogism may be illustrated in Figure 4.1

In the false syllogism, A and C could be quite distinct although still contained within B. To link them together goes beyond the original evidence. Because two things A and B are related to another thing, C, it does not *necessarily* mean that they are related together. In forming arguments, we too often jump to the conclusion that *some* means *all*.

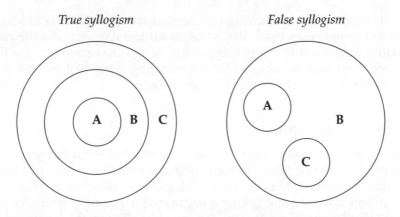

True syllogism   False syllogism

Figure 4.1 *The difference between true and false syllogisms*

Allowing the conclusion to go beyond the evidence can also take the form of assuming that because we are aware of the effect (the *consequent*), we also know the cause (the *antecedent*). But this assumption may be incorrect. An effect can have many different causes. This fallacy of the consequent, as it is termed, can be illustrated by the following example:

> If she wins the lottery, she would go to the West Indies.
> She has gone to the West Indies.
> Therefore she has won the lottery.

> ie If P then Q,
>   Q
> Therefore P.

But there are a number of other reasons why she could have gone to the West Indies besides winning the lottery. A clear inference can only be drawn if the cause is directly related to the effect, thus:

> If she wins the lottery she will go to the West Indies.
> She has won the lottery.
> Therefore she will go to the West Indies.

> ie if P then Q,
>   P
> Therefore Q.

A further danger in drawing conclusions from evidence is to forget that circumstances may alter cases. What has happened in the past will not necessarily happen again unless the circumstances are the same. You may be able to infer something from history but you cannot rely on that inference. Times change.

Begging the question

We beg the question when we take for granted what has yet to be proved. This can take the form of assuming the point in dispute without adequate reason; what the logicians call *petitio principii*.

If you spot anyone taking for granted a premise which is not contained in the conclusion you must challenge the assumption and ask for information about the premises upon which the conclusion is based. You can then assess whether or not the conclusion follows logically from those premises.

Challenging assumptions is a necessary part of thinking clearly. You should challenge your own assumptions as well as those made by others.

False analogy

Analogy forms the basis of much of our thinking. We notice that two cases resemble each other in certain respects and then infer an extension of the resemblance. Analogies also aid understanding of an unfamiliar topic.

Analogies can be used falsely as vivid arguments without any real evidence. Just because A is B, where both are familiar matters of fact, does not mean that X is Y, where X and Y are unfamiliar or abstract. When we argue by analogy we claim that if:

x has properties of p1, p2, p3 and f, and
y has properties of p1, p2 and p3, therefore
y also has the property of f.

This could be true unless y has a property incompatible with f, in which case the argument is unsound.

Analogies may be used to suggest a conclusion but they cannot establish it. They can be carried too far. Sometimes their relevance is more apparent than real.

Use argument by analogy to help support a case but do not rely upon it. Don't allow anyone else to get away with far-fetched analogies. They should be tested and their relevance should be proved.

Using words ambiguously

The Lewis Carroll approach – 'When I use a word it means just what I choose it to mean, neither more nor less' – is a favourite trick of those who aim to deceive. People use words that beg the question; that is, they define a word in a special way that supports their argument. They shift the meaning of words in different contexts. They may choose words which have the same meaning as each other but which show approval or disapproval. There is a well-known saying that the word 'firm' can be declined as follows: 'I am firm, You are obstinate, He is pigheaded.'

Chop logic

'Contrariwise,' continued Tweedledee, 'if it was so, it might be, and if it were so, it would be; but as it isn't, it ain't. That's logic'.

Chop logic is not quite as bad as that, but it can be equally misleading. It includes such debating tricks as:

● selecting instances favourable to a contention while ignoring those that conflict with it;
● twisting an argument advanced by opponents to mean something quite different from what was intended – putting words in someone's mouth;
● diverting opponents by throwing on them the burden of proving something they have not maintained;
● deliberately ignoring the point in dispute;
● introducing irrelevant matter into the argument;
● reiterating what has been denied and ignoring what has been asserted.

5

Coaching

Coaching is a personal (usually one-to-one), on-the-job approach used by managers and trainers to help people develop their skills and levels of competence. As a manager, you are there to get results through people; this means that you have a personal responsibility for ensuring that they acquire and develop the skills they need. Other people in the shape of training and management development specialists may help, but because by far the best way of learning is on the job, the onus is mainly on you.

The need for coaching may arise from formal or informal performance reviews but opportunities for coaching will emerge during normal day-to-day activities. Every time you delegate a new task to someone, a coaching opportunity is created to help the individual learn any new skills or techniques which are needed to do the job. Every time you provide feedback to an individual after a task has been completed, there is an opportunity to help that individual do better next time. Methods of giving feedback are described in Chapter 41.

AIMS

The aims of coaching are to:

- help people to become aware of how well they are doing, where they need to improve and what they need to learn;
- put controlled delegation into practice; in other words, managers can delegate new tasks or enlarged areas of work, provide guidance as necessary on how the tasks or work should be carried out and monitor performance in doing the work;
- get managers and individuals to use whatever situations arise as learning opportunities;
- enable guidance to be provided on how to carry out specific tasks as necessary, but always on the basis of helping people to learn rather than spoon-feeding them with instructions on what to do and how to do it.

THE COACHING SEQUENCE

Coaching can be carried out in the following stages:

1. Identify the areas of knowledge, skills or capabilities where learning needs to take place to qualify people to carry out the task, provide for continuous development, enhance transferable skills or improve performance.
2. Ensure that the person understands and accepts the need to learn.
3. Discuss with the person what needs to be learnt and the best way to undertake the learning.
4. Get the person to work out how they can manage their own learning while identifying where they will need help from you or someone else.
5. Provide encouragement and advice to the person in pursuing the self-learning programme.
6. Provide specific guidance as required where the person needs your help.
7. Agree how progress should be monitored and reviewed.

COACHING SKILLS

As Katherine Adams (Employee Development Bulletin, No. 72, December, 1995) writes:

> Coaching can only work with the willing participation of both learners and managers. It also requires an open and trusting relationship between the coach and the learner, and senior management support. Coaches may need special training in the skills required, they should be given specific responsibility for coaching, and their role needs to be suitably rewarded. Learning should be an explicit target of coaching along with others more directly related to the tasks being carried out. Finally, any system of coaching should be regularly monitored and evaluated.

EFFECTIVE COACHING

Coaching will be most effective when:

- The coach understands that his or her role is to help people to learn.
- Individuals are motivated to learn – they should be aware that their present level of knowledge or skill, or their behaviour needs to be improved if they are going to perform their work to their own and to others' satisfaction.
- Individuals are given guidance on what they should be learning and feedback on how they are doing.
- Learning is an active, not a passive, process – individuals need to be actively involved with their coach.
- The coach listens to individuals to understand what they want and need.
- The coach adopts a constructive approach, building on strengths and experience.

PLANNED COACHING

Coaching may be informal but it has to be planned. It is not simply checking from time to time on what people are doing and then advising them on how to do it better. Nor is it occasionally telling people where they have gone wrong and throwing in a lecture for good measure. As far as possible, coaching should take place within the framework of a general plan of the areas and direction in which individuals will benefit from further development. Coaching plans can and should be incorporated into the general development plans set out in a performance review as described in Chapter 36.

THE MANAGER AS COACH

Coaching enables you to provide motivation, structure and effective feedback as long as you have the required skills and commitment. As coaches, good managers believe that people can succeed and that they can contribute to their success. They can identify what people need to be able to do to improve their performance. They have to see this as an important part of the role – an enabling, empowering process which focuses on learning requirements.

6

Commitment – how to enhance it

Commitment is about attachment and loyalty. It has three components:

1. Identification with the organization – its purpose and values.
2. A desire to remain with the organization.
3. A willingness to work hard on behalf of the organization.

THE SIGNIFICANCE OF COMMITMENT

An American writer, Robert Walton (63), first highlighted the importance of commitment. His theme was that improved performance would result if the organization moved away from the traditional control-orientated approach to managing people. He argued that the approach should be replaced by a commitment strategy. He suggested that people respond best and most creatively when they are given broader responsibilities, encouraged to contribute and helped to achieve satisfaction in their work. Effective response over the long term is unlikely to happen when people are too tightly controlled by management, placed in narrowly defined jobs and treated like an unwelcome necessity. He expressed belief that in the new commitment-based organization:

> Jobs are designed to be broader than before, to combine planning and implementation, and to include efforts to upgrade operations, not just to maintain them... With management hierarchies relatively flat and differences in status minimized, control and lateral co-ordination depend on shared goals. And expertise rather than formal position determines influence.

Tom Peters (49) added weight to this belief in a commitment strategy. He wrote (in conjunction with Robert Waterman):

> Trust people and treat them like adults, enthuse them by lively and imaginative leadership, develop and demonstrate an obsession for quality, make them feel they own the business, and your workforce will respond with total commitment.

ENHANCING COMMITMENT

The steps you can take to enhance commitment include the following:

- Get people involved in discussing the purpose and values of the organization, listen to their constructive contributions and pass them on to higher management for incorporation in the organization's statement of purpose and values.
- Talk to team members informally as well as formally about what is going on in the department and plans for the future that will affect them.
- Involve team members in defining mutual expectations so that they 'own' and are committed to their objectives.
- Take whatever steps you can to improve the quality of working life in your department or team – the environment in which they work, the ways in which their jobs are designed, the style with which they are managed and the scope to participate – a 'culture of consent' rather than a 'command and control' situation.

● Help people to develop their skills and competencies to improve their 'employability' within and, indeed, outside the firm.

● Make no promises about 'a job for life', but emphasize, if this is true, that the company will do everything it can to increase employment opportunities and therefore security and will avoid compulsory redundancy if that is humanly possible.

Finally, bear in mind that in delivering any message about, for example, security, the frame of reference for those who receive the message will not necessarily coincide with your own. Your views may be received with open or hidden expressions of doubt and cynicism, even hostility. You have to work hard to create trust and this will be achieved more by your deeds than your words. Building trust is the only way in which commitment can be generated, and this will not be achieved if employees are simply treated as factors of production and in ways which are inconsistent with their status as the key business asset. And people will not feel committed to the organization unless they feel that they are valued by the organization.

7

Communicating

People recognize the need to communicate but find it difficult. Like Schopenhauer's hedgehogs, they want to get together, it's only their prickles that keep them apart.

Words may sound or look precise, but they are not. All sorts of barriers exist between the communicator and the receiver. Unless these barriers are overcome the message will be distorted or will not get through.

BARRIERS TO COMMUNICATION

Hearing what we want to hear

What we hear or understand when someone speaks to us is largely based on our own experience and background. Instead of hearing what people have told us, we hear what our minds tell us they have said. We have preconceptions about what people are going to say, and if what they say does not fit into our framework of reference we adjust it until it does. (Advice on how to listen is given later in this chapter.)

Ignoring conflicting information

We tend to ignore or reject communications that conflict with our own beliefs. If they are not rejected, some way is found of twisting and shaping their meaning to fit our preconceptions. When a message is inconsistent with existing beliefs, the receiver rejects its validity, avoids further exposure to it, easily forgets it and, in his or her memory, distorts what has been heard.

Perceptions about the communicator

It is difficult to separate what we hear from our feelings about the person who says it. Non-existent motives may be ascribed to the communicator. If we like people we are more likely to accept what they say – whether it is right or wrong – than if we dislike them.

Influence of the group

The group with which we identify influences our attitudes and feelings. What a group hears depends on its interests. Workers are more likely to listen to their colleagues, who share their experiences, than to outsiders such as managers or union officials.

Words mean different things to different people

Essentially, language is a method of using symbols to represent facts and feelings. Strictly speaking, we can't convey *meaning*, all we can do is to convey *words*. Do not assume that because something has a certain meaning to you, it will convey the same meaning to someone else.

Non-verbal communication

When we try to understand the meaning of what people say we listen to the words but we use other clues which convey meaning. We attend not only to *what* people say but to *how* they say it. We form impressions from what is called body language – eyes, shape of the mouth, the muscles of the face, even posture. We may feel that these tell us more about what someone is really saying than the words he or she uses. But there is enormous scope for misinterpretation.

Emotions

Our emotions colour our ability to convey or to receive the true message. When we are insecure or worried, what we hear seems more threatening than when we are secure and at peace with the world. When we are angry or depressed, we tend to reject what might otherwise seem like reasonable requests or good ideas. During heated argument, many things that are said may not be understood or may be badly distorted.

Noise

Any interference to communication is 'noise'. It can be literal noise which prevents the message being heard, or figurative in the shape of distracting or confused information which distorts or obscures the meaning.

Size

The larger and more complex the organization, the greater the problem of communication. The more levels of management and supervision through which a message has to pass, the greater the opportunity for distortion or misunderstanding.

OVERCOMING BARRIERS TO COMMUNICATION

Adjust to the world of the receiver

Try to predict the impact of what you are going to write or say on the receiver's feelings and attitudes. Tailor the message to fit the receiver's vocabulary, interests and values. Be aware of how the information might be misinterpreted because of prejudices, the influence of others and the tendency of people to reject what they do not want to hear.

Use feedback

Ensure that you get a message back from the receiver which tells you how much has been understood.

Use face-to-face communication

Whenever possible talk to people rather than write to them. That is how you get feedback. You can adjust or change your message according to reactions. You can also deliver it in a more human and understanding way – this can help to overcome prejudices. Verbal criticism can often be given in a more constructive manner than written reproof which always seems to be harsher.

Use reinforcement

You may have to present your message in a number of different ways to get it across. Re-emphasize the important points and follow up.

Use direct, simple language

This seems obvious. But many people clutter up what they say with jargon, long words and elaborate sentences.

Suit the actions to the word

Communications have to be credible to be effective. There is nothing worse than promising the earth and then failing to deliver. When you say you are going to do something, do it. Next time you are more likely to be believed.

Use different channels

Some communications have to be in writing to put the message across promptly and without any variations in the way they are delivered. But, wherever possible, supplement written communications with the spoken word. Conversely, an oral briefing should be reinforced in writing.

Reduce problems of size

If you can, reduce the number of levels of management. Encourage a reasonable degree of informality in communications. Ensure that activities are grouped together to ease communication on matters of mutual concern.

LISTENING SKILLS

There are many good writers and speakers but few good listeners. Most of us filter the spoken words addressed to us so that we absorb only some of them – frequently those we want to hear. Listening is an art which not many people cultivate. But it is a very necessary one, because a good listener will gather more information and achieve better rapport with the other person. And both these effects of good listening are essential to good communication.

People don't listen effectively because they are:

- unable to concentrate, for whatever reason;
- too preoccupied with themselves;
- over-concerned with what they are going to say next;
- uncertain about what they are listening to or why they are listening to it;
- unable to follow the points or arguments made by the speaker;
- simply not interested in what is being said.

Effective listeners:

- concentrate on the speaker, following not only words but also body language which, through the use of eyes or gestures, often underlines meaning and gives life to the message;
- respond quickly to points made by the speaker, if only in the shape of encouraging grunts;
- ask questions frequently to elucidate meaning and to give the speaker an opportunity to rephrase or underline a point;
- comment on the points made by the speaker, without inter-rupting the flow, in order to test understanding and demon-strate that the speaker and listener are still on the same wavelength. These comments may reflect back or summarize something the speaker has said, thus giving an opportunity for him to reconsider or elucidate the point made;
- make notes on the key points – even if the notes are not referred to later they will help to concentrate the mind;
- are continuously evaluating the messages being delivered to check that they are understood and relevant to the purpose of the meeting;
- are alert at all times to the nuances of what the speaker is saying;

- do not slump in their chairs – they lean forward, show interest and maintain contact through their oral responses and by means of body language;
- are prepared to let the speaker go on with the minimum of interruption.

8

Conflict management

Conflict is inevitable in organizations because the objectives, values and needs of groups and individuals do not always coincide. Conflict may be a sign of a healthy organization. Bland agreement on everything would be unnatural and enervating. There should be clashes of ideas about tasks and projects, and disagreements should not be suppressed. They should come out into the open because that is the only way to ensure that the issues are explored and conflicts are resolved.

There is such a thing as creative conflict – new or modified ideas, insights, approaches and solutions can be generated by a joint re-examination of the different points of view as long as this is based on an objective and rational exchange of information and ideas. But conflict becomes counter-productive when it is based on person-ality clashes, or when it is treated as an unseemly mess to be hurriedly cleared away, rather than as a problem to be worked through.

Conflict resolution can be concerned with conflict between groups or conflict between individuals.

HANDLING INTER-GROUP CONFLICT

There are three principal ways of resolving inter-group conflict: peaceful coexistence, compromise and problem-solving.

Peaceful coexistence

The aim here is to smooth out differences and emphasize the common ground. People are encouraged to learn to live together; there is a good deal of information, contact and exchange of views, and individuals move freely between groups (for example, between headquarters and the field, or between sales and manufacturing).

This is a pleasant ideal, but it may not be practicable in many situations. There is much evidence that conflict is not necessarily resolved by bringing people together. Improved communications and techniques such as briefing groups may appear to be good ideas but are useless if management has nothing to say that people want to hear. There is also the danger that the real issues, submerged for the moment in an atmosphere of superficial bonhomie, will surface again later.

Compromise

The issue is resolved by negotiation or bargaining and neither party wins or loses. This concept of splitting the difference is essentially pessimistic. The hallmark of this approach is that there is no 'right' or 'best' answer. Agreements only accommodate differences. Real issues are not likely to be solved.

Problem-solving

An attempt is made to find a genuine solution to the problem rather than just accommodating different points of view. This is where the apparent paradox of 'creative conflict' comes in. Conflict situations can be used to advantage to create better solutions.

If solutions are to be developed by problem-solving, they have to be generated by those who share the responsibility for seeing that the solutions work. The sequence of actions is: first, those concerned work to define the problem and agree on the objectives to be attained in reaching a solution; second, the group develops alternative solutions and debates their merits; third, agreement is reached on the preferred course of action and how it should be implemented.

HANDLING CONFLICT BETWEEN INDIVIDUALS

Handling interpersonal conflict can be even more difficult than resolving conflicts between groups. Whether the conflict is openly hostile or subtly covert, strong personal feelings may be involved. Yet, as James Ware and Louis Barnes (64) say:

> The ability to productively manage such conflict is critical to managerial success. Interpersonal differences often become sharpest when the organizational stakes seem to be high, but almost all organizations include their share of small issues blown into major conflicts. The manager's problem is to build on human differences of opinion while not letting them jeopardize overall performance, satisfaction and growth.

Ware and Barnes go on to say that interpersonal conflict, like intergroup conflict, is an organizational reality which is neither good nor bad. It can be destructive, but it can also play a productive role. 'Problems usually arise when potential conflict is artificially suppressed, or when it escalates beyond the control of the adversaries or third-party intermediaries.'

The reaction to interpersonal conflict may be the withdrawal of either party, leaving the other one to hold the field. This is the classic win/lose situation. The problem has been resolved by force, but this may not be the best solution if it represents one person's point of view which has ignored counter-arguments, and has, in fact, steamrollered over them. The winner may be triumphant but the loser will be aggrieved and either demotivated or resolved to fight again another day. There will have been a lull in, but not an end to, the conflict.

Another approach is to smooth over differences and pretend that the conflict does not exist, although no attempt has been made to tackle the root causes. Again, this is an unsatisfactory approach. The issue is likely to re-emerge and the battle will recommence.

Yet another approach is bargaining to reach a compromise. This means that both sides are prepared to lose as well as win some points and the aim is to reach a solution acceptable to both sides.

Bargaining, however, involves all sorts of tactical and often counter-productive games, and the parties are often more anxious to seek acceptable compromises than to achieve sound solutions.

Ware and Barnes identify two other approaches to managing interpersonal conflict: controlling, and constructive confrontation.

Controlling

Controlling can involve preventing interaction, or structuring the forms of interaction or reducing or changing external pressures.

Preventing interaction is a strategy for use when emotions are high. Conflict is controlled by keeping those apart in the hope that, although the differences still exist, the people involved have time to cool down and consider more constructive approaches. But this may only be a temporary expedient and the eventual confrontation could be even more explosive.

Structuring the forms of interaction can be a strategy when it is not possible to separate the parties. In these cases, ground rules can be developed to deal with the conflict concerning such behaviours as communicating information or dealing with specific issues. However, this may also be a temporary strategy if the strong underlying feelings are only suppressed rather than resolved.

Personal counselling is an approach which does not address the conflict itself but focuses on how the two people are reacting. Personal counselling gives people a chance to release pent-up tensions and may encourage them to think about new ways of resolving the conflict. But it does not address the essential nature of the conflict, which is the relationship between two people. That is why constructive confrontation offers the best hope of a long-term solution.

Constructive confrontation

Constructive confrontation is a method of bringing the individuals in conflict together, ideally with a third party whose function is to help build an exploratory and co-operative climate.

Constructive confrontation aims to get the parties involved to understand and explore the other's perceptions and feelings. It is a process of developing mutual understanding to produce a win/win situation. The issues will be confronted but on the basis of a joint analysis, with the help of the third party, of facts relating to the situation and the actual behaviour of those involved. Feelings will be expressed but they will be analysed by reference to specific events and behaviours rather than inferences or speculations about motives.

Third parties have a key role in this process, and it is not an easy one. They have to get agreement to the ground rules for discussions aimed at bringing out the facts and minimizing hostile behaviour. They must monitor the ways in which negative feelings are expressed and encourage the parties to produce new definitions of the problem and its cause or causes and new motives to reach a common solution. Third parties must avoid the temptation to support or appear to support either of those in contention. They should adopt a counselling approach, as follows:

- listen actively;
- observe as well as listen;
- help people to understand and define the problem by asking pertinent, open-ended questions;
- recognize feelings and allow them to be expressed;
- help people to define problems for themselves;
- encourage people to explore alternative solutions;
- get people to develop their own implementation plans but provide advice and help if asked.

CONCLUSIONS

Conflict, as has been said, is in itself not to be deplored: it is an inevitable concomitant of progress and change. What is regrettable is the failure to use conflict constructively. Effective problem-solving and constructive confrontation both resolve conflicts and open up channels of discussion and co-operative action.

Many years ago one of the pioneering writers on management, Mary Parker Follett (20), wrote something on managing conflict which is as valid today as it was then:

Differences can be made to contribute to the common cause if they are resolved by integration rather than domination or compromise.

9

Continuous improvement

The concept of continuous improvement is based on the assumption that continually striving to reach ever higher standards in every part of the organization will provide a series of incremental gains that will build superior performance. In Japan the process is called *kaizen*, which is a composite of the word *kai* meaning change, and *zen* meaning good or for the better. It consists of the organization creating an environment in which *all* employees can contribute to improving performance and overall effectiveness as a normal and continuing part of their job.

In an environment dedicated to continuous improvement, such as that developed at Nissan (67), the prime objective of managers and team leaders is to bring out new ideas and concepts from their staff. Their task is to create an environment in which new thinking is encouraged and welcomed. The management of Nissan believes that it is part of everyone's job to improve continually. This is embedded in the organization as a fundamental value not by exhortation but by practical steps such as workshops, where employees with ideas for new tooling or other changes can go to try them out.

The supervisor is expected to lead problem-solving and continuous improvement activities, but as experience develops, other team members will assume responsibility for improvement groups. It is accepted by managers and supervisors that they have no monopoly of wisdom on the best means of performing a task or making improvements. This is on the basis that the person actually doing the work is likely to know much more about the problem than they do.

By methods such as these and by constant emphasis at all levels on its importance, continuous improvement can become a way of life in an organization. It can, and should, be one of its key values, reflected in the way everyone behaves and underpinned by such processes as performance and reward management, where ability to stimulate and achieve improvements will be an important criterion for assessing and rewarding performance.

IMPLEMENTING CONTINUOUS IMPROVEMENT

The steps required to implement continuous improvement are:

1. Formulate and communicate the business strategy.
2. Define the key areas where a policy of continuous improvement will support the business strategy.
3. Appoint a member of the top management team to take charge.
4. Develop programmes for continuous improvement, with particular reference to process improvement, quality, and speeding up development, manufacturing and delivery times.
5. Provide facilities for identifying, reviewing and developing ideas for continuous improvement, eg improvement groups, team meetings, suggestion schemes.
6. Provide training in developing and implementing ideas.
7. Develop performance measures which enable progress to be monitored and assist in determining priorities for future developments.
8. Ensure that good ideas are recognized – the recognition need not necessarily be financial.
9. Communicate to everyone the aims of continuous improvement, how they are expected to contribute and what has been achieved.

10. Keep it simple. Avoid multiple initiatives and focus on developments which promise significant improvements.

The development of a culture of continuous improvement, however, is also fostered if the enterprise functions as a learning organization and implements continuous development policies.

THE LEARNING ORGANIZATION

A learning organization can be defined as an organization which facilitates the learning of all its members and continually transforms itself.

According to Alan Mumford (43), the characteristics of a learning organization are that it:

● encourages managers and staff to identify their own learning needs;
● provides a regular review of performance and learning for the individual;
● encourages employees to set challenging learning goals for themselves;
● provides feedback at the time on both performance and achieved learning;
● reviews the performance of managers in helping to develop others;
● assists employees to see learning opportunities on the job;
● seeks to provide new experiences from which people can learn;
● provides or facilitates on-the-job training;
● tolerates some mistakes, provided people try to learn from them;
● encourages managers to review, conclude and plan learning activities;
● encourages people to challenge traditional ways of working.

Charles Handy (23) points out that a learning organization can and should mean two things: an organization which learns and/or an organization which encourages learning in its people. He believes that a learning organization needs a formal way of asking questions, seeking out theories, testing them and reflecting upon them. The learning organization constantly reframes the world and its part in it. Members of the organization are encouraged to suggest improvements. The organization has to find answers to questions about its strengths and talents, its weaknesses and what sort of organization it wants to be. It also has to cultivate its 'negative capability', ie its capacity to learn from its mistakes.

Explicit steps are taken by learning organizations to learn from experience. They provide various forums such as development centres, team meetings, 'away day' conferences and workshops to enable people to reflect on what they have learned and what they still need to learn. Such reflections provide a basis for formulating organizational and individual improvement plans.

A learning organization will be concerned with the development of skills and competences at all levels, emphasizing the importance of learning by informal means on the job with the help and guidance of managers and colleagues. The importance will be recognized of what Alan Mumford calls 'incidental learning' – the learning that can be built around incidents in everyone's day-to-day working life and career. Performance management, as described in Chapter 36, is a process which can systematize this incidental learning by providing for the review of achievements in relation to agreed objectives and the analysis of the behaviours which have contributed to success or failure.

CONTINUOUS IMPROVEMENT CHECKLIST

1. Does the culture of the organization support and encourage new thinking and the involvement of employees at all levels in problem-solving and seeking improvements?
2. Is the capacity to involve people in seeking improvements and having new ideas accepted, recognized and rewarded appropriately?
3. Are people encouraged to challenge traditional ways of operating?
4. Are steps taken by the organization to ensure that the top management and employees at all levels have the 'space' and encouragement to reflect on their experiences and learn from them?
5. Are managers and individuals encouraged to identify their own learning needs and set learning goals for themselves?
6. Are managers and staff encouraged to see learning opportunities in their day-to-day work?

7. Are systematic efforts made by the organization and its managers to provide new experiences from which employees can learn?
8. Are people encouraged to learn from their mistakes as well as their successes?
9. Are forums (meetings, conferences, etc) provided for people to learn from their experiences and develop improvement plans?
10. Are managers encouraged to define and meet learning needs as they appear?

10

Controlling

Basically, you are seeking to control two areas – input and output – and the relationship between them, which is productivity or performance. All managers will know Murphy's two laws: if anything can go wrong, it will; and of the things that can't go wrong, some will.

The aim of good control is to protect your plans from the operation of these laws as far as possible; to detect trouble spots before they erupt; to prevent those accidents which are just waiting to happen. Prevention is better than cure.

ESSENTIALS OF CONTROL

Control is relative. It does not deal with absolutes, only with the difference between good and not-so-good performance.

The basis of control is measurement. It depends on accurate information about what is being achieved. This is then compared with what *should* have been achieved and with what has been achieved in the past. But that is only a starting point. Good control also identifies responsibility and points the way to action.

Effective control

If you want to exercise good control you need to:

1. *plan* what you aim to achieve;
2. *measure* regularly what has been achieved;
3. *compare* actual achievements with the plan;
4. *take action* to exploit opportunities revealed by this information or to correct deviations from the plan.

Note that control is not only a matter of putting things right. It also has a positive side – getting more or better things done on the basis of information received.

Problems of control

A good control system is not easy to set up. There are two essentials:

● To set appropriate and fair targets, standards and budgets. (This may be difficult where the scope for quantification is limited or if circumstances make forecasts unreliable.)
● To decide what information is crucial for control purposes and design reports which clearly convey that information to the people who need it and can use it to point the way to action. This also produces problems. Too many control systems generate a surfeit of indigestible data which go to the wrong people and are not acted upon. You can have too little information, but there is also such a thing as information overkill. There is, moreover, a tendency for some people to report good results and cover up poor results. In any case, the figures may not tell the whole story.

Overcoming the problem

There are five steps to take if you want to achieve good control:

1. Decide what you want to control.
2. Decide how you are going to measure and review performance.
3. Use ratio analysis to make comparisons and to identify variations and problems.

4. Set up a control system.
5. Manage by exception.

CONTROLLING INPUTS AND OUTPUTS

In controlling input and output, and hence productivity, an overview is essential. It is no good concentrating on inputs, mainly expressed as costs, unless you look at the benefits arising from these expenditures and the effectiveness with which the costs have been incurred. Cost benefit and cost-effectiveness studies are an essential part of the control process.

Input control

When you control inputs you should aim to measure and assess the performance of:

● *Money* – its productivity, flow, liquidity and conservation.
  You need to know what return you are getting on investments compared with the return you want.
  You should ensure that you have the cash and working capital to run the business. Cash-flow analysis is vital. One of the golden rules of management, as stated by Robert Heller, is 'cash in must exceed cash out'.
  You must conserve and provide the money needed to finance future trading and development projects and for capital investment.
  Management has to know how effectively its financial resources are being used to produce goods, services and profits and this requires continuous and close attention to the control of direct and indirect costs and overheads generally.

● *People* – the effectiveness of the people you employ in terms of their quality and performance.
● *Materials* – their availability, condition, convertibility and waste.
● *Equipment* – machine utilization and capability.

Output control

- *Quantitative control measures* – the units produced or sold, the amount of services provided, the sales turnover obtained and the profits achieved. Key performance measures will vary between organizations. You need to determine through analysis which are the crucial indicators of success or failure.
- *Qualitative control measures* – the level of service provided by an organization (eg a public corporation) or by a non-productive department within an organization (eg personnel). It is more difficult to select valid performance measures in these areas, but the attempt should be made.

Productivity control

Productivity is the relationship between input and output. Cost benefit studies are productivity studies in that they assess how much benefit (output) is obtained from a given cost (input).

Productivity is expressed by ratios. A productivity index can be produced as follows:

$$\text{Productivity Index} = \frac{\text{Output}}{\text{Input}} = \frac{\text{Performance achieved}}{\text{Resources consumed}} = \frac{\text{Effectiveness}}{\text{Efficiency}}$$

RATIO ANALYSIS

Expressing items as percentages or ratios of other items – ratio analysis – is the best way to measure and control inputs, outputs, productivity and the financial resources of the company generally. Ratios should not, however, be used in isolation. You should always take account of trends between present and past performance. And you should compare ratios within the business and between your business and other businesses. Most important, you should compare actual ratios with planned ratios.

It is essential to seek the *key* indicators in the form of ratios for your business. You will not want to collect sheets of ratios from every direction, but you should know when you look at a set of figures which one you have got to divide into the other to tell you what is really happening. It is no good just knowing how much sales have increased over the last period. You also need to know how the number of sales representatives has changed and the volume of sales per representative, this period compared with budget, the last period, and the same period last year.

The most important financial and productivity ratios are described below.

Return on capital employed

This is usually expressed as net profit as a percentage of capital. It tells you the extent to which an investment is paying off. It could apply to the whole business from the point of view of the shareholders, to part of the business, or to the specific return on an investment in capital equipment. When compared with the return you could get if you invested your money elsewhere, this ratio indicates the extent to which the investment is justified.

Economic value added

The economic value added (EVA) measure represents the difference between a company's post-tax operating profit and the cost of the capital invested in the business. The cost of capital includes the cost of equity – what shareholders expect to receive through capital gains. The theory of EVA is that it is not good enough for a company simply to make a profit. It has to justify the cost of its capital, equity included. If it is not covering that, it will not make good returns for investors. Most conventional measures of company performance, such as earnings per share, ignore the cost of capital in a business.

Earnings per share

Earnings per share is a measure of particular interest to investors. It is expressed as:

$$\frac{\text{Profits after interest, taxation and preference dividends but before extraordinary items}}{\text{The number of issued ordinary shares}} \times 100$$

Profit to sales ratio

This is the fundamental measure of the profitability of the company as a trading concern. It is expressed as a ratio:

$$\frac{\text{Net trading profit (ie the difference between expenses and income from sales)}}{\text{Sales revenue}}$$

Solvency ratios

These measure the company's short-term financial liabilities – its ability to pay its current liabilities as they fall due.

The 'current' ratio is calculated as follows:

$$\frac{\text{Current assets (stock, debtors and cash)}}{\text{Current liabilities (creditors and accrued charges)}}$$

If the current ratio is more than 1:1, the company has more current assets than current liabilities and, if it were forced to pay out all its current liabilities, would have sufficient current assets to do so.

If a really strict appraisal of a company's solvency is required, however, it is best to leave stock out of the current assets, and to take only the liquid assets into consideration. This is because if a company were forced to realize its stock quickly, it is doubtful if it would even recover its cost value. The ratio then becomes:

$$\frac{\text{Current assets excluding stock}}{\text{Current liabilities}}$$

This is sometimes called the 'acid test'. Ideally, the ratio should be at least 1:1 but there are cases where a ratio of somewhat less than 1:1 is acceptable. Too high a ratio, on the other hand, would mean that the company is not making sufficient use of its finances – cash by itself does not generate much profit.

Stock ratios

If the company holds too much stock it will be wasting its financial resources in an unused asset. If it holds too little stock it will lose sales revenue through not being able to service its customers.

To measure how much is being tied up in stock use the ratio:

$$\frac{\text{Stock}}{\text{Current assets}}$$

To measure how quickly the stock is turned over (stock turn) the ratio is:

$$\frac{\text{Sales}}{\text{Stock}}$$

The greater the stock turnover figure the better for the company. If the goods are being sold at a profit, the more that are sold the better the profit at the year end.

Other financial ratios

There are a number of other financial ratios you can use. Perhaps the most important are:

$$\frac{\text{Debtors}}{\text{Average daily sales}}$$

This measures how well management is speeding the flow of cash through the business, ie how many days' credit is being allowed to customers.

$$\frac{\text{Debtors}}{\text{Creditors}}$$

If creditors begin to outweigh debtors this may be a sign that the company is over-trading. The bad debt ratio (bad debts/sales) is also revealing.

$$\frac{\text{Current liabilities} - (\text{current assets minus stock})}{\text{Profit before tax and interest}} \times 365$$

This is the current liquidity ratio. It shows how many days it would take at current profit levels to pay off the deficit between current liabilities and liquid assets.

Productivity ratios

The most useful productivity ratio is:

$$\frac{\text{Results}}{\text{Resources}} \quad \text{ie} \quad \frac{\text{Sales}}{\text{Employees}}$$

The other main ratios are:

$$\frac{\text{Units produced or processed}}{\text{Number of employees}}$$

$$\frac{\text{Added value (ie sales revenue minus cost of sales)}}{\text{Number of employees}}$$

$$\frac{\text{Profit after tax}}{\text{Number of employees}}$$

Cost ratios

The best way to look at costs is to express them as a percentage of sales. Thus the fundamental measure is:

$$\frac{\text{Overheads}}{\text{Sales}} \times 100$$

Other measures include:

$$\frac{\text{Payroll costs}}{\text{Sales}} \times 100$$

$$\frac{\text{Cost of materials and bought in parts}}{\text{Sales}} \times 100$$

$$\frac{\text{Selling costs}}{\text{Sales}} \times 100$$

Use of ratios

Use ratios as you would use any other figures. They are no more than indicators. In themselves, they will not tell the whole story. You have to dig. A ratio is no more than a symptom. You need to find out the real cause of a variation or problem.

CONTROL SYSTEMS

What you need from a control system

Your basic requirement is reports that clearly identify areas of good and bad performance so that appropriate action can be taken.

At higher levels 'exception reporting' should be adopted so that significant deviations, on which action should be taken, can be highlighted. Overall summaries of performance against plan and of trends will also be necessary at this level, but these may disguise significant underlying deviations which would be pointed out in an exception report.

The reports themselves should:

● Contain measurements which are accurate, valid and reliable. Permit a direct and easy comparison between planned and actual performance.

● Analyse trends, comparing one period's performance with that of the previous period or of the same period the previous year and, where appropriate, summarizing the year to date position.

● Be given to the person who is responsible for the activity concerned.

● Arrive promptly, in time to allow the necessary action to be taken.

● Provide succinct explanations of any deviations from plan.

Measurements

Measurement is a good thing, but all figures need to be treated with caution. They may conceal more than they reveal. The weaknesses to look for are:

● *Non-representative reporting* – data selected which do not cover the key issues, disguise unfavourable results or over-emphasize favourable performance.

● *Not comparing like with like* – the 'apples and pears syndrome'. For example, a trend or projection which does not take account of changing or new factors which have altered or will alter the situation since the base data were collected.

● *Not starting from a common base*. This is a variant on the 'like with like' problem. Trend comparisons should be related to a common base in terms both of the period and the elements covered by the information.

● *Misleading averages.* Averages do not always tell you the whole story. They may conceal extremes in performance, which are significant.
● *Unintentional errors* – simple mistakes in calculation, presentation or observation.
● *Measurements out of context.* Almost any single measure is influenced by, or inseparable from, other measures. Figures in isolation may not mean very much. You have to know about relationships and underlying influences.

MANAGEMENT BY EXCEPTION

Management by exception is a system which rings alarm bells only when the manager's attention is needed. The principle was invented by the father of scientific management, Frederick Taylor (61). In 1911 he wrote in *Principles of Scientific Management:*

> Under the exception principle the manager should receive only condensed, summarized and invariably comparative reports covering, however, all of the elements entering into the management and even these summaries should all be carefully gone over by an assistant before they reach the manager, and have all the exceptions to the past averages or standards pointed out, both the especially good and the especially bad exceptions, thus giving him in a few minutes a full view of progress which is being made, or the reverse, and leaving him free to consider the broader lines of policy and to study the character and fitness of the important men under him.

Management by exception frees the boss to concentrate on the issues that matter. It gives the subordinate more scope to get on with his or her work while knowing that events out of the ordinary will be reported upwards.

Deciding what constitutes an exception is a useful exercise in itself. It means selecting the key events and measures which will show up good, bad or indifferent results and indicate whether or not performance is going according to plan.

The chosen indicators or ratios can be studied so that the significance of changes or trends is readily understood. More important, the possible causes of deviations can be analysed and kept in mind. Investigations will then be quickly launched in the right direction and swift remedial action can be taken.

Most of us have come across the boss or manager who seems to have the almost magic facility for studying a mass of figures and immediately spotting the one really important deviation or the item that does not ring true. It sometimes seems to be pure instinct, but of course it is not. Such managers are practising the art of management by exception, even if they never call it by that name. Their experience and analytical powers have told them what constitutes normal performance. But they can spot something out of the ordinary at a thousand paces. They *know* what the key indicators are and they look for them, hard. This is a skill that anyone can develop. And the effort of acquiring it is well worth while.

11

Co-ordinating

Co-ordinating – 'achieving unity of effort'– is not a separate function of a manager. The concept of co-ordination does not describe a *particular* set of operations but *all* operations which lead to a certain result.

Co-ordination is required because individual actions need to be synchronized. Some activities must follow one another in sequence. Others must go on at the same time and in the same direction in order to finish together.

HOW TO CO-ORDINATE

Obviously, you can achieve good co-ordination if you get people to work well together. This means integrating their activities, communicating well, exercising leadership, and team building (all subjects covered in individual chapters). But you should also pay attention to the specific techniques discussed below.

Planning

Co-ordinating should take place before the event rather than after it. Planning is the first step. This means deciding what should be done and when. It is a process of dividing the total task into a number of sequenced or related sub-tasks. Then you work out priorities and time scales.

Organizing

You know what should be done. You then decide who does it. When you divide work between people you should avoid breaking apart those tasks which are linked together and which you cannot separate cleanly from each other.

Your biggest problem will be deciding where the boundaries between distinct but related activities should be. If the boundary is either too rigid or insufficiently well defined, you may have co-ordination problems. Don't rely too much upon the formal organization as defined in job descriptions, charts and manuals. If you do, you will induce inflexibility and set up communication barriers, and these are fatal to co-ordination.

The informal organization which exists in all companies can help co-ordination. When people work together they develop a system of social relationships which cut across formal organizational boundaries. They create a network of informal groups which tend to discipline themselves. This frees management from detailed supervision and control and leaves it more time for planning, problem-solving and the overall monitoring of performance.

Delegating

The informal organization can help, but you still need to delegate work to individuals in a way that ensures they know what is expected of them *and* are aware of the need to liaise with others to achieve a co-ordinated result.

The art is to make everyone concerned understand the points on which they must link up with other people and the time in which such actions have to be completed. You should not have to *tell* people to co-ordinate; they should co-ordinate almost automatically. This they will do if you delegate not only specific tasks but also the job of working with others.

Communicating

You should not only communicate clearly what you want done, you should also encourage people to communicate with one another.

Avoid situations in which people can say: 'Why didn't someone tell me about this? If they had, I could have told them how to get out of the difficulty.' Nobody should be allowed to resort to James Forsyte's excuse that 'no one tells me anything.' It is up to people to find out what they need to know and not wait to be told.

Controlling

If you use the processes described above, and they work, theoretically you will not have to worry any more about co-ordination. But of course, life is not like that. You must monitor actions and results, spot problems and take swift corrective action when necessary. Co-ordination doesn't just happen. It has to be worked at, but avoid getting too involved. Allow people as much freedom as possible to develop horizontal relationships. These can facilitate co-ordination far more effectively than rigid and authoritarian control from above.

A CASE STUDY

There is no one right way of co-ordinating a number of activities. It all depends on the nature of those activities and the circumstances in which they are carried out; for example, the present organization structure, the existence of co-ordinating committees and the facility with which communication can take place between those involved. Ultimately, good co-ordination depends upon the will of everyone concerned – to co-ordinate or be co-ordinated. Mechanical devices such as committees will not necessarily do the trick.

An example of good co-ordination took place in a company which was developing a new product in a new market. Neither the product nor the market fitted conveniently into the existing divisional structure and it was therefore decided to appoint one man as project manager to get the product launched. He would have a staff of two – a brand manager and a secretary. The work of development, production, marketing, selling and customer servicing would be carried out by the relevant departments in various divisions of the company.

The project manager had the status and authority to get things done by each department. The board was right behind the project and had allocated the priorities and resources required. But the different activities had to be co-ordinated and only the project manager could do it.

The easy way out would have been to set up a massive co-ordinating committee and leave it at that. This would have failed. Projects of this complexity cannot be co-ordinated just by creating a committee.

The project manager developed a different approach which proved to be highly successful. His first objective was to make everyone concerned enthusiastic about the project. He wanted them to believe in its importance so that they would be committed to working closely with the other departments involved.

His next step was to hold separate discussions with departmental heads so that they completely understood the programme of work required in each area. With the help of a project planner he then drew up a chart showing the key events and activities, and the relationships between them and the sequence in which they needed to take place in order to complete the project. This chart was distributed to all the departmental heads supplemented by an explanatory brief on the work required at each stage of the programme. Only then did he call a meeting to iron out difficulties and to ensure that everyone knew what had to be done and when.

He set up a system of progress reports and held progress meetings with departmental heads. But these were only held as necessary and he did not rely upon them to achieve co-ordination. He depended much more on personal contacts with individual managers, reviewing problems, noting where adjustments to the programme were needed, and stimulating the managers to even greater efforts when required. It was time consuming, but it kept him closely in touch so that he could anticipate any likely delays, setbacks or failures in communication, and be in a position to take action. He used the chart as his main instrument for checking that the critical events took place as planned.

The successful co-ordination and completion of the project were not achieved by one method but by the judicious use of a combination of techniques relevant to the situation: motivating, team building, planning, integrating, monitoring and controlling.

12

Counselling

Counselling has been described by the Institute of Personnel Management (29) as: 'Any activity in the workplace where one individual uses a set of skills and techniques to help another individual to take responsibility for and to manage their own decision-making whether it is work related or personal.'

Counselling is central to the management and development of people. All managers engage in some activity which could be termed as counselling during their normal working life. It is therefore a natural component of management – an everyday activity which can arise from immediate feedback or play an important part in a formal performance review session (see Chapter 36).

One important aim as a manager is to encourage individuals to accept much of the responsibility for their own self-development. What people seek out for themselves, with some guidance as necessary, is likely to make a greater impact than anything handed out to them by their managers or by a trainer. Of course, you still have to make clear what you expect individuals to achieve. It is also necessary to ensure that people have the required training and guidance to enable them to meet your expectations. There will be occasions when you have to spell out how you expect the job to be done. But you will make no progress in developing the skills and abilities of your staff if you only *tell* them how to do things or how they should solve their work problems. Your job is to do as much as you can to help them to help themselves, because that is the best way for them to learn.

THE COUNSELLING PROCESS

The counselling process as described by the IPM consists of three stages:

- *Recognition and understanding* – recognizing the indicators of problems and issues.
- *Empowering* – enabling employees to recognize their own problem or situation and encouraging them to express it.
- *Resourcing* – managing the problem, which will include the decision on who is best able to act as counsellor: the manager, the specialist or an outside resource.

COUNSELLING STAGES

Egan (19) has suggested that the stages to be followed in counselling are:

1. *Listening, understanding and communicating.* This focuses on understanding the perspective of the other person and communicating that understanding. It is non-judgemental and concentrates on ensuring that both parties have the same understanding of the situation.
2. *Changing the picture.* Talking through an issue can help to change the individual's perspective and indicate a solution to the problem. But this does not always happen and as a counsellor you may have to use the 'tougher' skills of challenging and confronting, sharing the other's different perceptions and providing a different framework. The initial listening phase should have established an atmosphere of acceptance and openness which enables this tougher stage to take the process forward into action.

3. *Implementing action.* In this stage you resource the individual to take action. You become a facilitator, helping the individual to formulate action plans, and providing expertise and guidance as necessary. But it is not your role as a counsellor to tell the individual what action to take. Individuals must be helped to work out for themselves what needs to be done and how it should be done, although you should provide the resources required in the shape of coaching, training or the provision of better working facilities or systems. You can also be available to provide any additional guidance or help each individual requires.

COUNSELLING SKILLS

The counselling skills you need to develop are:

- *Problem identification* – recognizing that the problem exists.
- *Open questioning* – probing by open-ended, non-directive questions to identify the real focus of the problem rather than concentrating on its symptoms.
- *Listening* – the ability to listen actively to obtain the full story by probing, evaluating, interpreting and supporting.
- *Sensitivity* – to individual beliefs and values, some of which may be based on culture or religion.
- *Reflecting* – being able to restate the problem from the individual's point of view.
- *Empathy* – having regard for the feelings and anxieties of the individual.
- *Impartiality* – the ability to remain non-judgemental and to refrain from prescribing solutions.
- *Sincerity* – having a genuine attitude of interest and openness to the individual's problems.
- *Belief* – having the belief that individuals have the resources to solve their own problems, albeit with passive or active help.

13

Creativity and innovation

Walter Bagehot wrote: 'It is often said that men are ruled by their imagination; but it would be truer to say that they are governed by the weakness of their imagination.'

Unimaginative management is a sure way to failure. Creative thinking that leads to innovation aims to overcome the danger of being governed by this weakness.

CREATIVITY

Creative and logical thinking

Creative thinking is imaginative thinking. It produces new ideas, new ways of looking at things. It relates things or ideas which were previously unrelated. It is discontinuous and divergent. Edward de Bono (12) invented the phrase 'lateral thinking' for it and this term has stuck; it implies sideways leaps in the imagination rather than a continuous progression down a logical chain of reasoning.

Logical or analytical thinking is a step-by-step process. It is continuous, one step leading to the next until, ideally, you converge on the only possible solution. It is sometimes called 'convergent' thinking; de Bono refers to it as 'vertical thinking' because you go straight down the line from one state of information to another.

De Bono summed up the differences between vertical and lateral thinking as follows:

Vertical thinking	*Lateral thinking*
Chooses	Changes
Looks for what is right	Looks for what is different
One thing must follow directly from another	Makes deliberate jumps
Concentrates on relevance	Welcomes chance intrusions
Moves in the most likely directions	Explores the least likely

Creative thinking is not superior to logical thinking. It's just different. The best managers are both creative and logical. Eventually, however creative they have been, they have to make a decision. And logical thinking is necessary to ensure that it is the right decision.

The process of creativity

In *The Act of Creation*, Arthur Koestler (35) described the process of creativity as one of 'bisociation'; putting together two unconnected facts or ideas to form a single idea. The establishment of the relationship or bisociation is usually accompanied by a release of tension. There is a flash of illumination leading to a shout of 'Eureka!' or at least 'Aha!' As Koestler remarks, it is like the release of tension after the unexpected punch line of a joke – the 'haha' reaction. Or even the less dramatic release of tension when confronting a work of art.

If we assume that it is desirable to increase our capacity for creative thinking, there are three steps to take:

1. Understand the barriers to creative thinking.
2. Develop individual capacity for creative thinking.
3. Use the collective capacities of groups of people to develop new ideas by brainstorming.

Barriers to creative thinking

The main barriers to creative thinking are:

● Allowing your mind to be conditioned into following a dominant pattern – the mind is a patterning system and this means you can be trapped into a fixed way of looking at things, what de Bono calls a 'concept prison', or a 'tethering factor'.
● Restricting the free growth of your ideas within rigidly drawn boundaries which are treated as limiting conditions.
● Failure to identify and examine the assumptions you are making to ensure that they are not restricting the development of new ideas.
● Polarizing alternatives – reducing every decision to an 'either/or' when there may be other ways of looking at things.
● Being conditioned to think sequentially rather than laterally and looking for the 'best' idea, not different ideas. As de Bono says: 'It is better to have enough ideas for some of them to be wrong than always to be right by having no ideas at all.'
● Lack of effort in challenging the obvious – it is tempting to slip into the easy solution.
● Evaluating too quickly – jumping to conclusions and not giving yourself enough time to allow your imagination to range freely over other possible ways of looking at things.
● A tendency to conform – to give the answer expected.
● Fear of looking foolish or being put down.

How to develop your ability to think creatively

If you want to think more creatively, the first thing to do is to analyse yourself. Go through the list of barriers to creativity and ask yourself the question, 'Is this me?' If it is, think about ways in which you can overcome the difficulty, concentrating on:

● Breaking away from any restrictions.
● Opening up your mind to generate new ideas.
● Delaying judgement until you have thoroughly explored the alternative ideas.

Breaking away
To break away from the constraints on your ability to generate new ideas you should:

- Identify the dominant ideas influencing your thinking.
- Define the boundaries (ie past experience, precedents, policies, procedures, rules) within which you are working and try to get outside them by asking questions such as:
  - Are the constraints reasonable?
  - Is past experience reliable?
  - What's new about the present situation?
  - Is there another way?

- Bring your assumptions out into the open and challenge any which restrict your freedom to develop new ideas.
- Reject 'either/or' propositions – ask, 'Is there really a simple choice between alternatives?'
- Keep on asking 'Why?' (But bear in mind that if you do this too bluntly to other people you can antagonize them.)

Generating new ideas

To generate new ideas you have to open up your mind. If you have removed some of the constraints as suggested above you will be in a better position to:

- Look at the situation differently, exploring all possible angles.
- List as many alternative approaches as possible without seeking the 'one best way' (there is no such thing) and without indulging in premature evaluation (which can only lead to partial satisfaction).
- In de Bono's words, 'arrange discontinuity', deliberately set out to break the mould. The techniques for triggering off new ideas include:
  - free thinking, allowing your mind to wander over alternative and in many cases apparently irrelevant ways of looking at the situation;
  - deliberately exposing yourself to new influences in the form of people, articles, books, indeed anything which might give you a different insight, even though it might not be immediately relevant;
  - switching yourself or other people from problem to problem;
  - arranging for the cross-fertilization of ideas with other people;
  - using analogies to spark off ideas. The analogy should be suggested by the problem but should then be allowed to exist in its own right to indicate a different way of looking at the problem.

Delaying judgement

Your aim in creative thinking should be to separate the evaluation of ideas from their generation. The worst mistake you can make is to kill off new ideas too quickly. It is always easy to find 10 ways of saying 'no' to anything. For example:

- It won't work.
- We're already doing it.
- It's been tried before without success.
- It's not practical.
- It won't solve the problem.
- It's too risky.
- It's based on pure theory.
- It will cost too much.
- It will antagonize the customers/the boss/the union/the workers/the shareholders, etc.
- It will create more problems than it solves.

Some of these objections may be valid. But they should be held back until you have generated as many ideas as possible. Allow ideas to grow a little. Don't strangle them at birth.

It is too easy to say 'no', too easy to ridicule anything new or different. In creative thinking it is the end result that counts, and if you want it to be original you must not worry too much about the route you follow to get there. It doesn't matter if you stumble sometimes or take the wrong turning, as long as delays are not protracted and you arrive in the right place at the end.

As de Bono (12) says:

> In vertical thinking one has to be right at every step. So, no matter how many steps are taken, the end point (idea, solution, conclusion) is automatically right if all the intervening steps have been right... In lateral thinking one does not *have* to be right at each step, but one must be right at the *end*.

Delaying judgement is difficult. It goes against the grain. You have to make a conscious effort to hold back until the right moment arrives, which is when you feel that you have collected as many new ideas as you can in the time available.

Our training, our inhibitions, our reluctance to look foolish or to go out on a limb all work against us. We should certainly try to do it ourselves and persuade other people to go along with us. But we can help the processes of opening up, introducing discontinuity and releasing new ideas by the technique of brainstorming.

Brainstorming

Brainstorming has been defined as a means of getting a large number of ideas from a group of people in a short time. It is essentially a group activity which uses a formal setting to generate as many ideas as possible without pausing to evaluate them.

The main features of a brainstorming session are as follows:

1. A group of between six and twelve people is assembled. Some will be directly involved with the problem, some should be drawn from other areas from which they can bring different ideas and experience to bear on the problem. There is a chairman and a note-taker.
2. The chairman defines the rules, emphasizing that:

   – The aim is to get as many ideas as possible.
   – No attempt will be made to evaluate any ideas.
   – No one should feel inhibited about coming up with suggestions.

3. If necessary there is a warm-up session to familiarize the group with the procedure. For example, they could be asked to suggest how many uses they can think of for a paper clip.
4. The chairman states the problem, avoiding the trap of defining it too narrowly.
5. The chairman opens the session by a phrase such as 'In how many ways can we...?'
6. The chairman encourages people to contribute and prevents any attempt to evaluate ideas. From time to time he or she may restate the problem.
7. The note-taker condenses the ideas suggested and lists then on flip charts, not attempting to act as an editor or worrying about duplications at this stage. The session should not be tape recorded as this may inhibit ideas.
8. The chairman keeps on encouraging the group to contribute, trying to get people to freewheel and produce as many ideas as possible – good, bad, indifferent, sensible or silly. He or she keeps the pace going and never comments or allows

anyone else to comment on a contribution. Every idea is treated as relevant.

9. The chairman closes the meeting after 30 minutes or so – 45 minutes at most. The session must not be allowed to drag on.
10. Evaluation takes place later, possibly with a different group. At this session the aim is to:

   – Select ideas for immediate use.
   – Identify ideas for further exploration.
   – Review any different approaches which have been revealed by the session.

Brainstorming is a useful technique for releasing ideas, overcoming inhibitions, cross-fertilizing ideas and getting away from patterned thinking. It needs to be planned and executed carefully and proper evaluation is essential.

Use it selectively, where there seems to be ample scope for different ideas. It will not solve all your problems but can help you to crash through the barriers erected by the traditional approaches to decision-making.

Remember that however creative you are, what you finally decide on has to work. Brainstorming and other techniques for increasing creativity will help you to break new ground, but eventually you will have to think clearly and analytically about the pros and cons of the preferred solution before making your final decision.

INNOVATION

Innovation is the life-blood of an organization. There is nothing so stultifying to a company – or the people in it – as a belief that the old ways must be the best ways. An organization which tries to stand still will not survive.

Innovation requires a blend of creativity, clear thinking and the ability to get things done. It requires thinkers and doers to work closely together. Top management must create a climate in which managers have the scope to develop new ideas and the resources to implement them.

The success of innovative projects, therefore, can be seen to depend on two issues: the characteristics of the individual manager and the climate of the organization.

Organizational characteristics

The organizational characteristics which encourage innovation are:

- A free flow of information which allows executives to find ideas in unexpected places and pushes them to combine fragments of information.
- Close and frequent contact between departments, and an emphasis on lateral as well as vertical relationships providing resources, information and support.
- A tradition of working in teams and sharing credit.
- Senior executives who believe in innovation and will make the necessary resources available.
- Managers with the ability and desire to seize opportunities and to make time available for innovation.

Individual characteristics

To be an effective innovator you need:

- To have a clear initial view of the results you want to achieve – you should not worry too much to begin with about the ways of achieving them.
- To define clearly the aims and benefits of the project.
- To argue the case for the project persuasively.
- To elicit support not only from your boss but also from your colleagues and subordinates – you need to build a coalition in which everyone shares equally in the belief that the project is worth while.
- Courage – to take calculated risks and to weather the storm when the inevitable setbacks occur.
- To be good at getting people to act – mobilizing people to contribute fully to the project means using a participative management style.
- Power to mobilize support and resources and to achieve results.
- The ability to handle interference or opposition to the project – resistance can be open, but it often takes a passive or covert

form: criticism of the plan's details, foot-dragging, late responses to requests, or arguments over allocation of time and resources among projects. Covert resistance can be the most dangerous.

● The force of character to maintain momentum, especially after the initial enthusiasm for the project has waned and the team is involved in more tedious work.

14

Crisis management

WHAT IS CRISIS MANAGEMENT?

The phase 'crisis management' was coined by Robert Macnamara at the time of the Cuban missile crisis when we said: 'There is no longer any such thing as strategy, only crisis management.'

Crisis management is a phrase used most commonly in diplomatic circles but it is something that happens in any organization where the pressure of events – external or internal – forces management into making urgent decisions. These arise because a crisis is a turning-point or a time of danger and suspense, and, in this turbulent age, turning-points and dangerous moments are always with us.

Crisis management can be defined as:

> The process of dealing with a pressurized situation in a way which plans, organizes, directs and controls a number of interrelated operations and guides the decision-making process of those in charge to a rapid but unhurried resolution of the acute problem faced by the organization.

CAUSES OF CRISES

Crises are caused either by the actions of human beings or by natural disasters – fire, flood, earthquake, etc. If people are at the root of the crisis they may be deliberately inflicting harm on the organization from outside or, also externally, they may have taken actions which indirectly create a major problem. Internally, crises can be caused deliberately by people attempting to enforce their point of view or accidentally by some colossal misjudgement or a long history of compounded errors.

Crises may, however, be no more than sudden, unforeseen events which perhaps could have been anticipated. To dismiss strategy, as Macnamara did, is perhaps going too far, but Robert Burns did suggest that: 'The best laid schemes o' mice an' men gang aft a-gley', and this is as true today as when he wrote it in the eighteenth century.

In an ideal world, crises would not happen. You would know where you want to go and you would get there, with only minor deviations along the way. Problems would have been foreseen and contingency plans made to deal with them. This, of course, is not the way things are in real life. Murphy's law is always ready to strike again – if anything can go wrong it will.

Crises may appear to come suddenly, but this does not mean that they are unforeseeable. The Garcia Márquez novella, *Chronicle of a Death Foretold*, was written about a crisis, the murder of a young man, but, as the title implies, everyone knew it was going to happen only no one seemed able to stop it. Prior to a crisis there are often warning signs that disaster is about to strike. Even a volcanic explosion can be predicted.

There is a phenomenon which can be described as 'crisis slide'. Gradually, imperceptibly but inevitably, there is a build-up of events. Rain falls in ever-increasing volumes; the overflowing river is joined by equally overflowing streams, and the pressure increases. The force becomes progressively more irresistible until, under overwhelming pressure, the dam breaks. The crisis management process should, of course, have started as soon as observers had noticed the unusually heavy rainfall. Human error, however, creeps in and dams burst.

Steady slides down the slippery slope to an outright crisis can also happen, not because of human error, but because of human cussedness. If crisis management techniques are used coolly to assess potentially dangerous situations and bring the parties together in good time to discuss how to resolve the problems before they become critical, the dire effects of cussedness can be avoided. This can happen on the international scene as well as within organizations. Before Cuba, President Kennedy had been made aware of 60 nuclear near-disasters, including the launching of two missiles with nuclear warheads. He took steps not only to improve the US system of accident proofing but also to exchange information with the Russians. The Falklands crisis, however, was a sad story of a complete failure of the British both to understand how strongly the Argentines felt about the Malvinas and to appreciate that Galtieri was liable to go off the rails.

MANAGEMENT CRISES

In management all sorts of crises can happen: a takeover bid, a collapse in the foreign exchange rate, a drug which has disastrous side-effects, a competitive product which suddenly appears on the market and wipes the floor with a market leader brand, an innovation which renders a product obsolete, a sudden damaging strike, a dishonest senior executive who gets the company into the headlines, a fire or a flood, the departure of key members of the management team to competitors, and so on. The list is endless.

Tolstoy said of marriages: 'All happy families resemble one another, but each unhappy family is unhappy in its own way.' The same can be said of crises. Each crisis is a unique event and has to be dealt with accordingly. However, there are certain types of behaviour which are appropriate in all critical situations and there are some general principles that can be followed in crises involving negotiation or conflict. There are also a number of crisis management techniques that are generally applicable, subject to modification to suit particular circumstances.

CRISIS MANAGEMENT BEHAVIOUR

The most important thing to do in a crisis is to keep cool. As Kipling put it:

If you can keep your head when all about you
Are losing theirs and blaming it on you...
Yours is the Earth and everything that's in it
And – which is more – you'll be a Man, my son.

Perhaps the best exponent of this approach was Harold Macmillan who said at London Airport of a political crisis in his Cabinet: 'I thought the best thing to do was to settle up these little local difficulties, and then turn to the wider vision of the Commonwealth.' But another Prime Minister, James Callaghan, went too far when he said, also at London Airport (a great place for aphorisms), 'Crisis, what crisis?'

Statesmen, of course, have to give the impression of playing it cool. Henry Kissinger, who spent his whole diplomatic career in crisis management, said once: 'There cannot be a crisis next week. My schedule is already full.' But managers should play it cool too.

One of the arts of dealing with a crisis is to maintain the confidence of everyone around that you *are* managing it. Insouciance like Macmillan's, but not like Callaghan's, is one way of doing this. Another way is deliberately to give the impression that you are taking it easy – relaxing almost – when in actual fact you are working at top speed. Good crisis managers, in situations where all hell is let loose, and people and pieces of paper are being thrown about in all directions, and three telephones are ringing at once, will, from time to time, lean back in their chair, sip a cup of coffee, and idly gossip about last night's football game. They then resume work with redoubled energy. Robert Townsend (62) described this approach well in *Up the Organization* when he wrote: 'There is a time for engagement and a time for withdrawal. A time to contemplate it, and a time just to laugh at it.'

And in *The Right Stuff*, Tom Wolfe, in describing how Chuck Yeager (the man who broke the sound barrier for the first time with two broken ribs) influenced the crisis management style of airline pilots, wrote this about their approach:

> Anyone who travels very much on airlines in the United States soon gets to know the voice of the airline pilot... coming over the intercom... with a particular drawl, a particular folksiness, a particular down-home calmness that is so exaggerated it begins to parody itself (nevertheless! – it's reassuring)... the voice that tells you, as the airliner is caught in thunderheads and goes bolting up and down a thousand feet at a single gulp, to check your seat belt because 'it might get a little choppy'.

NEGOTIATING SITUATIONS

Crises concerning takeovers, industrial relations, legal disputes and other problems where the crunch has come because two sides have radically different views, will often involve negotiations. The normal negotiating tactics described in Chapter 33 will apply, although they may have to be speeded up.

In tense situations, special ploys may have to be used. For example, you can use the 'Trollope' ploy, which is the acceptance of an offer that has not been made in order to induce the adversary to accept the acceptance. Robert Kennedy coined this term, naming it after those Victorian heroines in the novels of Anthony Trollope who interpret a squeeze of the hand on the hero's part as a proposal of marriage and succeed in making this interpretation stick. It was used in the Cuban missile crisis where the ambiguity arose in communications from Mr Krushchev. He sent two letters, one implying a hard line about the American blockade, the other a mild and even yielding one. To deepen the confusion, it was not clear whether the 'hawklike' letter (which was received second) had been written before or after the 'dovelike' one. The American decision (the Trollope ploy) was to treat the dovelike letter as the true communication, ignoring the other hawklike one which was probably written second as the Russian's final position. As reported by Robert Kennedy, it was this creative use of ambiguity which enabled the settlement to be reached.

In negotiations it can indeed be said that a shadow of ambiguity over a situation may be as effective as real strength. It gives you more room to manoeuvre and more scope to vary your tactics.

WHEN TO FIGHT

In a crisis, the decision about when and how hard to fight is a matter of judgement. You can go in for aggressive brinkmanship or progressive appeasement, but either of these approaches will be inadequate if taken to an extreme.

At this stage it might be a good idea to remember Krushchev's message to Kennedy during the Cuban missile crisis: 'If people do not show wisdom, then in the final analysis they will come to a clash, like blind moles, and then reciprocal extermination will begin.'

The decision on tactics is never an easy one. It was said by Clausewitz that: 'War is nothing but the continuation of politics with the admixture of other means', and you should normally wait to launch an attack until you are certain that the normal process of peaceful negotiation is not going to get you anywhere.

The decision will also be affected by your ability to understand your opponent's strategy and tactics so that you can take pre-emptive action. Crisis management is very much about analysing other people's motives, intentions and ploys, and responding accordingly. Another adage from Clausewitz is worth bearing in mind: 'Despise the enemy strategically, respect him tactically.' In other words you may be quite certain that in the longer term your opponent will come to grief, but in the short term he may fight hard and you may have to fight back equally hard. Losing one battle may not lose the war but a succession of defeats must prejudice your chances, however just your cause and however superior your strategy.

Thomas Schelling (55), a leading commentator on crisis management, commented wisely on the fight or flight decision as follows:

> What is in dispute is usually not the momentary right of way, but everyone's expectations about how a participant will behave in the future. To yield is a signal that one can be expected to yield. To yield often or continuously may communicate an acknowledgement that that is one's role. To yield readily up to some limit, and then say 'enough', may guarantee that the first show of obduracy loses the game for both sides.

Crisis management may or may not take place within a well-defined strategy but, whatever happens, the tactics have got to be worked out on the basis of a complete understanding of the situation, especially those aspects of it which concern other people's intentions. If you yield, then, as Schelling says, take care to ensure that, because you have misunderstood or underestimated your opponent, he will not take advantage of it. Beware also of the possibility that both of you might lose in the end.

If you decide to fight, remember the following precepts of St Augustine and St Thomas Aquinas on what is a just war:

1. Just cause.
2. Right intention.
3. A reasonable chance of success.

4. If successful, a better situation than would prevail in the absence of action.
5. Force used (or threatened) should be proportional to the objective sought (or the evil repressed).
6. The intention should be to spare non-combatants or at least have a reasonable prospect of doing so.

CRISIS MANAGEMENT TECHNIQUES

In *The Conventions of Crisis*, Coral Bell (8) wrote:

> Looking back over the history of the postwar crisis as a whole, one is struck by a sense of how often the decision-makers seem to have been 'playing it off the cuff', acting on the promptings of intuition or temperament rather than plan or logic.

This highlights the biggest pitfall crisis managers can walk into in industry and commerce as well as in international affairs. All too easily they feel that instant and decisive action is required. Under acute pressure they do not look before they leap and they fall into the elephant trap.

Crisis management starts with avoiding action, keeping your finger on the pulse so that as soon as the pace hots up – at the first signs of the beginning of a crisis slide – you can take pre-emptive action. At this stage you have time to think, to consider contingency plans and to put them into effect.

If, however, in spite of all your efforts, you are faced with a crisis, the following is a checklist of the 10 steps you should take:

1. Sit back as coolly as you can and assess the situation. You may have to go through the analytical and thinking process five times as fast as usual, but do it. You need to establish:

    ● What exactly is happening.
    ● Why it is happening.
    ● What is likely to happen unless something is done about it.
    ● How quickly you *have* to act to prevent further damage.
    ● Who else is involved.
    ● Who is likely to be involved.
    ● What resources you have got – people, equipment, finance, back-up from other organizations, access to people with influence.

2. Draw up your preliminary plan of action – set it out step by step and prepare other contingency plans to deal with eventualities.

3. Line up a crisis management team to deal with the situation. Allocate roles and tasks and authorities to act (you may have to give emergency authority to some people).

4. Set up a crisis management centre (your office, the board room).

5. Set up a communications system so that you receive instant intelligence on what is happening and can put your messages across to the members of your team and anyone else whom you want to take action.

6. 'Load shed' when you can on the principle of the electrical system which sheds part of the load when the total load rises above a certain point. This means getting rid of any peripheral problems as quickly as possible.

7. Put items on the 'back burner', ie relegate problems to a non-crisis area where they can be dealt with at leisure.

8. Prepare your detailed plans, which will include:

    ● time-scales – act now or later;
    ● scope for a cooling-off period;
    ● longer-term solutions to be prepared and implemented at the right time;
    ● contingency plans to deal with new developments or emergencies.

9. Monitor continuously exactly what is happening. Ensure that you get the information you need fast so that you can react quickly but without panicking.

10. Evaluate actions and reactions continuously so that you can modify the plan and swiftly take corrective or pre-emptive steps.

QUALITIES OF A CRISIS MANAGER

Good crisis managers are decisive. They can react swiftly but their great skill is in being able to speed up the decision-making process. They will not miss out any steps in the standard problem-solving, decision-making sequence:

- define the situation;
- specify objectives;
- develop hypotheses;
- gather the facts;
- analyse the facts;
- consider possible courses of action;
- evaluate possible courses of action;
- decide and implement;
- monitor implementation.

Effective crisis managers will get through these stages more quickly, using their own experience and intelligence and that of their team.

Crisis managers buy time by putting issues on the back burner but, like all good managers, they can make things happen fast when they want to. They are good leaders – providing inspiration to their team, encouraging their efforts and giving them confidence in the successful outcome of the crisis management process.

Finally, and most important, they keep cool. They do not panic, they do not over-react, they do not lose their heads. In fact, they deliberately slow down the pace, when they can, to give the impression that everything is under control and it is all going according to plan.

To sum up, crisis management is no more than good management under pressure. The adrenalin may flow faster but this concentrates the mind wonderfully. Good managers thrive under pressure and they are the good crisis managers.

CRISIS MANAGEMENT TECHNIQUES – ORGANIZATIONAL

From an organizational viewpoint, crisis management is not a quick fix solution. It entails identifying, studying and forecasting crisis issues and setting forth specific ways that would enable the organization to prevent or cope with crisis. This is a long-term commitment. A systematic, orderly way is required to manage a crisis and many crises can be prevented – or at least coped with effectively – through early detection.

A crisis audit is a useful approach to adopt. It means identifying potential issues, assessing the probability that they will occur and estimating their likely impact. On the basis of this audit a contingency plan can be developed which sets out the main steps that should be taken to deal with the crisis and who will be involved in managing it.

15

Culture management

WHAT IS CORPORATE CULTURE?

Corporate culture is the pattern of shared beliefs, attitudes, assumptions and values in an organization. These may not have been articulated but in the absence of direct instructions shape the way people act and interact, and strongly influence the ways in which things get done. Corporate culture manifests itself in the form of:

- *Values* – beliefs on what is best or good for the organization and what sort of behaviour is desirable. They usually refer to such matters as the need for quality, customer care, teamwork, excellence, innovation, and concern for people.
- *Norms* – the unwritten rules of behaviour, the 'rules of the game', which provide informal guidelines on how to behave. Norms refer to such aspects of behaviour as how managers treat people, the work ethic, eg 'work hard, play hard', or how much importance is attached to status.
- *Organizational climate* – how people perceive (see and feel

about) the culture that has been created in their company or unit. It can be measured by the use of attitude surveys.

● *Management style* – the way in which managers behave as leaders and how they exercise authority. Managers can be autocratic or democratic, tough or soft, demanding or easy-going, directive or laissez-faire, distant or accessible, destructive or supportive, task orientated or people orientated, rigid or flexible, considerate or unfeeling, friendly or cold, keyed up or relaxed.

THE SIGNIFICANCE OF CULTURE

The significance of culture arises because it is rooted in deeply held beliefs. It reflects what has worked in the past, being composed of responses which have been accepted because they have met with success.

Corporate culture can work for an organization by creating an environment which is conducive to performance improvement and the management of change. It can work against an organization by erecting barriers which prevent the attainment of corporate strategies. These barriers include resistance to change and lack of commitment.

The concept of 'cultural fit' is important. It refers to the fact that if innovations do not fit the existing culture they will not work unless the culture is changed to fit them. And culture change can be a long haul, especially when it is deeply embedded.

WHAT IS CULTURE MANAGEMENT?

Culture management is the process of developing or reinforcing an appropriate culture in the organization; that is, one which helps it to fulfil its purpose. It is about reinforcing or embedding an existing appropriate (functional) culture or changing one that is not working well (a dysfunctional culture). It is a matter of analysis and diagnosis followed by the application of appropriate reinforcement or change levers.

Culture management is concerned with:

● *Culture change*, the development of attitudes, beliefs and values which will be congruent with the organization's mission, strategies, environment and technologies. The aim is to achieve significant changes in organizational climate, management style and behaviour which positively support the achievement of the organization's objectives.

● *Culture reinforcement*, which aims to preserve and reinforce what is good or functional about the present culture.

● *Change management*, which is concerned with enabling the culture to adapt successfully to change and gaining acceptance to changes in organization, systems, procedures and methods of work (see Chapter 3).

● *Enhancing commitment*, which is about increasing the commitment of members of the organization to its mission, strategies and values (see Chapter 6).

SUPPORTING AND CHANGING CULTURES

While it may not be possible to define an ideal structure or to prescribe how it can be developed, it is certain that embedded cultures exert considerable influence on organizational behaviour and therefore performance. If there *is* an appropriate and effective culture, it would be desirable to take steps to support or reinforce it. If the culture is inappropriate, attempts should be made to determine what needs to be changed and to develop and implement plans for change.

Culture analysis

In either case, the first step is to analyse the existing culture. This can be done through questionnaires, surveys and discussions in focus groups or workshops. It is often helpful to involve people in analysing the outcome of surveys, getting them to produce a diagnosis of the cultural issues facing the organization and to participate in the development and implementation of plans and programmes to deal with any issues.

Culture support and reinforcement

Culture support and reinforcement programmes aim to preserve and underpin what is good and functional about the present culture by:

- re-affirming existing values through discussions and communications;
- ensuring that values are put into practice (operationalizing them);
- using the core values defined for the organization (the value set) as headings for reviewing individual and team performance – emphasizing that people are expected to uphold the values;
- ensuring that induction procedures cover core values and how people are expected to achieve them;
- reinforcing induction training on further training courses set up as part of a continuous development programme.

Culture change

The process of managing cultural change can be modelled as three interlocking circles as shown in Figure 15.1.

The three key factors are:

- *Vision and commitment* – top management must articulate their vision of the culture they would like to have. They must then show their commitment by working within the articulated vision.
- *Communication* – people need to understand and work through the rationale of the reasons for culture change, what it means

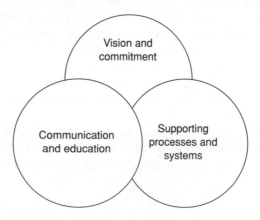

Figure 15.1 *The elements of culture change*

for them and how they, the organization and its other stake-holders will benefit.

- *Supporting processes and systems* – education and training, performance management, reward systems.

The circles interlock because each of these elements must move forward together in harmony to achieve successful culture change.

In normal circumstances, cultural change programmes tend to focus on one or two particular areas which it is felt need to be given priority. They rarely, if ever, try to cover every aspect of organizational culture. The areas might, for example, be performance, commitment, quality, customer service or teamwork. In each case the underpinning values would need to be defined. It would probably be necessary to prioritize by deciding which areas need the most urgent attention. There is a limit to how much can be done at once. The effectiveness of culture change programmes largely depends on the quality of change management processes as described in Chapter 3.

Levers for change

Having identified what needs to be done and the priorities, the next step is to consider what levers for change exist and how they can be used. The levers could include, as appropriate:

- *performance* – performance-related or competency-related pay schemes; performance management processes; gain-sharing; leadership training, skills development;
- *commitment* – communication, participation and involvement programmes; developing a climate of co-operation and trust; clarifying the psychological contract;
- *quality* – total quality programmes;
- *customer service* – customer care programmes;
- *teamwork* – teambuilding; team performance management; team rewards;
- *values* – gaining understanding, acceptance and commitment through involvement in defining values, performance management processes and employee development interventions.

16

Customer care

The achievement of high standards of customer care is generally recognized as an essential element in achieving competitive edge. Customer care is concerned with looking after customers to ensure that their wants, needs and expectations are met or exceeded, thus creating customer satisfaction and loyalty. It refers to everything an organization does when it provides services to its customers. It is also about delighting customers. The aim is not just to meet their needs but to go further – to give them something valuable which they did not expect, which, perhaps, they did not even know they wanted.

AIMS OF CUSTOMER CARE

The aims of customer care are:

1. to improve customer service by managing all customer contacts to mutual benefit;
2. to persuade customers to purchase again – not to switch brands or change to another supplier;

3. to increase the profitability of a business or the effectiveness of a service provider organization.

WHY CUSTOMER CARE?

It was Jan Carlson of Scandinavian Airlines System (SAS) who popularized the phrase 'moments of truth', pointing out that whenever customers came into contact with any part of the organization, the whole is judged by the bit they have seen. Customer care can therefore enhance the organization's reputation generally.

The need to improve levels of customer care also arises from competitive pressures. Companies compete on the quality of the goods and services they offer, and this extends not only to the products and services themselves but also to the ways in which the service is delivered.

THE MEANING OF CUSTOMER SERVICE

Customer service is to a certain degree intangible because it is about performance – the manner in which the service is delivered, as well as about outcomes – what the customer actually gets.

The main factors determining the level of customer service as listed by Pasuram *et al* (46) are:

1. *Reliability* – consistency of performance and dependability;
2. *Responsiveness* – the willingness or readiness to provide service;
3. *Competence* – having the required skills and knowledge to perform the service;
4. *Access* – approachability and ease of contact;
5. *Courtesy* – politeness, respect, consideration and friendliness of contact personnel;
6. *Communication* – keeping the customers informed in language they can understand and listening to them;
7. *Credibility* – trustworthiness, believability, honesty;
8. *Security* – freedom from danger, risk or doubt;
9. *Understanding/knowing the customer* – making the effort to understand the customer's needs;
10. *Tangibles* – the physical evidence of service.

ESTABLISHING CUSTOMER EXPECTATIONS

When developing customer care initiatives it is necessary to establish what the customer expects in terms of 'deliverables': conformity to specifications, quality, price, reliability in service, delivery dates, price and after-sales service. The two fundamental questions to be answered are: (1) what services do existing and potential customers want? and (2) what service is provided by competitors?

Establishing customer expectations can be done by surveying customers. Abbey Life sent out questionnaires to 1,000 clients in each of its business sections. On the credit side, this revealed that customers were satisfied with the time it took for their letters to be answered. But there was dissatisfaction with replies, which customers felt did not fully answer their questions. The company now believes it has solved this problem.

Customer expectations can also be assessed by using market research techniques such as opinion surveys and focus groups.

Further information can be obtained from data the organization may already have in the form of analyses of customer complaints and questions. The opinion of staff about what *their* customers want is worth having. Industry data published by trade associations and in journals is another source.

SETTING CUSTOMER SERVICE STANDARDS

Customer service standards are related to the key aspects of customer service which have been revealed by surveys of customer expectations and present arrangements. The aim is to distil the information to identify critical customer service success factors. These are likely to fall into several main categories:

- speed of response and processing of orders, enquiries, complaints, requests for service or spare parts;
- quality of response to enquiries or complaints;
- backlog of enquiries or complaints;
- in call centres, call pick up and lost call rate;
- number of complaints (as a proportion of total orders);
- time taken between order and delivery;
- the extent to which customer expectations have been met in service delivery;
- customer reactions to service and perceptions of service quality.

MEASURING AND MONITORING CUSTOMER SERVICE LEVELS

The measurement of quality service levels is the basis for monitoring and managing customer care. The starting point is to define standards as described above. The next step is to decide how to measure and monitor the achievement of those standards so that corrective action can be taken. In the formative stages of developing a customer care strategy, measurements indicate where the priorities lie by highlighting areas for concern. The main measurement and monitoring techniques are customer questionnaires, customer surveys, mystery shopping and benchmarking.

DEVELOPING A CUSTOMER CARE STRATEGY

Customer care strategies indicate the intentions of the organization concerning the maintenance and improvement of customer service levels. They emphasize the customer orientation of the business and the part everyone is expected to play.

The customer care strategy sets out the organization's intentions with regard to:

- the analysis of customer expectations and reactions;
- setting standards;
- measuring and monitoring performance against the standards;
- providing information to staff on the importance of customer care (a communication strategy);
- providing leadership to staff;
- training staff;
- rewarding teams and individuals for good performance;
- helping and supporting people to improve performance;
- attending to the needs of both internal and external customers;
- generally developing a customer care culture which includes managing change, especially the transition from the existing to the desired.

17

Delegating

You can't do everything yourself, so you have to delegate. At first sight delegation looks simple. Just tell people what you want them to do and then let them do it. But there is more to it than that.

It may be that you would wish to delegate everything except what your subordinate cannot do. But you cannot then withdraw. You have arranged for someone else to do the job, but you have not passed on the responsibility for it. You are always accountable to your superior for what your subordinate does. Hence, as is often said, you can't delegate responsibility.

Delegation is difficult. It is perhaps the hardest task that managers have to do. The problem is achieving the right balance between delegating too much or too little and between over- or under-supervision. When you give people a job to do you have to make sure that it is done. And you have to do that without breathing down their neck, wasting your time and theirs, and getting in the way. There has to be trust as well as guidance and supervision.

ADVANTAGES OF DELEGATION

- It relieves you of routine and less critical tasks.
- If frees you for more important work – planning, organizing, motivating and controlling.
- It extends your capacity to manage.
- It reduces delay in decision-making – as long as authority is delegated close to the point of action.
- It allows decisions to be taken at the level where the details are known.
- It develops the capacity of staff to make decisions, achieve objectives and take responsibility.

THE PROCESS OF DELEGATION

Delegation is a process which can follow a sequence from total control (no freedom of action for the individual to whom work has been allocated) to full devolution (the individual is completely empowered to carry out the work), as illustrated in Figure 17.1.

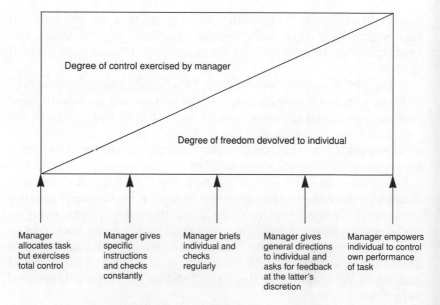

Figure 17.1 *The delegation sequence*

WHEN TO DELEGATE

You should delegate when:

● You have more work than you can effectively carry out yourself.
● You cannot allocate sufficient time to your priority tasks.
● You want to develop your subordinate.
● The job can be done adequately by your subordinate.

HOW TO DELEGATE

When you delegate you have to decide:

● What to delegate.
● To whom you delegate – choosing who does the work.
● How to inform or brief your subordinate – giving out the work.
● How you will guide and develop your subordinate.
● How you will monitor his or her performance.

What to delegate

You delegate tasks that you don't need to do yourself. You are not just ridding yourself of the difficult, tedious or unrewarding tasks. Neither are you trying to win for yourself an easier life. Delegation will, in fact, make your life more difficult, but also more rewarding.

Clearly, you delegate routine and repetitive tasks which you cannot reasonably be expected to do yourself – as long as you use the time you have won productively.

You also delegate specialist tasks to those who have the skills and know-how to do them. You cannot do it all yourself. Nor can you be expected to know it all yourself. You have to know how to select and use expertise. There will be no problem as long as you make it clear what you want from the experts and ask – if necessary force – them to present it to you in a usable way. As a manager you must know what specialists can do for you and you should be knowledgeable enough about the subject to understand whether or not what they produce is worth having.

Choosing who does the work

Ideally, the person you choose to do the work should have the knowledge, skills, motivation and time needed to get it done to your complete satisfaction. Frequently, however, you will have to use someone who has less than ideal experience, knowledge or skills. In these cases you should try to select an individual who has intelligence, natural aptitude and, above all, willingness to learn how to do the job with help and guidance. This is how people develop, and the development of your staff should be your conscious aim whenever you delegate.

You are looking for someone you can trust. You don't want to over-supervise, so you have to believe that the person you select will get on with it and have the sense to come to you when stuck or before making a bad mistake.

How do you know whom you can trust? The best way is to try people out first on smaller and less important tasks, increasingly giving them more scope so that they learn how far they can go and you can observe how they do it. If they get on well, their sense of responsibility and powers of judgement will increase and improve and you will be able to trust them with more demanding and responsible tasks.

Giving out the work

When you delegate you should ensure that your subordinates understand:

● Why the work needs to be done.
● What they are expected to do.
● The date by which they are expected to do it.
● The authority they have to make decisions.
● The problems they must refer back.
● The progress or completion reports they should submit.
● How you propose to guide and monitor them.
● The resources and help they will have to complete the work.

Subordinates may need guidance on how the work should be done. The extent to which you spell it out will clearly depend on how much they already know about how to do the work. You don't want to give directions in such laborious detail that you run the risk of stifling initiative. As long as you are sure they will do the job without breaking the law, exceeding the budget, embarrassing you or seriously upsetting people, let them get on with it. Follow Robert Heller's golden rule: 'If you can't do something yourself, find someone who can – and then let him do it in his own sweet way.'

You can make a distinction between *hard* and *soft* delegation. Hard delegation takes place when you tell someone exactly what to do, how to do it and when you want the results. You spell it out, confirm it in writing and make a note in your diary of the date when you expect the job to be completed. And then you follow up regularly.

Soft delegation takes place when you agree generally what has to be achieved and leave your subordinate to get on with it. You should still agree limits of authority, define the decisions to be referred to you, say what exception reports you want (see Chapter 10), and indicate when and how you will review progress. Then you sit back until the results are due and observe from afar, only coming closer for periodical progress meetings, or when the exception reports suggests that something needs looking into, or when a problem or decision is referred to you.

You should always delegate by the results you expect. Even if you do not need to specify *exactly* how the results should be achieved, it is a good idea when delegating a problem to ask your subordinates how they propose to solve it. You then have the opportunity to provide guidance at the outset; guidance at a later stage may be seen as interference.

Guidance and development

Delegation not only helps you to get your work done; it can be used to improve your subordinates' performance and therefore your trust in their ability to carry out more responsible work. Instruction, training and development are part of the process of delegation.

Monitoring performance

At first you may have to monitor your subordinates' performance carefully. But the sooner you can relax and watch progress informally the better.

You will have set target dates, and you should keep a reminder of these in your diary so that you can ensure they are achieved. Don't allow your subordinates to become careless about meeting deadlines.

Without being oppressive, you should ensure that progress reports are made when required and that you discuss deviations from the original plan in good time. You will have clearly indicated to your subordinates the extent of their authority to act without further reference to you. They must therefore expect to be reprimanded if on any occasion they exceed their brief or fail to keep you informed. You don't want any surprises and your subordinates must understand that you will not tolerate being kept in the dark.

Try to restrain yourself from undue interference in the way the work is being done. It is, after all, the results that count. Of course, you must step in if there is any danger of things going off the rails. The Nelson touch is all right if your subordinate is a Nelson, but how many Nelsons have you got? Rash decisions, over-expenditure and ignoring defined and reasonable constraints and rules must be prevented.

There is a delicate balance to be achieved between hedging people around with restrictions which may appear petty and allowing them licence to do what they like. You must use your knowledge of your subordinates and the circumstances to decide where the balance should be struck. The best delegators are those who have a comprehensive understanding of the strengths and weaknesses of their staff and the situation in which they are working.

Above all, avoid 'river banking'. This happens when a boss gives a subordinate a task which is more or less impossible to do. As the subordinate is 'going down' for the third time the boss is observed in a remote and safe position on the river bank saying: 'It's easy really, all you need to do is to try a bit harder.'

THE THOUGHTS OF SOME SUCCESSFUL DELEGATORS

John H Johnson, editor and publisher of Johnson Publishing Company, chief executive officer of Supreme Life Insurance Company and on the board of many large US corporations, said of his delegation techniques: 'I want to be big and I want to be bigger and I can't do it all by myself. So I try to do only those things that I can't get anyone else to do.'

Franklin D Roosevelt used a particularly ruthless technique based on competition, when he requested his aides to find some information. One of his aides told the story as follows: 'He would call you in, and he'd ask you to get the story on some complicated business and you'd come back after a couple of days of hard labour and present the juicy morsel you'd uncovered under a stone somewhere and *then* you'd find out he knew all about it, along with something else you *didn't* know. Where he got this information from he wouldn't mention, usually, but after he had done this to you once or twice you got damn careful about your information.'

Robert Townsend's approach to delegation when he was chairman of Avis was to emphasize the need to delegate 'as many important matters as you can because that creates a climate in which people grow'.

Robert Magaven, when he started as the head of Safeway Food Stores, told his division managers: 'I don't know anything about the grocery business but you fellows do. From now on, you're running your division as if it were your own business. You don't take orders from anyone but me and I'm not going to give you orders. I'm going to hold you responsible.'

Franklin Moore related the following example of strong delegation: Ralf Cordiner, the head of General Electric in the US for 10 years, had a vice president who wanted to see him urgently about a problem. The vice president explained his problem, and the choices he thought he had. 'Now, Mr Cordiner,' he said, 'What should I do?' 'Do?' Cordiner answered, 'You'd damn well better get on an airplane and get back to your office and decide. And if you can't decide we'd better get someone who can.'

Peter Drucker (17), writing about responsibility, referred to a newspaper interview with a young American infantry captain in the Vietnam jungle. The reported asked: 'How in this confused situation can you retain command?' The captain replied: 'Around here, I am the only guy who is responsible. If these men don't know what to do when they run into an enemy in the jungle, I'm too far away to tell them. My job is to make sure they know. What they do depends on the situation which only they can judge. The responsibility is always mine, but the decision lies with whoever is on the spot.'

A CASE STUDY

A group of researchers studying how managers delegate found that the following was happening in one of the companies they were studying:

In the situations in which the men we were interviewing found themselves, the boss was usually a hurried, and sometimes a harried, man. He gave out broad, briefly stated assignments, expecting his subordinates to make sense out of them. He also expected them to decide what information they needed, to obtain that information and then to go ahead and carry out their assignments. In the case of repetitive tasks, the typical boss assumed that after a few trials his subordinates would know for themselves when a job needed doing.

Frequently the boss wasn't sure himself about which issues needed attention in his department. And although he knew what eventually had to be accomplished, often he had less idea than his subordinates about the approaches to take. It wasn't unusual, therefore, for the boss to be vague or even impatient when approached with questions about the job while it was going on. Usually he was much more assertive in describing what he wanted after a job was done than while it was in progress.

The production director came out of the board of directors' meeting where he had been roundly criticized for not getting the most out of his organization. He immediately called a meeting of his subordinates and told them: 'I don't intend to subject myself to such humiliation again. You men are paid to do your jobs; it's not up to me to do them for you. I don't know how you spend your time and I don't intend to try to find out. You know your responsibilities, and these figures bear out that you haven't discharged them properly. If the next report doesn't show a marked improvement, there will be some new faces around here.'

18

Developing people

INVESTING IN PEOPLE

The chairman of an advertising firm once said that his 'inventory goes up and down in the lift'. His prime resource – his working capital – was people. The same applies in any other sort of organization. Money matters, but the human beings who work there matter even more.

If you want to take a pragmatic view of people, regard them as an investment. They cost money to acquire and maintain and they should provide a return on that outlay; their value increases as they become more effective in their jobs and capable of taking on greater responsibility. In accounting terms, people may be treated like any other asset on the balance sheet, taking into account acquisition costs and their increasing value as they gain experience.

THE MANAGER'S CONTRIBUTION TO EFFECTIVE DEVELOPMENT

The following are 10 ways in which you can contribute to the effective development of your staff:

1. Determine the standards of performance required for each of the jobs you control.
2. Analyse the competences (knowledge and skills) relevant to the achievement of these standards. If necessary, seek help from specialized trainers to carry out this analysis.
3. Agree with the individuals concerned what these standards and competences are.
4. Review with these individuals their performance so that agreement can be reached on any gaps to be filled between what they can do and what they should be able to do.
5. Every time you give someone an instruction, treat it as a training opportunity. Encourage individuals to tell you how they would do the job. If they get it wrong, help them to work out the best way for themselves, progressively giving them less guidance so that they learn to stand on their own feet.
6. Allow for the learning curve. Don't expect too much, but do require trainees to improve at a pace which matches their natural aptitudes. Only bear down hard on people if they are clearly not trying – without any excuse.
7. Train and develop by example. Give people the opportunity to learn from the way you do things. Remember the truth of the saying that managers learn best how to manage by managing under a good manager. This principle applies equally well to other categories of job holders.
8. Remember that the prime responsibility for training and developing your staff rests with you. Your results depend on their competence. You neglect your training responsibilities at your peril. And you must not rely on the training department to do it for you. They can provide advice and help but cannot replace your capacity to train on the job.
9. Plan the training for your staff in accordance with a regular review of their training needs.
10. Remember to use a variety of training techniques such as job instruction, assignments, coaching, guided reading and computer-based training.

MANAGEMENT DEVELOPMENT

Management development is about improving the performance of existing managers, giving them opportunities for growth and development, and ensuring, as far as possible, that management succession is provided for.

Managers need to be given the opportunity to develop themselves. As Peter Drucker (16) wrote in *The Practice of Management*:

> Development is always self-development. Nothing could be more absurd than for the enterprise to assume responsibility for the development of a man. The responsibility rests with the individual, his abilities, his efforts... Every manager in a business has the opportunity to encourage self-development or to stifle it, to direct it or to misdirect it. He should be specifically assigned the responsibility for helping all men working with him to focus, direct and apply their self-development efforts productively. And every company can provide systematic development changes to its managers.

In Douglas McGregor's phrase, managers are grown – they are neither born nor made. And your role is to provide conditions favourable to foster growth. As McGregor (39) wrote in *The Human Side of Enterprise*:

> The job environment of the individual is the most important variable affecting his development. Unless that environment is conducive to his growth, none of the other things we do to him or for him will be effective. That is why the 'agricultural' approach to management development is preferable to the 'manufacturing' approach. The latter leads, among other things, to the unrealistic expectations that we can create and develop managers in the classroom.

There are two main activities in management development – performance management, discussed in Chapter 36, and planned experience, discussed below.

Planned experience

People learn mainly through experience. Surely, therefore, it is worth spending a little of your time planning the experience of anyone with potential for development.

Planning people's experience means giving them extra tasks to do which provide a challenge or extend them into a new area. It could be a project which they have to complete themselves or they could be included in a project team looking at a new development or problem which cuts across organizational boundaries. Projects which enlarge experience in unfamiliar areas, for example, a marketing executive in finance or vice versa, are particularly useful. Planned experience will work better if it is accompanied by coaching so that those undergoing it can receive the maximum benefit from expert advice.

COACHING

As mentioned in the introduction, the best way to learn how to manage is to manage, under the guidance of a good manager. Coaching is an informal but deliberate way of providing this guidance. It should be linked to performance management and the counselling that takes place as part of that process. Coaching skills are described in Chapter 5.

19

Effective speaking

A manager's job usually includes giving formal or informal presentations at meetings, and addressing groups of people at conferences or training sessions. To be able to speak well in public is therefore a necessary management skill which you should acquire and develop.

The three keys to effective speaking are:

● overcoming nervousness;
● thorough preparation;
● good delivery.

OVERCOMING NERVOUSNESS

Some nervousness is a good thing. It makes you prepare, makes you think and makes the adrenalin flow, thus raising performance. But excessive nervousness ruins your effectiveness and must be controlled.

The common reasons for excessive nervousness are: fear of

failure, fear of looking foolish, fear of breakdown, a sense of inferiority and dread of the isolation of the speaker. To overcome it there are three things to remember and six things to do.

Three things to remember about nervousness

● Everyone is nervous. It is natural and, for the reasons mentioned earlier, a good thing.
● Speaking standards are generally low. You can do better than the other person.
● You have something to contribute. Otherwise why should you have been asked to speak?

Six thing to do about nervousness

● *Practise.* Take every opportunity you can get to speak in public. The more you do it, the more confident you will become. Solicit constructive criticism and act on it.
● *Know your subject.* Get the facts, examples and illustrations which you need to put across.
● *Know your audience.* Who is going to be there? What are they expecting to hear? What will they want to get out of listening to you?
● *Know your objective.* Make sure that you know what you want to achieve. Visualize, if you can, each member of your audience going away having learned something new which he or she is going to put into practical use.
● *Prepare.*
● *Rehearse.*

PREPARATION

Allow yourself ample time for preparation in two ways. First, leave yourself plenty of low-pressure time; start thinking early – in your bath, on the way to work, mowing your lawn, any place where you can freely develop new ideas on the subject. Second, you should leave yourself lots of time actually to prepare the talk. There are eight stages of preparation.

1. Agreeing to talk

Do not agree to talk unless you know you have something to contribute to *this audience* on *this subject*.

2. Getting informed

Collect facts and arguments for your talk by: brainstorming and writing down all the points as they occur; reading up the subject; talking to colleagues and friends and keeping cuttings and files on subjects you may have to speak on.

3. Deciding what to say

Start by defining your objective. It is to persuade, inform, interest or inspire? Then decide the main message you want to put across. Adopt the 'rule of three'. Few people can absorb more than three new ideas at a time. Simplify your presentation to ensure that the three main points you want to convey come over loud and clear. Finally, select the facts and arguments which best support your message.

Never try to do too much. The most fatal mistake speakers can make is to tell everything they know. Select and simplify using the rule of three.

4. Structuring your presentation

Good structure is vital. It provides for continuity, makes your thoughts easy to follow, give the talk perspective and balance and, above all, enables you to ram your message home.

The classic method of structuring a talk is to 'tell them what you are going to say – say it – tell them what you have said'. This is the rule of three in action again, as applied to attention span. Your audience will probably only listen to one-third of what you say. If you say it three times in three different ways they will at least hear you once.

You were no doubt told at school that an essay should have a beginning, a middle and an end. Exactly the same principle applies to a talk.

Tackle the middle of your talk first and:

● Write the main message on separate postcards.
● List the points you want to make against each main message.
● Illustrate the points with facts, evidence, examples and introduce local colour.
● Arrange the cards in different sequences to help you to decide on the best way to achieve impact and a logical flow of ideas.

Then turn to the opening of your talk. Your objectives should be to create attention, arouse interest and inspire confidence. Give your audience a trailer to what you are going to say. Underline the objective of your presentation – what *they* will get out of it.

Finally, think about how you are going to close your talk. First and last impressions are very important. End on a high note.

Think carefully about length, reinforcement and continuity. Never talk for more than 40 minutes at a time. Twenty or thirty minutes is better. Very few speakers can keep people's attention for long. An audience is usually very interested to begin with (unless you make a mess of your opening) but interest declines steadily until people realize that you are approaching the end. Then they perk up. Hence the importance of your conclusion.

To keep their attention throughout, give interim summaries which reinforce what you are saying and, above all, hammer home your key points at intervals throughout your talk.

Continuity is equally important. You should build your argument progressively until you come to a positive and overwhelming conclusion. Provide signposts, interim summaries and bridging sections which lead your audience naturally from one point to the next.

5. Prepare your notes

The best sort of notes are the postcards used in preparing the talk. Each card should cover one section and include the main headings. Avoid using too many words on each; they will only confuse you.

Cards of this type can easily be referred to during your talk and should not distract your audience. It is quite a good idea, however, to write out your opening and closing remarks, in full, on separate cards. You can then learn these by heart, ensuring a confident start and a positive end to your presentation.

6. Prepare visual aids

As your audience will only absorb one-third of what you say, if that, reinforce your message with visual aids. Appeal to more than one sense at a time. Flip charts, slides and so on all provide good back-up, but don't overdo them and keep them simple. Too many visuals can be distracting, and too many words, or an over-elaborate presentation, will distract, bore and confuse your audience.

7. Rehearse

Rehearsal is vital. It instils confidence, helps you to get your timing right, enables you to polish your opening and closing remarks and to co-ordinate your talk and visual aids.

Rehearse the talk to yourself several times and note how long each section takes. Get used to expanding your notes without waffling. Never write down your talk in full and read it during rehearsal. This will guarantee a stilted and lifeless presentation.

Practise giving your talk out loud – standing up, if that is the way you are going to present it. Some people like to tape record themselves but that can be off-putting. It is better to get someone to hear you and provide constructive criticism. It may be hard to take but it could do you a world of good.

Finally, try to rehearse in the actual room in which you are going to speak, using your visual aids and with someone listening at the back to make sure you are audible.

8. Check and prepare arrangements on site

Check the visibility of your visual aids. Make sure that you know how to use them. Test and focus the overhead or slide projector. Brief your film projector operator and get him or her to run through the film to ensure there are no snags.

If you are using slides in a carousel go through the lot to check that the sequence is right and none is upside down.

Be prepared for something to go wrong with your equipment. You may have to do without it at short notice. That is why you should not rely too much on visual aids.

Before you start your talk, check that your notes and visual aids are in the right order and to hand. There is nothing worse than a speaker who mixes up his or her speech and fumbles helplessly for the next slide.

DELIVERY

With thorough preparation you will not fail. You will not break down. But the way you deliver the talk will affect the impact you make. Good delivery depends on technique and manner.

Technique

Your *voice* should reach the people at the back. If you don't know that you can be heard, ask. It is distracting if someone shouts 'speak up'. Vary the pace, pitch and emphasis of your delivery. Pause before making a key point, to highlight it, and again afterwards to allow it to sink in. Try to be conversational. Avoid a stilted delivery. This is one reason why you should *never* read your talk. If you are your natural self the audience is more likely to be on your side.

Light relief is a good thing if it comes naturally. People are easily bored if they feel they are being lectured, but you should never tell jokes unless you are good at telling jokes. Don't drag them in because you feel you must. Many effective and enjoyable speakers never use them.

Your *words* and *sentences* should be simple and short.

Your *eyes* are an important link with your audience. Look at them, measure their reaction and adjust to it. Don't fret if people look at their watches; it's when they start shaking them to see if they've stopped that you should start to worry.

Use *hands* for gesture and emphasis only. Avoid fidgeting. Don't put your hands in your pockets.

Stand naturally and upright. Do not stand casually. Be and look like someone in command. If you pace up and down like a caged tiger you will distract your audience. They will be waiting for you to trip over some equipment or fall off the edge of the platform.

Manner

Relax and show that you are relaxed. Convey an air of quiet confidence. Relaxation and confidence will come with thorough preparation and practice.

Don't preach or pontificate to your audience. They will resent it and turn against you.

Show sincerity and conviction. Obvious sincerity, belief in your message, positive conviction and enthusiasm in putting your message across count more than any technique.

CONCLUSION

- You can learn to become an effective speaker with practice. Seize every opportunity to develop your skills.
- Nervousness can be controlled by preparation and knowledge of technique.
- Good preparation is more than half the battle.
- Technique is there to help you to exploit your personality and style to the full, not to obliterate them.

20

Empowering people

WHAT IS EMPOWERMENT?

Empowerment is the process of giving people more scope or 'power' to exercise control over, and take responsibility for, their work. It means getting people to use their own judgement in the interests of the organization and its customers. Jan Carlson, Chief Executive of Scandinavian Airline Systems, as quoted by Jane Pickard (52), says that: 'The purpose of empowerment is to free someone from rigorous control by instructions and orders and give them freedom to take responsibility for their ideas and actions, to release hidden resources which would otherwise remain inaccessible.'

Empowerment provides greater 'space' for individuals to use their abilities by enabling and encouraging them to take decisions close to the point of impact.

BASIS

The basis for the belief that empowerment is a valid approach to improving organizational effectiveness is that people who are nearest to the problem are best able to judge its solution, provided they have a framework within which to make their decisions.

Assumptions about the empowered organization

Charles Handy (23) has suggested that the assumptions behind the concept of the empowered organization are:

- *Competence* – the belief that individual employees can be expected to perform to the limit of their competence with the minimum of supervision.
- *Trust* – it is necessary not only to believe in people's competence but also to trust them to get on with the job.
- *Teamwork* – few organizational problems can be solved by one person acting alone. The sheer rate of change and turbulence means that as new challenges and problems appear, people must naturally group together in flexible teams without barriers of status or hierarchy, to solve the problems within the framework of the organization's goals and values. The organization is held together by these beliefs and values – by people who are committed to one another and to common goals.

But Handy has more recently made an interesting distinction between empowerment and subsidiarity: 'Empowerment implies that someone on high is giving away power. Subsidiarity on the other hand, implies that the power belongs, in the first place, lower down or further out. You take it away as a last resort' (24).

Reasons for empowerment

The reasons for empowerment are that it:

- can speed up decision-making processes and reaction times;
- releases the creative and innovative capacities of employees;
- provides for greater job satisfaction, motivation and commitment;
- gives people more responsibility;
- enables employees to gain a greater sense of achievement from their work;
- reduces operational costs by eliminating unnecessary layers of management, staff functions and quality control and checking operations.

Replacing the command organization

A 'command' organization is one in which decision-making is centralized, reliance is placed on the authority of managers to 'get things done', management believes it always knows best (however far away it is from the scene of action – the client or the customer), and the contributions of staff are taken for granted rather than welcomed.

In contrast, the empowered organization makes much better use of the ability and enthusiasm of its employees. It has the potential to improve continuously by a series of small and large steps, day after day, and at all levels, feeding the learning from its experience back, to make it work better.

The command organization can be likened to a dinosaur with its tiny brain impotently issuing instructions to its massive body. The empowered organization is more like a shoal of fish, moving rapidly and consistently and adjusting through instantly understood signals.

THE PROCESS OF EMPOWERMENT

Empowerment can be achieved through:

● structural means – organizational and work grouping;
● the behaviour or style of individual managers;
● enlisting the support of employees in tackling immediate organizational issues;
● gaining the 'hearts and minds' of people.

Structural empowerment – organizational

An empowered organization is likely to have a flat structure with the minimum number of management layers. A multi-layered structure filters the two-way flow of information and hinders decision-making from penetrating as far down the organization as it should.

Structural empowerment – work group

As suggested by Christian Schumacher (56) of *Small is Beautiful* fame, empowerment can be achieved at the work group level by applying the following principles:

1. Work should be organized around basic operations to form 'whole tasks'.
2. The basic organizational unit should be the primary work group (ie 4–20 people).
3. Each work group should include a designated leader.
4. Each work group and its leader should, as far as possible, plan and organize its own work.
5. Each work group should be able fully to evaluate its performance against agreed standards of excellence.
6. Jobs should be structured so that work group members can personally plan, execute and evaluate at least one operation in the process.
7. All work group members should have the opportunity to participate in the group's processes of planning, problem-solving and evaluation.

Management style

Managers empower the members of their teams, not by giving up control but by changing the way control is exercised. They have to learn to delegate more and to allow individuals and teams more scope to plan, act and monitor their own performance.

But they still have the responsibility to provide guidance and support to their staff as required. They must also help them to develop the skills and competences they need to function effectively in an empowered organization.

Involvement in issues

Empowerment can be achieved by involving people in developing their own solutions to specific issues. This can be done by expecting teams not simply to propose ways forward or to hope that someone else will do something, but actually to solve the problem in their part of the organization, in accordance with the resources they have and the constraints within which they work.

At General Electric, the Chief Executive, Jack Welch, arranged for employees at all levels to get together and work out how to improve the ways in which work was carried out. His aim was 'to give people a voice, give them a say, give them a chance to participate'. In describing these 'work-outs' he also said that:

Ultimately, we're talking about redefining the relationship between boss and subordinate. I want to get to the point where people challenge their bosses every day: 'Why do you require me to do wasteful things? Why don't you let me do things you shouldn't be doing so you can move on and create? That's the job of the leader – to create, not to control. Trust me to do my job and don't make me waste all my time trying to deal with you on control issues' (66).

Hearts and minds

Empowerment is about engaging both the hearts and minds of people so that they can take the opportunities made available to them for increased responsibility.

At management level this is achieved by sharing strategic vision and corporate values throughout the organization, creating the assumption of competence and furthering the trust without which an empowered organization cannot operate.

TEN WAYS OF EMPOWERING PEOPLE

1. Delegate more.
2. Involve people in setting their targets and standards of performance and in deciding on performance measures.
3. Allow individuals and teams more scope to plan, act and monitor their own performance.
4. Involve people in developing their own solutions to problems.
5. Create self-managed teams – ones that set their own objectives and standards and manage their own performance.
6. Give people a voice in deciding what needs to be done.
7. Help people to learn from their mistakes.
8. Encourage continuous development so that people can both grow in their roles and grow their roles.
9. Share your vision and plans with the members of your team.
10. Trust people and treat them as adults (Tom Peters).

21

Getting on

Getting on is first about knowing what you can do – your strengths and weaknesses. Then you can decide what you want to do and set out to do it.

You can start in the right direction, therefore, by trying to analyse yourself and the situation which you are in.

Beyond that there are certain actions you can take which will help you to get on. Some are obvious, others less so. How you apply them must depend on your assessment of where you are and what you can do. With due acknowledgement to the two men who have written the most sense on this subject – Peter Drucker and Robert Townsend – the list of steps to take is set out below under four main headings:

- Knowing yourself.
- Knowing what you want.
- Developing and deploying the skills required to get what you want.
- Displaying the personal qualities and behaving in the ways that will contribute to your success.

KNOWING YOURSELF

Carlyle once described the saying 'know thyself' as an impossible precept. He felt that to 'know what thou canst work at' would be better advice. Therefore, the starting point in career management is what you can do – your strengths and your weaknesses. This means developing self-awareness by analysing your achievements, skills and knowledge and by assessing your own performance.

Achievement, skills and knowledge

The questions to ask yourself are:

1. *What have I achieved so far?* Answer this question by looking back on your life and list the key events, happenings, incidents and turning points that have taken place. Whenever you have succeeded in doing something new or better than ever before, analyse the factors which contributed to that success. Was it initiative, hard work, determination, the correct application of skills and knowledge based on a searching analysis of the situation, the ability to work in a team, the exercise of leadership, the capacity to seize an opportunity (another and better word for luck) and exploit it, the ability to articulate a need and get into action to satisfy it, the ability to make things happen – or any other factor you can think of?

2. *When have I failed to achieve what I wanted?* You do not want to dwell too much on failure but it can be treated positively, as long as you analyse dispassionately where you went wrong and assess what you might have been able to do to put it right.

3. *What am I good or bad at doing?* What are your distinctive competences? Consider these in terms of professional, technical or managerial know-how as well as the exercise of such skills as communicating, decision-making, problem-solving, teamworking, exercising leadership, delegating, co-ordinating, meeting deadlines, managing time, planning, organizing and controlling work, dealing with crises.

4. *How well do I know my chosen area of expertise?* Have you got the right qualifications? Have you acquired the right know-how through study, training and relevant experience?

5. *What sort of person am I?* (This is the most difficult question of all to answer truthfully.) The following is a checklist of the

points you should consider, based on Cattell's classification of primary personality factors. In each case, assess the extent to which either of the paired descriptions applies to you:

- *Outgoing* – warm-hearted, easy-going, participating, extroverted; or
- *Reserved* – detached, critical, cool, introverted.

- *Intellectual* – good at abstract thinking; or
- *Non-intellectual* – better at concrete thinking.

- *Emotionally stable* – calm, able to face reality; or
- *Affected by feelings* – emotionally unstable, easily upset.

- *Assertive* – independent, aggressive, stubborn; or
- *Submissive* – mild, obedient, conforming.

- *Enthusiastic* – lively, happy-go-lucky, heedless, talkative; or
- *Sober* – prudent, serious, taciturn.

- *Conscientious* – persevering, staid, rule-bound; or
- *Expedient* – 'a law unto yourself', bypasses obligations.

- *Venturesome* – bold, uninhibited, spontaneous; or
- *Shy* – restrained, different, timid.

- *Tender-minded* – dependent, over-protected, sensitive; or
- *Though-minded* – self-reliant, realistic, a no-nonsense approach.

- *Suspicious* – self-opinionated, distrustful, hard to fool; or
- *Trusting* – free of suspicion or jealousy, adaptable, easy to get on with.

- *Imaginative* – speculative, careless of practical matters, wrapped up in inner urgencies; or
- *Practical* – inclined to action rather than speculation, regulated by external realities, careful, conventional.

- *Shrewd* – calculating, penetrating, worldly; or
- *Artless* – guileless, ingenuous, natural.

- *Apprehensive* – a worrier, depressive, troubled; or
- *Confident* – self-assured, serene, placid.

- *Experimenting* – critical, liberal, analytical, free-thinking; or
- *Conservative* – respecter of established ideas, tolerant of traditional practices.

- *Self-sufficient* – resilient, resourceful, prefers own decisions; or
- *Group-dependent* – a 'joiner', happiest in a group, reliant on the support of others.

- *Controlled* – socially precise, self-disciplined, compulsive; or
- *Casual* – careless of protocol, untidy, follows own inclinations.

- *Tense* – driven, overwrought, fretful; or
- *Relaxed* – tranquil, unfrustrated, calm.

Assess your managerial competences

While self-awareness is the basis for a more specific assessment of your strengths and weaknesses as a manager, you need also to consider your basic managerial qualities and the competences required to operate effectively.

In analysing your effectiveness as a manager it is useful to look at the criteria used by major organizations in measuring the competence of their managers at their assessment or development centres (two- to three-day affairs where managers are subjected to a number of tests and undertake various exercises to demonstrate their skills).

The following are the typical criteria expressed as competence requirements used by organizations when they assess the capabilities of their managers:

- *Achievement/results orientation.* The desire to get things done well and the ability to set and meet challenging goals, create own measures of excellence and constantly seek ways of improving performance.
- *Business awareness.* The capacity continually to identify and explore business opportunities, understand the business opportunities and priorities of the organization and constantly to seek methods of ensuring that the organization becomes more business-like.
- *Communication.* The ability to communicate clearly and persuasively, orally or in writing.
- *Customer focus.* The exercise of unceasing care in looking after the interests of external and internal customers to ensure that their wants, needs and expectations are met or exceeded.

- *Developing others.* The desire and capacity to foster the development of members of his or her team, providing feedback, support, encouragement and coaching.
- *Flexibility.* The ability to adapt to and work effectively in different situations and to carry out a variety of tasks.
- *Leadership.* The capacity to inspire individuals to give of their best to achieve a desired result and to maintain effective relationships with individuals and the team as a whole.
- *Planning.* The ability to decide on courses of action, ensuring that the resources required to implement the action will be available and scheduling the programme of work required to achieve a defined end-result.
- *Problem-solving.* The capacity to analyse situations, diagnose problems, identify the key issues, establish and evaluate alternative courses of action and produce a logical, practical and acceptable solution.
- *Teamwork.* The ability to work co-operatively and flexibly with other members of the team with a full understanding of the role to be played as a team member.

You can assess your competence as a manager against these criteria giving yourself marks between 1 and 10 for each item relating to a classification along these lines:

A = outstanding (9–10 points)
B = very effective (7–8 points)
C = satisfactory (5–6 points)
D = barely satisfactory (3–4 points)
E = unsatisfactory (0–2 points)

On completing this assessment, note the particularly high and low scores in each list and draw up a schedule of your strengths and weaknesses as a manager. You can complete this 'SWOT' analysis (Strengths and Weaknesses, Opportunities and Threats) by considering your opportunities for advancement in your present organization (or elsewhere) and assessing any threats that might prevent you from realizing your ambitions.

KNOWING WHAT YOU WANT

1. Find out what you are good at doing and then do it.

133

2. Analyse not only your strengths but also your weaknesses: 'There is nothing that helps a man in his conduct through life more than a knowledge of his own characteristic weaknesses' (William Hazlitt).
3. Decide what you want to do and then go for it. Believe that if you really want something you can get it, and act accordingly.
4. Set demanding targets and deadlines for yourself. 'People grow according to the demands they make on themselves' (Drucker). But don't over-commit yourself. Be realistic about what you can achieve.
5. Pursue excellence. 'If you can't do it excellently don't do it at all' (Townsend).
6. Focus on what *you* can contribute. 'To ask "what can I contribute?" is to look for the unused potential in a job' (Drucker).
7. Get your priorities right. Adapt Drucker's rules for identifying them:

   - pick the future as against the past;
   - focus on opportunities rather than on problems;
   - choose your own direction – rather than climb on the bandwagon;
   - aim high, aim for something that will make a difference rather than something that is 'safe' and easy to do.

8. Be specific about what you want to do yourself and what you want others to do for you.
9. Keep it simple. Concentrate. Consider all your tasks and eliminate the irrelevant ones. Slough off old activities before you start new ones. 'Concentration is the key to economic results... no other principle of effectiveness is violated as constantly today as the basic principle of concentration... Our motto seems to be: "let's do a little bit of everything" ' (Drucker).
10. Take the broad view but don't ignore the significant detail: 'Ill can he rule the great, that cannot reach the small' (Spenser). It is sometimes necessary to penetrate beneath the surface to find out what is really happening – on the shop floor or in the field. But do this selectively.
11. Adapt to changing demands. 'The executive who keeps on doing what he has done successfully before is almost bound to fail' (Drucker).

DEVELOP SKILLS

Every chapter in this book refers to an area of management skill that you need to develop if you want to get on. The key areas are:

- Communicating – express yourself clearly, concisely and persuasively.
- Problem-solving – adopt a logical approach to problem-solving but don't forget that lateral thinking can be very productive of new ideas.
- Decision-making – develop the analytical skills and confidence in yourself to enable you to make incisive judgements.
- Listening – listen to ideas and act on the good ones. Hear what is said, let the other person know that you have heard, show an interest, let him feel important.
- Motivating – understand what your people can do and what makes them tick, make clear what you expect them to do, setting standards which are grounded on the requirement of the task and not personal, reward them or otherwise according to their contribution.
- Staffing – select people for their strengths, accept that everyone has some weakness or other, don't go for mediocrity.
- Managing yourself – achieve control over your work day. Separate the essentials from the inessentials that litter your desk. Know how to simplify your workload – where appropriate cut corners.

PERSONAL QUALITIES AND BEHAVIOUR

- Be enthusiastic and show it.
- Innovate and create – come up with new ideas and react positively to other people's ideas. Don't sulk if your ideas are not accepted. Try again another way.
- Show willing – there is nothing worse than the person who always moans when he is given something to do. Don't say: 'How can I possibly do that?' Instead, respond immediately with something like this: 'Right, this is what I propose to do – is that what you want?'
- Be positive – in the words of the old Bing Crosby song: 'accentuate the positive and eliminate the negative'.

- Work hard – people who get on are hard workers. But they don't work for work's sake. Effectiveness is never a function of how late you stay in the office. It's what you do while you are there that counts.

- Present yourself well – life is not all about making a good impression but you might as well make sure that your achievements are known and appreciated. And if people are impressed by executives who are decisive, punctual and answer promptly, why not impress them that way? More good than harm will come of it.

- Be ambitious – 'A man's reach should exceed his grasp, or what's a heaven for?' (Robert Browning). But don't overdo it. Don't appear to be more concerned about your future status than with present effectiveness.

- Be courageous – take calculated risks, believe in what you are doing and stick to your guns.

- Be assertive but not aggressive.

- Put your points across firmly and succinctly.

- Don't talk too much. Never over-commit yourself. Save up what you want to say until the right moment. Keep your powder dry. Don't shoot your mouth off. 'Whereof one cannot speak, thereon one must remain silent' (Wittgenstein).

- Learn to cope with stress. You won't avoid it and you have to live with it. If problems are coming at you thick and fast, try to slow down. Relax. Take a little time off. Give yourself a chance to put the situation into perspective.

- If things go wrong, bounce back. Accept reverses calmly. Think about what you need to do and then get into action – fast. There is nothing like purposeful activity in these circumstances.

- Get people to trust you – you will do this if you never lie or even shade the truth, if you avoid playing politics and if you always deliver what you promise.

- Accept constructive criticism.

- 'Admit your own mistakes openly, even joyfully' (Townsend, 62). Never make an excuse. Accept the responsibility *and* the blame if you make a mistake.

22

Handling negative behaviour

Managers and team leaders sometimes come across negative behaviour from one of the members of their team. This may take the form of lack of interest in the work, unwillingness to co-operate with you or other members of the team, complaining about the work or working conditions, grumbling at being asked to carry out a perfectly reasonable task, objecting strongly to being asked to do something extra (or even refusing to do it) – 'it's not in my job description', or, in extreme cases, insolence. People exhibiting negative behaviour may be quietly resentful rather than openly disruptive. They are negative, mutter away in the background at meetings and lack enthusiasm.

As a manager you can tolerate a certain amount of negative behaviour as long as the individual works reasonably well and does not upset other team members. You have simply to say to yourself, 'It takes all sorts...' and put up with it, although you might quietly say during a review meeting, 'You're doing a good job but...'. If, however, you do take this line, you have to be specific. You must cite actual instances. It is no good making generalized accusations which will either be openly denied or internalized by the receiver, making him or her even more resentful.

If the negative behaviour means that the individual's contribution is not acceptable or *is* disruptive then you must take action. Negative people are often quiet but are usually angry about something; their negative behaviour is an easy way of expressing their anger. To deal with the problem it is necessary to find out what has made the person angry.

CAUSES OF NEGATIVE BEHAVIOUR

The causes could include one or more of the following:

- a real or imagined slight from you or a colleague;
- a feeling of being put upon;
- a belief that the contribution made by the person is neither appreciated nor rewarded properly in terms of pay or promotion;
- resentment at what was perceived to be unfair criticism;
- anger directed at the company or you because what was considered to be a reasonable request was turned down, eg for leave or a transfer, or because of an unfair accusation, eg overclaiming travel expenses.

DEALING WITH THE PROBLEM

It is because there can be such a variety of real or imagined causes of negative behaviour that dealing with it becomes one of the most difficult tasks a manager has to undertake. If the action taken is crude or insensitive, the negative behaviour will only be intensified. This might end up in invoking the disciplinary procedure, which should be your last resort.

In one sense, it is easier to deal with an actual example of negative behaviour. This can be handled on the spot. If the problem is one of general attitude rather than specific actions it is more difficult to cope with. When individuals are accused of being, for example, generally unenthusiastic or uncooperative, they can simply go into denial, and accuse you of being prejudiced. Their negative behaviour may be reinforced.

If you have to deal with this sort of problem it is best to do it informally, either when it arises or at any point during the year when you feel that something has to be done about it. An annual formal appraisal meeting is not the right time, especially if it produces ratings which are linked to a pay increase. Raising the issue then will only put individuals on the defensive and a productive discussion will be impossible.

The discussion may be informal but it should have three clear objectives:

1. To discuss the situation with individuals, the aim being if possible to get them to recognize for themselves that they are behaving negatively. If this cannot be achieved, then the objective is to bring to the attention of individuals your belief that their behaviour is unacceptable in certain ways.
2. To establish the reasons for the individuals' negative behaviour so far as this is feasible.
3. To discuss and agree any actions individuals could take to behave more positively, or what you or the organization could do to remove the causes of the behaviour.

Discussing the problem

Start by asking generally how individuals feel about their work. Do they have any problems in carrying it out? Are they happy with the support they get from you or their colleagues? Are they satisfied that they are pulling their weight to the best of their ability?

You may find that this generalized start provides the basis for the next two stages – identifying the causes and remedies. It is best if individuals identify for themselves that there is a problem. But in many, if not the majority of cases, this is unlikely to happen. Individuals may not recognize that they are behaving negatively or will not be prepared to admit it.

You will then have to bring to their attention the problem as you see it. You should indicate truthfully that you are concerned because they seem to be unhappy and you wish to know if they feel that you or the organization is treating them unfairly so that you can try to put things right. Give them time to say their piece and then give a rational explanation, dealing with specific grievances. If they are not satisfied with your explanation you can say that they will be given the opportunity to discuss the problem with higher authority, thus indicating that you recognize that your judgement is not final.

If the response you get to these initial points does not bring out into the open the problem as you see it, then you have to explain how the individual's behaviour gives the impression of being negative. Be as specific as possible about the behaviour, bringing up actual instances. For example, a discussion could be based on the following questions: 'Do you recall yesterday's team meeting?' 'How did you think it went?' 'How helpful do you think you were in dealing with the problem?' 'Do you remember saying...?' 'How helpful do you think that remark was?' 'Would it surprise you to learn that I felt you had not been particularly helpful in the following ways...?'

Of course, even if this careful approach is adopted, there will be occasions when individuals refuse to admit that there is anything wrong with their behaviour. If you reach this impasse, then you have no alternative but to spell out to them your perceptions of where they have gone wrong. But do this in a positive way: 'Then I think that it is only fair for me to point out to you that your contribution (to the meeting) would have been more helpful if you had...'.

Establishing causes

If the negative behaviour is because of a real or imagined grievance about what you or colleagues or the organization has done, then you have to get individuals to spell this out as precisely as possible. At this point, your job is to listen, not to judge. People can be just as angry about imaginary as about real slights. You have to find out how they perceive the problem before you can deal with it.

It may emerge during the discussion that the problem has nothing to do with you or the company. It may be family troubles or worries about health or finance. If this is the case, you can be sympathetic and may be able to suggest remedies in the form of counselling or practical advice from within or outside the organization.

If the perceived problem is you, colleagues or the organization, try to get chapter and verse on what it is so that you are in a position to take remedial action or to explain the real facts of the case.

Taking remedial action

If the problem rests with the individual, the objective is, of course, to get them to recognize for themselves that remedial action is necessary and what they need to do about it – with your help as necessary. In this situation you might suggest counselling or recommend a source of advice. But be careful, you don't want to imply that there is something wrong with them. You should go no further than suggesting that individuals may find this helpful – they don't *need* it but they could *benefit* from it. You should be careful about offering counselling advice yourself. This is often better done by professional counsellors. But if you do feel that it is appropriate to offer advice, refer to the approaches to counselling as described in Chapter 12.

If there is anything specific that the parties involved in the situation can do, then the line to take is that *we* can tackle this problem together: 'This is what I will do', 'This is what the company will do', 'What do you think you should do?' If there is no response to the last question, then this is the point where you have to spell out the action you think they need to take. Be as specific as possible and try to express your wishes as suggestions, not commands. A joint problem-solving approach is always best.

TEN APPROACHES TO MANAGING NEGATIVE BEHAVIOUR

1. Define the type of negative behaviour which is being exhibited. Make notes of examples.
2. Discuss the behaviour with the individual as soon as possible, aiming to reach agreement about what it is and the impact it makes.
3. If agreement is not obtained, give actual examples of behaviour and explain why you believe them to be negative.
4. Discuss and so far as possible agree reasons for the negative behaviour, including those attributed to the individual, yourself and the organization.
5. Discuss and agree possible remedies – actions on the part of the individual, yourself or the organization.
6. Monitor the actions taken and the results obtained.
7. If improvement is not achieved and the negative behaviour is

significantly affecting the performance of the individual and the team, then invoke the disciplinary procedure.

8. Start with a verbal warning, indicating the ways in which behaviour must improve, and give a time-scale and offers of further support and help as required.

9. If there is no improvement, issue a formal warning, setting out as specifically as possible what must be achieved over a defined period of time, indicating the disciplinary action that could be taken.

10. If the negative behaviour persists and continues seriously to affect performance, take the disciplinary action. If you have no alternative but to dismiss someone, the approach you should adopt is given on page 200.

23

How things go wrong and how to put them right

Things can go wrong through events beyond your control or through incompetence. It is difficult and very rare for anyone to admit that they are incompetent, but this is why things most frequently go adrift. It is therefore useful to know something about the causes of incompetence so that you can put them right. You should also know about trouble-shooting so that you can tackle problems, whether or not they are of your own making Theodore Roosevelt once said: 'Do what you can, with what you have, where you are.' The trouble is, people don't always take this advice. Things go wrong because people do less than they are capable of, misuse their resources or choose an inappropriate time or place in which to do it. Situations are misjudged and the wrong action is taken.

STUDIES OF INCOMPETENCE

There have been two interesting analyses of incompetence which, if studied, will give you some clues about how to avoid or at least minimize mistakes. The first of these is *The Peter Principle* by Dr Lawrence J Peter (48); the second is *On the Psychology of Military Incompetence* by Norman F Dixon (15).

The Peter Principle

In *The Peter Principle*, Dr Lawrence Peter suggested that in a hierarchy, individuals tend to rise to the level of their own incompetence. This somewhat pessimistic view was based on his experience that the system encourages this to happen because people are told that if they are doing their job efficiently and with ease, the job lacks challenge and they should move up. However, as Peter says, 'The problem is that when you find something you can't do very well, that is where you stay, bungling your job, frustrating your co-workers, and eroding the effectiveness of the organization.'

The Peter Principle has only been accepted as common parlance because it reflects a fundamental problem when assessing potential. We know, or we think we know, that someone is good at his or her present job. But does this predict success in the next one up? Perhaps yes, perhaps no; however, we cannot be sure because the skills needed by, for example, a first-rate research scientist are quite different from those required by the leader of a research team. Technical competence does not necessarily indicate managerial competence.

Beating the Peter Principle – for yourself

Can the Peter Principle be beaten? The answer is yes, but with difficulty. People don't usually refuse promotion. If they do, they become suspect. It is thought that they should be made of sterner stuff. It is, however, perfectly reasonable to check on what is involved if you are promoted. You should obtain precise answers to questions on what you will be expected to achieve, the resources you will be given to achieve it and the problems you will meet. If you think these demands are unreasonable, discuss the job to see if they can be modified.

Don't take a job unless you are satisfied that you can do it, or at least that you can learn how to do it within an acceptable period of time. You can quite properly ask what training and help you will be given in the early stages. If your predecessor failed, you can ask what went wrong so that you can avoid making the same mistakes.

Beating the Peter Principle – for others

If you are in a position of offering promotion or a new job, you have to be aware of the Peter Principle and how to circumvent it. You need to match the capacities of the candidate to the demands of the job, and your starting point for this process should be an analysis in depth of the skills required. These should be classified under the headings of MATCH:

1. *Managerial* – making things happen, leading, inspiring and motivating people, team building and maintaining morale, co-ordinating and directing effort, using resources productively, and controlling events to achieve the required results.
2. *Analytical* – dissecting problems and coming up with the right conclusions about what is happening and what should happen.
3. *Technical/professional* – an understanding not only of all the tricks of the trade but also of how to use other people's knowledge effectively.
4. *Communications* – putting the message across.
5. *Human resource management/personal* – the ability to persuade, enthuse and motivate, trustworthiness, integrity, dedication.

When you have drawn up the specifications, measure the candidate against each of these criteria. Obtain whatever evidence you can about his or her performance in the present job which gives any indication of potential competence in these areas. Ask for information on successes and failures and why they occurred.

This matching process should identify any potential weaknesses. You can then discuss these and decide on any help the individual needs in the shape of coaching, training or further experience.

Monitor the progress of the individual carefully in the initial months. Your aim should be to spot dangerous tendencies in good time so that swift remedial action can be taken.

Military incompetence

Normal Dixon suggests that there are two basic types of military incompetence. The first group includes Generals Elphinstone (first Afghan war), Raglan (the Crimean War), Butler (Boer War), and Percival (Singapore). These were all mild, courteous and peaceful men, paralysed by the burden of decision-making under fire. The second group includes people like Haig, Joffre, and a number of the other First World War generals. They are characterized by over-weening ambition coupled with a terrifying insensitivity to the suffering of others. Far from being paralysed by decisions, they were active, but active in vain, devious, scheming and dishonest ways. Alastair Mant in *Leaders We Deserve* quotes the example of the catastrophic results achieved in the Crimean War when an incompetent in the first group (Raglan) has authority over someone in the second group (the Earl of Cardigan, reputed by one contemporary to possess the 'brains of a horse').

The elements of military incompetence are listed by Norman Dixon as:

● Serious wastage of human resources.
● Fundamental conservatism and clinging to outworn tradition or to past successes.
● Tendency to reject or ignore information which is unpalatable or which conflicts with preconceptions (eg company yes men).
● Tendency to underestimate the enemy.
● Indecisiveness and a tendency to abdicate from the role of decision-maker.
● Obstinate persistence in a given task despite strong contrary evidence.
● Failure to exploit a situation gained and a tendency to 'pull punches'.
● Failure to make adequate reconnaissance.
● A predilection for frontal assults, often against the enemy's strongest point (reference the gross overcrowding of once profitable markets).
● Belief in brute force rather than the clever ruse.
● Failure to make use of surprise or deception.
● Undue readiness to find scapegoats.
● Suppression or distortion of news from the Front, usually deemed necessary for morale or security.
● Belief in mystical forces – fate, bad luck, etc.

Examples of all these can be found in the actions or inactions of business leaders and managers:

1. *Wasting resources.* Most factories and offices are overstaffed, to the tune of 10 per cent or more.

2. *Conservatism.* 'That's the way it has always worked.' We have been market leaders for the last 20 years, why change?
3. *Rejecting unpalatable information.* 'What did you say about our losing market share? I don't believe it; these desk surveys are always inaccurate.'
4. *Underestimating the enemy.* 'What's this? Bloggs & Co have introduced a new product in our range. And you think it will compete? Forget it. They're useless. They couldn't run a winkle stall.'
5. *Indecisiveness.* 'We need to think a bit more about this.' 'I need more information.' 'I sometimes think that if you put problems like this in the "too difficult" section of your pending tray, they will go away.' 'It seems to me that we have several alternative routes (*sic*) ahead of us. Let's call a meeting next week or sometime to look at the pros and cons.' 'This is something for the Board.'
6. *Obstinate persistence.* 'Don't confuse me with the facts.' 'That's the way it's going to be.'
7. *Failure to exploit a situation.* 'Okay, you think we're going to exceed budget on our launch and you want to accelerate the programme. But let's not get too excited, we mustn't over-stretch ourselves.'
8. *Failure to reconnoitre.* 'I don't believe in market research.'
9. *A predilection for frontal assaults.* 'Bloggs are doing particularly well in widgets. Yes, I appreciate we know nothing about widgets, but we can soon find out. Let's get in there fast and topple them from their perch.'
10. *A belief in brute force.* 'Tell the union they can either take 5 per cent or do the other thing... What's this about a productivity package? I don't believe in messing about. It's a straight offer or nothing... They'll come out? I don't believe it, not with unemployment levels round here topping 15 per cent.'
11. *A failure to make use of surprise.* 'I don't like playing about. Let's get this show on the road... You think we'll get off to a better start if we keep the competition guessing? Forget it, we're miles better than they are!'
12. *Scapegoating.* 'It's not us, it's the rate of exchange.' 'This xxxx government has screwed us up!' 'Why am I surrounded by incompetent fools?'
13. *Suppression of news.* 'Don't tell them about how well we're doing. They'll only ask for more money.'

14. *A belief in mystical forces.* 'I just *feel* in my bones we must do this thing.'

WHY THINGS GO WRONG – A SUMMARY

The main reasons for things going wrong are:

- inability to learn from mistakes;
- sheer incompetence through over-promotion;
- poor selection, inadequate training;
- over-confidence;
- under-confidence;
- carelessness;
- laziness;
- lack of foresight.

WHAT CAN YOU DO ABOUT IT?

Inability to learn from mistakes

Remember Murphy's Law, which states that if anything can go wrong it will. Mistakes will happen. The unforgivable thing is to make the same mistake twice. You learn from your mistakes by analysing what went wrong – no excuses, no alibis – and making notes of what to do and what not to do next time.

Incompetence

This is something you should minimize in your subordinates by a constant drive to improve selection and performance standards and by training and coaching aimed at correcting specified weaknesses.

If you have doubts about your own ability, analyse your own strengths and weaknesses and grab every opportunity you can to get extra training and advice from people you believe in. If that still does not work, get out in good time.

Poor selection, inadequate training

If you pick the wrong person for the job they will underperform and make mistakes. You must ensure that you specify exactly what you want in terms of experience, qualifications, knowledge, skills and personality and that you do not settle for second best. Your interview should be planned systematically to find out what the candidate has to offer under each of the headings of your specification. Ensure by probing questions that you establish whether or not the experience is of the right sort and at the right level. Ask for details of achievements. Check that the candidate has had a progressive career with no record of failures or mysterious gaps. Check by telephone with the present or previous employer that the candidate has told you the truth about his job, period of employment and, where appropriate, reason for leaving.

If you have failed to provide proper induction training, or to take the right steps to identify and meet the individual's training needs, you should not be surprised if he is not up to the job. Guidance on approaches to developing your staff is given in Chapter 18.

Over-confidence

This is the most difficult problem to eradicate. It is always said in the Royal Air Force that the most accident-prone pilots are the over-confident ones. You need confidence in yourself and your staff. How can it be controlled from going over the edge?

It takes time to understand or demonstrate that misjudgements occur because you are so certain that you know all the answers that no attempt is made to foresee or take care of the unexpected. Over-confident people tend to have tunnel vision – they can see quite clearly to the end but they take no notice of what is happening on either side or beyond. And if they see the light at the end of the tunnel they may not appreciate that it is the light of the oncoming train.

Under-confidence

This can be overcome as long as the individual is fundamentally competent. People who lack confidence often need help from someone who can underline achievements and provide encouragement to do more of the same. Mentors can help, as can a deliberate policy of extending people steadily so that they are not suddenly faced with a daunting leap in the level of work they have to do. Start by giving the under-confident tasks that are well within their capabilities and progressively increase demands, but only in achievable steps.

Carelessness

This is a universal problem. It can happen through over-confidence, but we all make mistakes under pressure or because we think the task is easier than it is. Sadly, reputations can be damaged, even destroyed by relatively minor mistakes. If you submit a report to your board with a glaring arithmetical error in it, the credibility of your whole report may be damaged, even if the mistake, although obvious, was not significant. Never submit a report or write a key letter without checking every figure and every fact at least once. If possible, ask someone else to do it as well.

Laziness

No one would ever admit to being lazy. But lazy people do exist, either because they are naturally indolent or they have not been given sufficient leadership and a well-defined role in the organization. If one of your staff is lazy, put the boot in. It cannot be tolerated.

Lack of foresight

This is a common reason for errors. As a manager, one of your prime responsibilities is to think ahead. You must try to anticipate all the eventualities and make contingency plans accordingly. You won't get it right every time and you may find yourself occasionally in a crisis-management situation. But you will at least be better prepared if thought has been given to some of the eventualities, even if you could not anticipate them all.

TROUBLE-SHOOTING

No matter what you do, things will sometimes go wrong. As a manager, you will often be called upon to put them right, or to employ other people to do it for you.

Trouble-shooting requires diagnostic ability, to size up the difficulties; know-how, to select the required solution and decide how to implement it; and managerial skill, to put the solution into effect. It can be divided into three main parts:

- Planning the campaign.
- Diagnosis.
- Cure.

PLANNING THE CAMPAIGN

Even if you decide to do it yourself without using management consultants, you can still take a leaf out of the consultant's book. A good management consultant will go through the following stages:

- Analysis of the present situation – what has happened and why.
- Development of alternative solutions to the problem.
- Decision as to the preferred solution, stating the costs and benefits of implementing it.
- Defining a method of proceeding – how and over what time-scale should the solution be implemented, who does it and with what resources. If a staged implementation is preferred, the stages will be defined and a programme worked out.

The most important task at the planning stage is to define the problem, clarify objectives and terms of reference. A problem defined is a problem half solved. And it is the difficult half. The rest should follow quite naturally if an analytical approach is adopted.

Once you know what the problem is you can define what you want done and prepare terms of reference for those who are conducting the investigation, including yourself. These should set out the problem, how and by whom it is to be tackled, what is to be achieved and by when. All those concerned in the exercise should know what these terms of reference are.

The next step is to programme the trouble-shooting assignment. Four points need to be decided: the information you need, where you get it from, how you obtain it and who receives it. Draw up lists of facts required and the people who can supply them. Remember you will have to deal with opinion as well as fact; all data are subject to interpretation. List those who are likely to understand what has happened and why; those who might have good ideas about what to do next.

Then draw up your programme. Give notice that you require information. Warn people in plenty of time that you want to discuss particular points with them and that you expect them to have thought about the subject *and* have supporting evidence to hand.

DIAGNOSIS

Diagnosis means finding out *what* is happening – the symptom – and then digging to establish *why* it is happening – the cause. There may be a mass of evidence. The skilled diagnostician dissects the facts, sorts out what is relevant to the problem and refines it all down until he or she reveals the crucial pieces of information which show the cause of the problem and point to its solution.

Analytical ability – being able to sort the wheat from the chaff – is a key element in diagnosis. It is a matter of getting the facts and then submitting each one to a critical examination, in order to determine which is significant.

During the process of diagnosis you must remain open-minded. You should not allow yourself to have preconceptions or to be over-influenced by anyone's opinion. Listen and observe, but suspend judgement until you can arrange all the facts against all the opinions.

At the same time, do whatever you can to enlist the interest and support of those involved. If you can minimize their natural fears and suspicions, those close to the problem will reveal ideas and facts which might otherwise be concealed from you.

TROUBLE-SHOOTING CHECKLIST

Base your diagnosis on an analysis of the factors likely to have contributed to the problem: people, systems, structure and circumstances.

People

1. Have mistakes been made? If so, why? Is it because staff are inadequate in themselves or is it because they have been badly managed or trained?
2. If management is at fault, was the problem one of system, structure or the managers themselves?
3. If the people doing the job are inadequate why were they selected in the first place?

Systems

4. To what extent are poor systems or procedures to blame for the problem?
5. Is the fault in the systems themselves? Are they badly designed or inappropriate?
6. Or is it the fault of the people who operate or manage the systems?

Structure

7. How far has the organization or management structure contributed to the problem?
8. Do people know what is expected of them?
9. Are activities grouped together logically, so that adequate control can be exercised over them?
10. Are managers and supervisors clear about their responsibilities for maintaining control and do they exercise these responsibilities effectively?

Circumstances

11. To what extent, if any, is the problem a result of circumstances beyond the control of those concerned? For example, have external economic pressures or changing government policies had a detrimental effect?
12. If there have been external pressures, has there been a failure to anticipate or to react quickly enough to them?
13. Have adequate resources (people, money and materials) been made available, and if not, why not?

CURE

The diagnosis should point the way to the cure. But this may still mean that you have to evaluate different ways of dealing with the problem. There is seldom 'one best way', only a choice between alternatives. You have to narrow them down until you reach the one which, *on balance*, is better than the others.

Your diagnosis should have established the extent to which the problem is one of people, systems, structure or circumstances. Fallible human beings may well be at the bottom of it. If so, remember not to indulge in indiscriminate criticism. Your job is to be constructive; to build people up, not to destroy them.

Avoid being too theoretical. Take account of circumstances – including the ability of the people available now to deal with the problem, or, if you have doubts, the availability of people from elsewhere who can be deployed effectively. Your recommendation should be practical in the sense that it can be made to work with resources which are readily available and within acceptable timescales.

You must make clear not only what needs to be done but *how* it is to be done. Assess costs as well as benefits and demonstrate that the benefits outweigh the costs. Resources have to be allocated, a timescale set and, above all, specific responsibility given to people to get the work done. Your recommendations have to be realistic in the sense that they can be phased in without undue disruption and without spending more time and money than is justified by the results.

Take care when you apportion blame to individuals. Some may clearly be inadequate and have to be replaced. Others may be the victims of poor management, poor training or circumstances beyond their control. Their help may be essential in overcoming the trouble. It is unwise to destroy their confidence or their willingness to help.

USING MANAGEMENT CONSULTANTS TO TROUBLE SHOOT

A management consultant has been described, or dismissed, as someone with a briefcase 50 miles from home. Robert Townsend (62) has suggested that consultants are people 'who borrow your watch to tell you what time it is and then walk off with it'.

Calling in consultants in desperation can indeed be an expensive and time-wasting exercise. But they have their uses. They bring experience and expertise in diagnosis. They can act as an extra pair of hands when suitable people are not available from within the organization. And, as a third party, they can sometimes see the wood through the trees and solve problems or unlock ideas within the company which, sadly, are often inhibited by structural or managerial constraints.

There are, however, a number of rules, as set out opposite, which you should be aware of when contemplating bringing in consultants.

DO	DON'T
Get tenders from two or three firms and compare, not only their fees, but their understanding of your problem and the practical suggestions they have on how to tackle it.	Be bamboozled by a smooth principal who is employed mainly as a salesperson.
	Go for a big firm simply because it has a good reputation. It may not have the particular expertise you want.
Check on the experience of the firm and, most important, of the consultant who is going to carry out the assignment.	Accept any old consultant who comes along. Many redundant executives have set up as consultants without having a clue about how to do it. There is a lot of skill in being an effective consultant. Check that the firm is a member of the Management Consultants Association or that the principal is a member of the Institute of Management Consultants (for UK-based firms). These provide a guarantee of professional status.
Brief the firm very carefully on the terms of reference.	
Get a clear statement of the proposed programme, total estimated costs (fees *plus* expenses) and who is actually going to carry out the assignment.	
Meet and assess the consultant who is going to carry out the work.	
Insist on regular progress meetings.	Allow the consultant to change the programme without prior consultation.
Ensure that the outcome of the assignment is a practical proposal which you can implement yourself, or with the minimum of further help.	Leave the consultant to his or her own devices for too long. Keep in touch. Appoint a member of your staff to liaise or even to work with the consultant.

24

Improving business performance

AIMS

The aims of programmes to improve business performance are to:

- increase shareholder value;
- ensure that every activity conducted in the organization creates added value;
- develop an effective organization which achieves its goals to the satisfaction of its other stakeholders;
- address specific issues concerning profitability, productivity, costs and operating efficiency.

Meeting the needs of shareholders

It is essential to align the interests of shareholders with corporate performance. This will be measured by shareholder value analysis, and the key measure that has emerged in recent years is economic value added (EVA). This measures the difference between a company's post-tax operating profit and the cost of the capital invested in the business. The cost of capital includes the cost of equity – what shareholders expect to receive through capital gains. The concept of EVA is based on the proposition that it is not good enough for a company simply to make a profit. It has to justify the cost of its capital, equity included. If it does not do that, it will not provide a satisfactory return to its investors.

Increasing shareholder value

In his book *Mean Business*, Albert Dunlop makes the point that business is simple and needs to follow four simple rules:

1. Get the right management team – as small as is feasible.
2. Cut costs to improve the profit and loss account.
3. Focus on the core business and dispose of non-core assets to improve the balance sheet.
4. Get a real strategy; one that requires setting a few, major, attainable goals and then tenaciously pursuing them.

Improving business performance

The starting point for a drive to improve business performance will be the four rules set out above. The next step is to benchmark what other organizations are doing in order to set standards. This can provide the basis for the specific programmes described in this chapter concerned with profit and productivity improvement, cost cutting, business process re-engineering and turning round the business. Your part in improving business performance depends heavily on the degree to which you are aware of business needs as discussed at the end of this chapter.

BENCHMARKING

To establish how well – or badly – you are doing and to identify areas for improvement, it pays to compare your organization with its best-performing peers. You need to study what the 'best-in-class' companies are doing – how well they perform generally in comparison with your business and how well they are carrying out specific activities and processes.

Asked what he thought of his wife, James Thurber replied: 'Compared with what?' Whatever we are comparing – products, processes, output levels, performance standards – we all seek yardsticks or measures to enable meaningful comparisons to take place. This is what benchmarking is about.

What is benchmarking?

Xerox, one of the first firms to carry out regular benchmarking surveys, defines benchmarking as:

> A continuous, systematic process of evaluating companies recognized as industry leaders, to determine business and work processes that represent 'best practice' and establish rational performance goals.

The main benchmarking activities are:

1. *Competitive analysis* – the systematic analysis of competitor activity so that you can improve your performance.
2. *Best practice* – looking for best practice associated with the way companies do things.
3. *Performance comparison* – a means of assessing company and department performance.
4. *Standard setting* – a means of providing guidance on setting appropriate and stretching performance standards.

Why benchmark?

The purpose of benchmarking is to identify areas for improvement and to stimulate change. Its underlying logic is compelling: unless you know what the competition is doing, and how customers rate your efforts on a comparative basis, how can you establish meaningful goals for improvement? Without benchmarks, the impact of improvement programmes can be a lottery; raising standards to an industry average, for example, is not the same as leap-frogging rivals. Benchmarking helps to set targets which enable companies to achieve sustainable competitive advantage.

What do you benchmark?

Anything which drives or measures performance can be benchmarked. Examples include productivity, product quality, standards of service delivery, cycle times, pay, fund management performance and product characteristics.

Benchmarking sometimes concentrates on overall performance indices and ratios but it often produces the best results when it compares operational or process performance levels so that specific standards and targets for improvement can be set. When valid and reliable comparative data is available on, say, delivery times, managers who will not accept that it is possible to improve their performance can be told: 'If they can do it, then so can you.'

With whom do you benchmark?

Ideally you benchmark with direct competitors, especially those who are operating in similar circumstances to your own. But direct competitors may not be willing to exchange information. In any case, useful comparisons can be made with out-of-sector companies. Xerox, for example, looked at mail specialists L L Bean when it was evaluating customer service.

In some circumstances it may be valuable to benchmark within the organization, thus spreading best practice from one internal unit to another.

How do you benchmark?

Some organizations get outside help, but it is possible to run your own benchmarking exercise. This could consist of the following stages:

1. *Planning* – make decisions about what is to be benchmarked. You cannot do everything at once, so you must focus on those things which are likely to deliver the greatest returns – the drivers of performance.
2. *Collecting data* – decide on sources of data (other organizations and databases or publications). Approach the selected organizations, making sure you get to the right people, ask the right questions and evaluate the information you receive. You need to be reasonably certain that it is factual rather than propaganda material.

3. *Analysing results* – compare the figures and solutions provided by different organizations, ensuring that as far as possible you are comparing like with like. Make allowances for any significant operational differences which might affect the performance data. Assess as dispassionately as you can what can be learnt and applied within your own organization, bearing in mind that other people's solutions will not necessarily transplant successfully into your own organization.

4. *Implementing changes* – decide what improvements need to be made, and plan and execute the change. The change management process will be helped if the people affected have been involved in the planning, analysis and decision-making stages.

5. *Reviewing progress* – take stock of how the change programme is progressing and take corrective action as required. If may be necessary to obtain new information from different sources or to check on the validity of the data you have received.

What factors should be taken into account?

The following factors should be taken into account in analysing and using benchmark data:

● Benchmarking is likely to be most effective if the company has a clear vision of where it wants to go and well-articulated strategies for realizing that vision. It should know what its critical success factors are – the key drivers of organizational performance. Even if like-for-like comparisons can be made between the results achieved by different companies, the ways in which the leading performers have achieved their results may still be unclear. This is why benchmarking should cover processes as well as outcomes.

● What works well in one place will not necessarily work well elsewhere.

● Even if you get good reliable information from a number of sources, it still requires considerable skill to translate this into terms which will be meaningful in your organization.

● Make sure that organizations provide information on what they are actually achieving, not just their intentions for the future.

● There is often as much to be learnt from the failures and bad practices of comparator organizations (if you can find out about them) as there is from their successes.

PROFIT IMPROVEMENT

Profit is the result, not the objective, of efficient management. On its own, profit, as shown on the balance sheet, is not necessarily an accurate measure of success in business. Profit figures can be influenced by factors quite distinct from the trading performance of the company. These include how research and development is treated in the accounts, how stocks and work in progress are valued and how the flow of funds resulting from investments and realization of investments is dealt with.

The president of International Harvester once said: 'All you have to do in business is to make some stuff and sell it to someone else for more than you paid for it.' And the controller of Bethlehem Steel stated: 'We're not in business to make steel, we're not in business to build ships, we're not in business to erect buildings. We're in business to make money.'

Both these statements are, of course, gross over-simplifications, but at least they emphasize the importance of the flow of money. As Robert Heller (26) has said: 'Business and managers don't earn profits, they earn money.' And he has emphasized that the first rule of business is that cash in must exceed cash out. Profit improvement is about increasing the flow of money into the business and reducing the flow of money out. It is not about maximizing an abstraction called profit, which is subject to so many extraneous influences. Perhaps we should think of it as performance improvement measured in financial terms rather than profit improvement. But profit improvement is what most people call it, and this is the term used here, with the reservations expressed above.

FACTORS AFFECTING PROFIT IMPROVEMENT

The three key factors are sales, costs and effectiveness.

Sales

The maximization of sales revenue depends largely on good marketing, although the importance of delivering quality and high levels of service cannot be overestimated. There are two approaches to marketing. One is to assess the market in terms of what existing and potential customers will buy. This means an analysis of existing wants and buying patterns along with possible future needs. The other is to assess the scope for creating wants which do not exist at the moment, by developing and offering new products or services.

A company can maximize its market penetration by moving into market development (new markets for existing products), product development (improved or new products for existing markets) or diversification (new products for new markets). Good marketing ensures that the company and its products are presented to customers by advertising, merchandising and public relations in a way which will best promote sales.

Finally, good marketing ensures that prices match what customers can be persuaded to pay, with the objective of maximizing contribution to profits and direct overheads. Maximizing profit means getting the right balance between high margins and high sales volume. Sales depend on good marketing but do not necessarily follow from it. A well-trained, well-motivated and well-controlled sales force is an essential ingredient.

The final, but often neglected, ingredient is distribution. Effective marketing and selling will go for nought if order processing is inefficient, if the turn-round of customer orders takes too long, if the wrong distribution channels are used from the point of view of speed, reliability and cost, or if customer queries and complaints are not dealt with properly.

Costs

One of the many wise things Peter Drucker has said (17) is that cost, after all, does not exist by itself. It is always incurred – in intent, at least – for the sake of a result. What matters therefore is not the absolute cost level but the relationship between efforts and their results. The approach to cost reduction as described later in this chapter should therefore be to distinguish between those costs which are producing results and those which are not. Indiscriminate attacks on all costs – the 10 per cent slash approach – are counter-productive. On a selective basis, it may be better to cut something out altogether than to try to make a series of marginal cost reductions. As Drucker says: 'There is little point in trying to do cheaply what should not be done at all.'

Effectiveness

The objective should be effectiveness rather than just efficiency: to do the right things rather than merely to do things right. Effectiveness should be aimed for in the areas of:

● *Productivity* – getting more for less, whether it is human resources (output per head), capital (return on investment) or equipment (output per unit).
● *Finance* – tightening credit policies, cracking down on bad debts, controlling quantity and settlement discounts, optimizing cash-holdings while gaining maximum interest on surplus cash, and reducing interest payments on bank overdrafts to a minimum.
● *Inventory* – keeping the amount tied up in working capital to the minimum consistent with the need to satisfy customer demand.
● *Buying* – using supplier's warehouse space by 'calling off' at specified intervals, ensuring that competitive bids are obtained for all new or renewed contracts, specifying to buyers how they should use 'clout' to get good terms, resisting the temptation to over-order, having clearly laid down policies on mark-ups.

Approach to profit improvement

Profit improvement should be a continuous exercise. It should not be left until a crisis forces you to think about it. Start with an analysis of your current situation. Look at the whole product range for each market and assess the relative profitability and potential of all products and markets. Try to spot those which are fading and the up-and-coming ones. For fading products or markets, consider whether remedial or surgical treatment is appropriate. For up-and-coming products or markets, work out how their progress can be assured and, possibly, accelerated.

Use the 80/20 rule (Pareto's Law) to suggest the 20 per cent of your products/markets which generate 80 per cent of your profits. Concentrate on maximizing the effectiveness of the 20 per cent of areas where the impact will be greatest.

Identify those factors within the business which are restraining its potential and, in Drucker's words, 'convert into opportunity what everybody else considers dangers'. Build on strengths.

Then look ahead. Project trends, anticipate problems and, where appropriate, innovate so that you can challenge the future rather than being overwhelmed by it.

Above all, bear in mind the results of the following highly pertinent research carried out by William Hall (22). Hall looked at 64 companies in depth to determine which had the best hopes of surviving in a hostile environment. Writing in the *Harvard Business Review*, he identified two key factors. The best business survivors are, first, those which can deliver their products at the lowest cost, and second, those which have the highest 'differentiated position'. This means having the product which customers perceive most clearly as being different from and, in important respects, better than that of the competition.

PRODUCTIVITY IMPROVEMENT

The benefits of improved productivity

Work measurement programmes usually show that staff not on an incentive scheme perform at about 50 to 60 per cent of the standard that can reasonably be expected from an average worker.

It has been established that productivity audits of manufacturing and distribution activities consistently pinpoint opportunities of improving output by from 25 to 40 per cent with much the same plant and human resources. Similarly, clerical work measurement programmes can almost always save more than 15 per cent of staff without affecting input or quality. The scope for improvement is tremendous and so is the pay-off, as the analysis in Table 24.1 shows.

Table 24.1 *Scope for productivity improvement*

Payroll as a percentage of sales	Percentage increase in profit before tax* from improvement in productivity of:			
	5%	10%	20%	40%
20	20	40	80	160
30	30	60	20	240
40	40	80	60	320
50	50	100	200	500

*Assumes a return on sales of 5%

The pay-off from improving productivity is high, but how can you achieve it?

The first thing to do is to overcome apathy. Both managers and the workforce must be persuaded somehow that they have a common interest in increasing output per head. This is a difficult exercise. It requires considerable powers of leadership from the top and this means positive programmes for motivating and involving all concerned to obtain their commitment to improvement. Gainsharing schemes which share the outcomes of increased productivity are a valuable means of obtaining commitment.

A continuous drive for productivity is required and a productivity improvement programme based on a productivity audit should be the instrument.

Productivity improvement programme

The objective of a productivity improvement programme should be to achieve a significant change for the better in the relationship between outputs and inputs or, to put it another way, an improvement in the following ratio:

Performance achieved:Resources consumed

What are the factors of success?

A successful productivity improvement campaign depends on:

- a well-planned programme based on a productivity audit, with positive objectives and a clearly defined timetable;
- a commitment on the part of management and supervisors to the programme;
- the involvement of employees in the programme so that they are prepared, with suitable safeguards concerning their future, to participate in implementing it;
- a recognition that the benefits resulting from the programme should be shared among everyone concerned.

These are demanding criteria and they are not easily achieved. Things can go wrong. Managers, supervisors and other employees may all be suspicious of the programme. They will see it as either a device for exposing their inadequacies, an instrument for producing unacceptable change or a threat to their livelihood. These are emotional reactions and, once emotion comes in at the door, reason goes out of the window. So communication, education, involvement and persuasion are essential aspects of the programme.

Even if your powers of persuasion are great and you manage to involve employees in the programme sufficiently to overcome their natural resistance to change, there are a number of mistakes to be avoided in implementing productivity improvements. These include:

- making recommendations based on inaccurate information;
- making recommendations on new equipment, methods or procedures without properly evaluating the cost-effectiveness of the proposal;
- making recommendations without properly evaluating the impact of changes on other departments;
- proposing changes without giving sufficient consideration to the reactions of those involved.

These are common, but avoidable, errors. Those responsible for productivity improvement programmes will be much less likely to commit them if they are made aware of the dangers in advance. This is why it is important to be quite clear about who runs the programme and how it should be conducted.

Who runs the programme?

The programme for improving productivity must be run by top management. They should set the objectives, define terms of reference, appoint the executive responsible for the programme, provide him or her with the resources required and monitor the results achieved.

A senior manager responsible directly to the chief executive should be in charge of the programme. Never use a committee. It will spend its time talking, not doing. The employment of outside consultants will have to be considered. You should normally only use them as 'an extra pair of hands' providing expertise and resources not necessarily available within the organization. But they should be kept under control. They are there to work under the direction of the productivity executive, not to pursue their own line.

Consultants are often used as hatchet men or women to put forward the unpleasant recommendations that no one else wants to make. This is a pity. If you believe in productivity, you should realize that its achievement may not always be a comfortable process. You ought to be prepared to take justified action yourself and not rely on others to do it for you.

When you have decided who runs the programme, make sure that they know what you want them to achieve and that they adopt a systematic approach.

Implementing improvements

It will be much easier to implement improvements in productivity if the objectives of your programme are understood and accepted by all concerned. Clear direction from the top and a systematic approach to conducting investigations are also important. But you will fail to achieve the results you want if you cannot get your workforce involved in the programme.

If you can get your staff involved, they are more likely to identify with the results. This will reduce their natural resistance to change and ensure their co-operation. It will become their programme rather than something imposed upon them. In other words, they will own it.

COST CUTTING

Costs always require to be controlled. You should start with the assumption that costs are too high and that they can be reduced. This assumption is based on the knowledge that some companies have not only survived but flourished after drastic cost-cutting exercises. When you remove the fat that always exists, you get a leaner and more powerful organization.

Cost cutting requires these basic approaches:

1. Decide where and what to cut.
2. Plan to cut.
3. Conduct the cost-reduction.

What to cut

Your attack on costs should concentrate on these six areas:

1. *Payroll costs* – in labour-intensive companies payroll costs may exceed 50 per cent of income. Over-staffing, especially in service and staff departments, is a major contributory cause of excessively high costs.
2. *Manufacturing costs* – these are the actual costs incurred in making products; they reflect labour, material and operating costs but also, most importantly, the way in which the product has been designed.
3. *Selling costs* – these may be largely accounted for by the sales force, which is covered under payroll costs. But the figure will also include advertising, promotions, public relations, packaging and display material.
4. *Development costs* – these are the costs of developing new products, markets, processes and materials, and of acquiring new businesses.
5. *Material and inventory costs* – the cost of buying materials and bought-in parts and of maintaining optimum stock levels.
6. *Operating costs* – all the other costs incurred in operating the business; these will include space, computers and their systems, the provision of plant and equipment, and all the services required to keep the organization going.

Waste

Any examination of costs should aim to identify wasteful practices. The areas where they can occur need to be identified before conducting a cost-reduction exercise so that attention can be directed to likely trouble spots. Concentrate both on company practices or procedures which lead to waste or pointless costs and on areas where staff can waste time or incur unnecessary expenditure.

The company can be wasteful in any or all of the following ways:

- over-complex procedures
- too much checking and verifying of work
- too many and/or too large committees
- too many layers of management
- bottlenecks and inefficient work flows or procurement procedures
- delays in decision-making because authority is not delegated down the line
- over-rigid adherence to rules and regulations.

Time-wasting practices by staff include arriving late or leaving early, prolonged tea or meal breaks, unnecessary breaks for any other reason, and dealing with personal matters in company time.

Cost-creating practices also include extravagant use of the company's facilities and equipment, such as photocopying machines, telephones and stationery, and even spending too much time on the internet or generating unnecessary e-mail messages.

Planning to cut costs

First, you build cost effectiveness into your plans, possibly basing them on a business process re-engineering exercise as described later in this chapter. In manufacturing, value analysis techniques as described below can be used to remove unnecessary cost elements and improve the value–cost relationship, which means a product that provides the necessary function with the essential qualities at minimum cost.

Then you introduce or improve procedures which define what costs you can incur and, at a later stage, control expenditure against budget. Zero-base budgeting, which involves having to justify every item on the budget from scratch, is a useful technique for taking every expense and shaking it to make sure that it is justified.

Plans

Plans should be based on cost/benefit studies which aim to get the best ratio between expenditure and results, ie to minimize costs and maximize benefits. The emphasis should be on realism. It is good to be forward-looking and entrepreneurial. But if you are like that, you are always in danger of becoming euphoric about the future, overestimating the benefits and underestimating the costs. At the planning stage you must be realistic about costs. Don't accept averages and assumed overhead rates. Get actuals. Find out what you are really going to spend and add at least 10 per cent for contingencies. Allow for inflation too.

You should be equally realistic about likely benefits. Carry out 'sensitivity analysis' to determine the effects on profit and costs of optimistic, realistic and pessimistic forecasts of performance.

Design

Ensure that when products, systems or services are designed, at every stage the costs of what you are going to do are evaluated. Use value analysis techniques for this purpose. Value analysis takes each part of the product, service or system and subjects it to detailed examination to see if there is any way in which its costs could be reduced without affecting quality. You start with the assumption that anything you use or do can be bought, made or operated at less cost.

Value analysis in manufacturing is often carried out by a committee using brainstorming techniques to consider alternative, less costly ways of achieving the functions for which the article is being manufactured. These functions cover the use to which the article is being put, and therefore consideration has to be given to marketing and pricing as well as manufacturing costs. But, given a definition of use, the main aim of value analysis is to reduce the costs of materials, processing and labour. The following is a checklist of points to be covered:

1. Does its use contribute to value?
2. Is its cost proportionate to its usefulness?
3. Does it need all its features?
4. Is there a better alternative which will meet its intended use?
5. Can a usable part be made by a less costly method?
6. Can a standard and less costly part be used instead?
7. Will another dependable supplier provide it at less cost?
8. Can alternative and cheaper materials or components be used?
9. Can it be manufactured with the use of less skilled labour or less expensive machinery or equipment?
10. Can it be manufactured in a way which will reduce the number of standard labour hours required?
11. Can its design be simplified to reduce manufacturing costs?
12. Can the tolerances specified be modified to ease manufacture and reduce reject rates?

Although value analysis was first developed as a design engineering technique, the approach is equally applicable to the design of any system or service where the component parts can be costed.

The cost-reduction exercise

A cost-reduction exercise is a planned campaign aimed at cutting costs by a specified amount. It requires three steps:

1. *Setting targets* either for immediate cuts in crisis conditions or for specific reductions in the short term (defined in weeks rather than months). Targets may be set in specific areas, eg a 10 per cent cut in staff; or they may be for a more comprehensive overhead reduction or a productivity increase.

   Productivity targets expressed in financial terms, such as 'reduce costs per unit of output by 3 per cent', may be less immediate but they could usefully be incorporated in a set of cost-reduction targets as longer-term objectives. The message must be got across that unit costs are there to be attacked at all times because, after all, they aggregate into total costs. Wherever possible, get down to basics – the shop floor and the general office. That is where the main costs are incurred. Keep it simple. Look at specific items. Use value analysis. Compare and contrast to identify places where costs are excessive.

2. *Deciding where to cut*, which will probably be in manpower costs or wasteful practices. It is remarkable how often departmental managers who scream with pain when they are told to cut their staff by 10 per cent cope quite well afterwards. Experience has shown that organizations can easily cut staff numbers by 15 per cent without reducing effectiveness if they take steps to ensure that the remaining staff are employed more efficiently.

3. *Deciding how to cut* – allocating responsibilities and then drawing up and implementing the programme.

RE-ENGINEERING THE BUSINESS

Even when a business is functioning well there is much to be said for conducting a thorough analysis and review of the key business processes to ensure that they will be capable of sustaining growth and the creation of added value. Business processes re-engineering is a method of conducting such a review.

Business process re-engineering (BPR) is essentially about business *process*, which can be defined as:

> The collection of activities that takes one or more kinds of input and creates an output that is of value to the customer.

This 'order fulfilment' is a process which starts with an order as its input and results in the delivery of the ordered goods. This delivery is the value that the process creates. This is much wider than simply a selling or distribution activity. Business process re-engineering does not look at related functions as separate entities. Instead it examines the process that contains and links those functions together from initiation to completion.

Approaches to business process re-engineering

The chief tool of business process re-engineering is a clean sheet of paper. Re-engineers start from the future and work backwards. They are unconstrained by existing methods, people or departments. In effect they ask: 'If we were a new company, how would we run the place?' Then they take what are usually drastic steps to make the company conform to the vision.

Conventional process structures are fragmented and piecemeal. Work tends to be organized as a sequence of narrowly defined tasks. The people carrying out these tasks are then aggregated into departments and managers are installed to administer them. Control systems funnel information up the hierarchy to the few who are presumed to know what to do with it.

Re-engineering takes a much broader and radical view. It looks at the fundamental processes of a business from a cross-functional perspective. Its aim is to achieve integration. It breaks away from conventional wisdom and the constraints of organizational boundaries. It uses information technology not to automate an existing process but to facilitate a new one. Expert systems, for example, are used to enable people to use accumulated and systematized knowledge to make decisions on the spot without having to refer to higher authority or bring in specialists.

Re-engineers ask two fundamental questions: 'Why?' and 'What if?' In that respect they are following in the footsteps of good methods engineers, who use critical examination techniques to challenge assumptions, indeed to question the very existence of an activity, and only when they receive a satisfactory answer, to explore better (ie quicker, less costly, more efficient) ways of doing it. The critical examination questions they ask are:

- What is done? Why do it?
- How is it done? Why do it that way?

- Where is it done? Why do it there?
- When is it done? Why do it then?
- Who does it? Why that person?

The difference between this traditional and often very effective approach and business process re-engineering is that the latter carries out an even more fundamental look at business processes across the organization. This examination is driven by top management as a means of achieving radical change affecting the whole business or a major part of it. Method study tended to be more piecemeal and not integrated with a business strategy for comprehensive change and improvement. Another significant difference is that business process re-engineering is much more concerned with exploiting the power of information technology. Again, however, systems design in BPR cuts across functional boundaries and, in contrast to the traditional approach to systems analysis, is focused on producing new and fully integrated solutions.

The considerations which should be taken into account in a BPR exercise are described below.

Get the strategy straight first
One of the mottoes of BPR is: 'Don't fix stuff you shouldn't be doing in the first place.' Re-engineering is about processes and operations; only strategy can tell you which ones matter. It is necessary to start with a long hard look at what business the organization is in and how it intends to make money out of it. It is equally important to identify the core competencies of the organization and ensure that the business is built round them.

Lead from the top
The one crucial factor for success in re-engineering is executive leadership with real vision. Moreover, because re-engineering is cross-functional, it must be driven by people with the authority to oversee a process from end to end and top to bottom. There should be a core team of functional heads led by the chief executive.

Create a sense of urgency
Re-engineering will break apart under political pressure or peter out after a few easy gains unless the case for doing it is compelling, urgent and constantly refreshed.

Methodology

Business process re-engineering cannot be planned meticulously and accomplished in small and cautious steps. It tends to be an all-or-nothing proposition, often with an uncertain result. It is therefore a high-risk undertaking and not worth attempting unless there is a pressing need to rethink what the organization is doing overall or in a major area.

Process re-engineering should not spend too much time studying existing work flows. However, the review process should aim to identify points of leverage where new thinking will provide the greatest benefit.

TURNING ROUND ORGANIZATIONS

Organizations can get into trouble in terms of generating cash and added value for all sorts of reasons. Complacency, poor leadership, marketing and financial management are typical causes. Low productivity or competitive products or services (out of date, poor quality or too costly) are also common reasons for a crisis. Shareholder value is diminishing and the institutions take action to replace the existing chief executive and, possibly, other members of top management. A new broom is appointed with a brief to 'turn round' the business, ie bring it back into profitability and deliver higher value to shareholders. Sometimes a management consultancy which specializes in this type of 'turnaround' exercise is brought in.

Stuart Wallis, who specializes in turnarounds, described his approach in *The Director*, May 1996. He describes the 10 steps it is necessary to take to achieve a good result.

1. *Meet the people* – get to know as many people as possible and get their ideas on strengths and weaknesses, opportunities and threats and what needs to be done. Then produce your first action list.
2. *Hold a senior staff get-together* to present and discuss your action list and agree on an action programme. You have to present your actions openly and forcefully but be prepared to listen.
3. *Pick your dream team* – decide on your ideal organization structure and who is suitable within the organization to fill the key positions. Fill the gaps by recruitment and let the others go.

4. *Ensure that communication channels are open* – this applies to both internal and external channels.
5. *Promote quality* – develop a quality culture, challenging anything which is not of the best.
6. *Keep it simple* – ensure that operating statements contain all the information required on one sheet of paper and expressed in language that non-accountants can understand.
7. *Let cash be king* – keep tight control on cash by speedy collection of debts, proper control of stocks and creditors, tight controls on expenses and capital expenditure.
8. *Have a clear idea of where you are going* – be certain of where you are going in terms of market share and market positioning and then decide on the necessary building blocks and identify the pitfalls. Deal with the latter first.
9. *Get the balance sheet right* – ensure that the assets and liabilities are correctly valued, that the cost of reorganization is funded and that bankers, institutions and your accountants are informed of your proposed actions.
10. *Don't forget what you are doing it for* – ensure that the share-holders' and your employees' best interests are being served and check constantly actions to ensure that they are delivering the required results. If they are not, 'Either change direction or resign immediately'.

BUSINESS AWARENESS

Business awareness is a managerial competence which is frequently included in performance management and 360° feed-back appraisal schemes. To demonstrate that you are fully competent in this area you need to:

- continually identify and explore business opportunities;
- understand the business priorities of the organization;
- appreciate the organizational core competencies and critical success factors;
- anticipate and seek to understand the needs of customers;
- establish and maintain good relationships with customers;
- meet customer expectations as far as possible;
- constantly seek methods of ensuring that the organization becomes more business-like in such areas as communication, cost control and operational efficiency.

25

Influencing skills

Managers are constantly having to exert influence – on their bosses, their colleagues, their staff and their clients, customers and suppliers. They must know about persuading people, presenting cases and resolving problems when exerting influence.

PERSUADING PEOPLE

A manager's job is 60 per cent getting it right and 40 per cent putting it across. Managers spend a lot of time persuading other people to accept their ideas and suggestions.

Persuasion is just another word for selling. You may feel that good ideas should sell themselves, but life is not like that. Everyone resists change and anything new is certain to be treated with suspicion. So it's worth learning a few simple rules that will help you to sell your ideas more effectively.

SIX RULES FOR EFFECTIVE PERSUASION

1. *Define your objective and get the facts.* Decide what you want to achieve and why. Assemble all the facts you need to support your case. Eliminate emotional arguments so that you and others can judge the proposition on the facts alone.

2. *Find out what 'they' want.* Never underestimate people's natural resistance to change. But bear in mind that such resistance is proportional, not to the total extent of the change, but to the extent to which it affects them personally. When asked to accept a proposition, the first questions people ask themselves are: 'How does this affect me?' 'What do I stand to lose?' 'What do I stand to gain?' These questions must be answered before persuasion can start.

   The key to all persuasion and selling is to see your proposition from the other person's point of view. If you can really put yourself into the other person's shoes you will be able to foresee objections and present your ideas in the way most attractive to him or her.

   You must find out how people look at things – what they want. Listen to what they have to say. Don't talk too much. Ask questions. If they ask you a question reply with another question. Find out what they are after. Then present your case in a way that highlights its benefits to them, or at least reduces any objections or fears.

3. *Prepare a simple and attractive presentation.* Your presentation should be as simple and straightforward as possible. Emphasize the benefits. Don't bury the selling points. Lead them in gently so there are no surprises. Anticipate objections.

4. *Make them a party to your ideas.* Get them to contribute, if at all possible. Find some common ground in order to start off with agreement. Don't antagonize them. Avoid defeating them in arguments. Help them to preserve their self-esteem. Always leave a way out.

5. *Positively sell the benefits.* Show conviction. You are not going to sell anything if you don't believe in it and communicate that belief. To persuade effectively you have to sell yourself. You must spell out the benefits. *What* you are proposing is of less interest to the individuals concerned than the effects of that proposal on them.

6. *Clinch and take action.* Choose the right moment to clinch the proposal and get out. Make sure that you are not pushing too

hard, but when you reach your objective don't stay and risk losing it. Take prompt follow-up action. There is no point in going to all the trouble of getting agreement if you let matters slide afterwards.

CASE PRESENTATION

As a manager, you will frequently have to make out a case for what you think should be done. You have to persuade people to believe in your views and accept your recommendations. To do this, you must have a clear idea of what you want, and you have to show that you believe in it yourself. Above all, the effectiveness of your presentation will depend upon the care with which you have prepared it.

Preparation

Thorough preparation is vital. You must think through not only what should be done and why, but also how people will react. Only then can you decide how to make your case: stressing the benefits without underestimating the costs, and anticipating objections.

You should think of the questions your audience is likely to raise, and answer them in advance, or at least have your answers ready. The most likely questions are:

What – is the proposal?
     – will be the benefit?
     – will it cost?
     – are the facts, figures, forecasts and assumptions upon which the proposal is based?
     – are the alternatives?
Why – should we change what we are doing now?
     – is this proposal or solution better than the alternatives?
How – is the change to be made?
     – are the snags to be overcome?
     – have the alternatives been examined?
     – am I affected by the change?
Who – will be affected by the change and what will be their reaction?

- is likely to have the strongest views for or against the change, and why?
- will implement the proposal?

When – should this be done?

To make your case you have to do three things:

1. Show that it is based on a thorough analysis of the facts and that the alternatives were properly evaluated before the conclusion was reached. If you have made assumptions, you must demonstrate that these are reasonable on the basis of relevant experience and justifiable projections, which allow for the unexpected. Bear in mind Robert Heller's words (26) that 'a proposal is only as strong as its weakest assumption'.
2. Spell out the benefits – to the company *and* the individuals to whom the case is being made. Wherever possible, express benefits in financial terms. Abstract benefits, such as customer satisfaction or workers' morale, are difficult to sell. But don't produce 'funny numbers' – financial justification which will not stand up to examination.
3. Reveal costs. Don't try to disguise them in any way. And be realistic. Your proposition will be destroyed if anyone can show that you have underestimated the costs.

Remember, boards want to know in precise terms what they will get for their money. Most boards are cautious, being unwilling and often unable to take much risk. For this reason, it is difficult to make a case for experiments or pilot schemes unless the board, committee or individual can see what the benefits and the ultimate bill will be.

Presentation

Your proposal will often be made in two stages: a written report followed by an oral presentation. The quality of the latter will often tip the balance in your favour (or against you). Effective speaking and writing reports are dealt with in Chapters 19 and 43 respectively, but it is appropriate to note at this stage some special points you should bear in mind when making a case orally in front of an audience:

1. Your presentation should not just consist of a repetition of the facts in the written report. It should be used to put across the main points of the argument, leaving out the detail.

2. Do not assume that your audience has read the written report or understood it. While you are talking, try to avoid referring to the report. This may switch people's attention from what you are saying. Use visual aids, preferably a flip chart, to emphasize the main points. But don't overdo them – it is possible to be too slick. The audience will be convinced by you, not by your elegant visual aids.

3. Make sure your opening secures people's attention. They must be immediately interested in your presentation. Begin by outlining your plan, its benefits and costs, and let the audience know how you are going to develop your case.

4. Bring out the disadvantages and the alternative courses of action so that you are not suspected of concealing or missing something.

5. Avoid being drawn into too much detail. Be succinct and to the point.

6. An emphatic summing up is imperative. It should convey with complete clarity what you want the board, committee or individual to do.

The effectiveness of your presentation will be largely dependent on how well you have prepared – not only putting your facts, figures and arguments clearly down on paper but also deciding what you are going to say at the meeting and how you are going to say it. The more important the case, the more carefully you should rehearse the presentation.

Checklist

1. Do you know exactly what you want?
2. Do you really believe in your case?
3. Have you obtained and checked all the facts that support your case?
4. What are the strongest arguments for your case?
5. Why must the present situation be changed?
6. Who else will be affected? Unions, other divisions or departments?
7. What are the arguments against your plan?
8. What alternatives are there to your plan?
9. To whom are you presenting your plan? Have you done any lobbying?

10. Have you discussed the finances with the experts?
11. Do you know who are your probable allies and who are likely to be your opponents?
12. Have you prepared handouts of any complicated figures?
13. Have you discussed the best time to present your case?
14. Your ideas were good when you first thought of them: are they still as good?

RESOLVING PROBLEMS WHEN INFLUENCING PEOPLE

You may believe that you are simply presenting a set of facts or clear and useful recommendations to other people which they will understand completely and act upon without hesitation. But the barriers to communication mentioned in Chapter 7 may mean that it does not always work out as planned. As suggested by Steibel (58), the four steps you can take to resolve potential problems are as follows:

1. Determine whether the problem is a misunderstanding (a failure to understand each other accurately) or a true disagreement (a failure to agree even when both parties understand one another). It is not necessarily possible to resolve a true disagreement by understanding each other better. People generally believe that an argument is a battle to understand who is correct. More often, it is a battle to decide who is more stubborn.
2. Create the person's next move. It is not a question of deciding what we want to do but what we want the other person to do. Your goal is to get results, not indulge in emotions. Break the problem into manageable pieces and deal with them one step at a time.
3. Use their own perceptions to convince people because they decide what to do on the basis of their own perceptions, not yours.
4. Predict the other person's response – everything we say should be focused on that likely response.

26

Leadership

Leadership is the process of inspiring individuals to give of their best to achieve a desired result. It is about getting people to move in the right direction, gaining their commitment, and motivating them to achieve their goals. According to Warren Bennis and Bert Nanus (9): 'Managers do things right, leaders do the right things.'

THE ROLES OF THE LEADER

Leaders have two essential roles. They have to:

1. *Achieve the task* – that is why their group exists. Leaders ensure that the group's purpose is fulfilled. If it is not, the result is frustration, disharmony, criticism and eventually, perhaps, disintegration of the group.
2. *Maintain effective relationships* – between themselves and the members of the group, and between the people within the group. These relationships are effective if they contribute to achieving the task. They can be divided into those concerned with the team and its morale and sense of common purpose,

and those concerned with individuals and how they are motivated.

John Adair (1), the expert on leadership, suggested some time ago that these demands are best expressed as three areas of need which leaders are there to satisfy. These are: (1) *task needs* – to get the job done; (2) *individual needs* – to harmonize the needs of the individual with the needs of the task and the group; and (3) *group needs* – to build and maintain team spirit.

Other more recent research, including that conducted by the Industrial Society as described later in this chapter, has expanded and refined this model, but it still rings true as a basic description of what leadership is about.

LEADERSHIP STYLES

Leaders adopt different styles which can be classified as:

- *Charismatic/non-charismatic.* Charismatic leaders rely on their personality, their inspirational qualities and their 'aura'. They are often visionary leaders who are achievement orientated, calculated risk takers and good communicators. Non-charismatic leaders rely mainly on their know-how (authority goes to the person who knows), their quiet confidence and their cool, analytical approach to dealing with problems.
- *Autocratic/democratic.* Autocratic leaders impose their decisions, using their position to force people to do as they are told. Democratic leaders encourage people to participate and involve themselves in decision-taking.
- *Enabler/controller.* Enablers inspire people with their vision of the future and empower them to accomplish team goals. Controllers manipulate people to obtain their compliance.
- *Transactional/transformational.* Transactional leaders trade money, jobs and security for compliance. Transformational leaders motivate people to strive for higher-level goals.

THE IMPACT OF THE SITUATION

The situation in which leaders and their teams function will influence the approaches that leaders adopt. There is no such thing as an ideal leadership style. It all depends. The factors affecting the degree to which a style is appropriate will be the type of organization, the nature of the task, the characteristics of the group and, importantly, the personality of the leader. A task-orientated approach (autocratic, controlling, transactional) may be best in emergency or crisis situations, or when the leader has power, formal backing and a relatively well-structured task. In these circumstances the group is more ready to be directed and told what to do. In less well-structured or ambiguous situations, where results depend on the group working well together with a common sense of purpose, leaders who are more concerned with maintaining good relationships (democratic, enablers, transformational) are more likely to obtain good results.

However, commentators such as Charles Handy are concerned that intelligent organizations have to be run by persuasion and consent. He suggests that the heroic leader of the past 'knew all, could do all and could solve every problem'. Now, the post-heroic leader has come to the fore, who 'asks how every problem can be solved in a way that develops other people's capacity to handle it'.

LEADERSHIP QUALITIES

The qualities required of leaders may vary somewhat in different situations, but research into, and analysis of, effective leaders have identified a number of generic characteristics which good leaders are likely to have. John Adair lists the following qualities:

- *enthusiasm* – to get things done which they can communicate to other people;
- *confidence* – belief in themselves which again people can sense (but this must not be over-confidence, which leads to arrogance);
- *toughness* – resilient, tenacious and demanding high standards, seeking respect but not necessarily popularity;
- *integrity* – being true to oneself – personal wholeness, soundness and honesty which inspire trust;
- *warmth* – in personal relationships, caring for people and being considerate;
- *humility* – willingness to listen and take the blame; not being arrogant and overbearing.

WHAT ORGANIZATIONS REQUIRE OF LEADERS

Research conducted by the Industrial Society (28) and published in 1997 showed what organizations required of leaders and how these requirements fit into today's structures and cultures. What organizations want is:

- leaders who will make the right space for people to perform well without having to be watched over – not bosses;
- flat structures where people can be trusted to work with minimal supervision;
- a wide range of people who are able to 'take a lead', step into a leadership role when necessary and consistently behave in a responsible way;
- a culture where people can be responsive to customer demands and agile in the face of changing technology.

BEHAVIOURS PEOPLE VALUE IN LEADERS

The respondents to the Industrial Society survey were asked to rank the importance of 35 factors in leader behaviour. The top 10 factors, in rank order, are as follows:

1. Shows enthusiasm.
2. Supports other people.
3. Recognizes individual effort.
4. Listens to individuals' ideas and problems.
5. Provides direction.
6. Demonstrates personal integrity.
7. Practises what he/she preaches.
8. Encourages teamwork.
9. Actively encourages feedback.
10. Develops other people.

LEADERSHIP CHECKLIST

The task

- What needs to be done and why?
- What results have to be achieved and by when?

- What problems have to be overcome?
- To what extent are these problems straightforward?
- Is there a crisis situation?
- What has to be done now to deal with the crisis?
- What are these priorities?
- What pressures are likely to be exerted?

The individual

- What are his/her strengths and weaknesses?
- What are likely to be the best ways of motivating him/her?
- What tasks is he/she best at doing?
- Is there scope to increase flexibility by developing new skills?
- How well does he/she perform in achieving targets and performance standards?
- Are there any areas where there is a need to develop skill or competence?
- How can I provide the individual with the sort of support and guidance which will improve his/her performance?

The team

- How well is the team organized?
- Does the team work well together?
- How can the commitment and motivation of the team be achieved?
- What is the team good and not so good at doing?
- What can I do to improve the performance of the team?
- Are team members flexible – capable of carrying out different tasks?
- Is there scope to empower the team so that it can take on greater responsibility for setting standards, monitoring performance and taking corrective action?
- Can the team be encouraged to work together to produce ideas for improving performance?

CASE STUDIES

The following are descriptions of the leadership style deployed by three highly effective managers. In each case the style was influenced by three factors: the environment, the people involved, and the personality of the manager.

Edward Smith

Ted Smith was the planning manager in a large engineering works. He had some 200 people working in the departments under his control who dealt with process planning, shop loading and production control. It was a highly responsible job and his staff included highly qualified engineers as well as large numbers of clerks doing routine work.

Ted's job was to make sure that his departments ran like clockwork. Everyone had to know exactly what to do and when they had to do it. Close co-operation between the three areas under his control was essential. Charismatic-type leadership was out. He had to be cool, calm, measured and a little bit distant. Everyone in the department had to believe he knew what he was doing and what he wanted.

He therefore held regular meetings with all his subordinates at which he quickly and efficiently reviewed progress, gave instructions and, as and when necessary, discussed problems. At these meetings he was prepared to switch quickly from being someone who knew exactly what he wanted and who expected people to do exactly as they were told (because it was sensible and right for them to do so) to someone who was prepared to listen to different views, weigh them up and decide. Sometimes he would deliberately throw his managers a problem and tell them to go away and solve it, and let him know the outcome of their actions.

Ted also ensured that his managers transmitted the content of these meetings down to first line supervisor level. And the latter were encouraged to meet their sections regularly. He emphasized throughout the need for teamwork and demonstrated his commitment by ensuring that at inter-departmental meetings problems of lack of co-operation or poor communications were given priority. The only time he was ever seen to express anger was when work suffered because of feuds between departments.

Elwyn Jones

Elwyn Jones was the personnel director of a large conglomerate in the food industry with over 80,000 employees. The firm had grown fast by acquisition and was highly decentralized. Staff were deliberately kept to a minimum at headquarters and Jones had only four executives responsible directly to him. He was, however, also responsible for the implementation of group personnel policies in each of the divisions and on these matters the divisional personnel directors were responsible to him.

Jones was not in a position to dictate to divisions what he wanted them to do. He could only influence them, and he felt that he had to get genuine acceptance for new policies before they could be introduced. He therefore had to consult on any changes or innovations he wished to introduce and, in most cases, he had to solicit cooperation on the testing of new ideas.

With his headquarters staff, Jones adopted a highly informal, almost permissive approach. He gave them broad guidelines on how they should develop their ideas in the divisions but encouraged them to think and act for themselves. He never called a formal meeting. He was more likely to withdraw to the local pub where, under the watchful eyes of 'big fat Nellie' behind the bar, he consumed pink gins with his colleagues and discussed strategies on entirely equal terms. He adopted precisely the same approach with the divisional personnel directors, although once or twice a year they all got together in a country hotel (one recommended by the *Good Food Guide*, of course) and spent a pleasant couple of days talking generally about their mutual interests.

James Robinson

Jim Robinson was the managing director of a medium-sized business (1,000 employees) in the fast-moving consumer goods sector of industry. He had come up the hard way and his experience had always been in similar firms. Business was highly competitive and the pressures on maintaining, never mind increasing, market share were considerable. Tough decisions about products, markets and people had to be made often and quickly. There was a non-executive chairman and three outside non-executive directors on the board, but they let Robinson get on with it as long as he delivered the results they wanted – which he did.

Robinson was a despot, although a benevolent one. He knew much more about the business as a whole than any of the other four executive directors, and the chairman and the key institutions (who were represented by the non-executive directors on the board) relied implicitly on his judgement.

Robinson's management style was rumbustious. He did not suffer fools gladly and he cracked down on any repeated inefficiencies or mistakes. He made the key decisions himself. At meetings of the executive directors he would sometimes say that he wanted the views of those present but stated quite clearly that he had already made up his mind and would need a lot of convincing to change it.

But his deep understanding of the business and his ability to think faster on his feet than anyone else meant that, while his autocratic behaviour was sometimes resented at the time, those subjected to it would say on almost every occasion 'you've got to give it to the old so-and-so – he knows his stuff and he's right'. He led, they followed. This was simply because they knew he could accomplish whatever was required in the volatile environment in which they worked.

27

Managing morale

The word *morale* has a slightly old-fashioned ring about it, associated with the military and those head teachers who talk, or used to talk, about 'esprit de corps'. But it is a term which is frequently used. It is a helpful one because it describes generally the feelings and attitudes of groups of people about their organization and their work. Morale is sometimes defined as being about group cohesion, about the feelings shared among a group concerning the situation it is in – what it is there to do and the extent to which its members believe generally that it is worthwhile and should be supported by their joint effort. If morale is high, commitment, enthusiasm and teamwork is more likely to be high. If it is low, people are likely to be uncooperative, argumentative in a negative way, and prone to conflict – with each other as well as management.

ASSESSING MORALE

Organizations can assess morale by the use of attitude or opinion surveys which ask questions about such things as:

- how well the organization is managed;
- the quality of the organization as an employer;
- the fairness with which people are treated by the organization and their bosses;
- the extent to which people like working for the organization;
- the amount of responsibility people are given;
- satisfaction with the current job;
- the extent to which the job makes the best use of skills and abilities;
- the support provided by bosses and colleagues;
- the extent to which achievements are recognized.

Such surveys can focus on particular departments or groups of employees, but they are best prepared and administered by experts, often from outside the company. Held regularly, they can measure changes in attitudes and morale over the years and indicate where steps need to be taken to improve.

Of course, if you keep your finger on the pulse by talking *and* listening to people and by observing what is going on, you can produce a good picture of the state of morale in your department or team. High morale will be indicated by enthusiasm, interest in and dedication to the task, effective teamwork and a willingness to discuss and resolve problems openly and without undue emotion. Poor morale will be evidenced by conflict, an excessive number of grievances, absenteeism, lateness, uncooperative behaviour, interpersonal disputes, errors, and failure to provide good service to customers.

IMPROVING MORALE

The best way to improve morale is to identify the reasons for the problem by talking and listening to people and then focus on corrective action. This action should be considered, planned and implemented with the active involvement of the team. Your task – not an easy one – is to convince them that they will benefit personally from participating in this process.

The following are examples of the action that can be taken in different circumstances:

- *lack of co-operation* – get people to re-examine jointly what they *and* their colleagues are there to do, and establish how they can improve things by establishing mutually agreed aims and methods of working together;

- *conflict* – get team members together to define the problem and agree on the objectives to be attained in reaching a solution; then get the group to develop alternative solutions and debate their merits; finally, get the group to agree on the preferred course of action and how it should be implemented;
- *lack of commitment* – ensure that the team is involved in setting objectives, decision-making, monitoring performance and taking corrective action.

Note that there are no universal prescriptions for improving morale. You can generally adopt a 'hearts and minds' to winning over people, but ultimately what you do and how you do it will depend on the situation you are in.

28

Managing the psychological contract

Managing people is to a large extent about exercising leadership and developing motivation and commitment. But this all takes place within the context of the psychological contract, which refers to the beliefs people have about how they and others are expected to behave.

THE NATURE AND IMPORTANCE OF THE PSYCHOLOGICAL CONTRACT

A psychological contract consists of understandings about the behaviour employers expect from their employees on the one hand and the behaviour employees expect from their employer on the other. The essence of the psychological contract is that it consists of *unwritten* expectations. It is based on assumptions which may be held by one party but not the other. Psychological contracts are implied and inferred rather than stated and agreed.

The psychological contract is important because it creates attitudes and emotions which form and govern behaviour. Problems can arise with the employment relationship if there are misunderstandings, which are only too likely to occur.

EMPLOYEE EXPECTATIONS

Employees may expect the following from their employers:

- to be treated fairly as human beings;
- to be provided with work which uses their abilities;
- to be rewarded equitably in accordance with their contribution;
- to be able to display competence;
- to have opportunities for further growth;
- to have security in employment;
- to know what is expected of them;
- to be given feedback (preferably positive) on how they are doing.

EMPLOYER EXPECTATIONS

Employers may expect the following from their employees:

- to be fully committed to the organization and its values;
- to work hard;
- to be loyal – 'to put themselves out';
- to be compliant;
- to be competent;
- to enhance the image of the organization with its customers, clients and suppliers.

CLARIFYING THE PSYCHOLOGICAL CONTRACT

Marked differences between the mutual expectations of employees and employers can damage the employment relationship. They can create confusion, conflict, dissatisfaction and poor morale.

As a line manager you can make an important contribution to clarifying the psychological contract by taking the following steps:

- during *recruitment interviews* – spelling out as clearly as possible what the job entails, not painting too glowing a picture and not glossing over the demands it will make on the job holder (this is sometimes called a 'realistic job preview');
- in *induction programmes* – telling new starters about the organization's values and what they are expected to do to uphold them;
- through *performance management* – getting agreement on the objectives and standards of performance an employee is expected to attain; the aim is to get employees to 'own', ie to be committed to, those objectives and standards;
- through *mutual contact* – making the best use of semi-formal and informal contacts with team members to discuss and clarify mutual expectations;
- by adopting a general approach of *transparency* – ensuring that on matters which affect them employees know what is happening, why it is happening and how it will affect them;
- by *involving* team members in discussions about work plans and problems;
- by managing *payment systems* so as to achieve equity, fairness and consistency in all aspects of financial reward;
- by providing *feedback* to employees on how well they are doing;
- by *encouraging* team members to create personal development plans and helping them to develop their skills, improve their potential and increase their employability.

29

Managing under-performers

WHY POOR PERFORMANCE OCCURS

Poor performance may arise because individuals lack the skills and/or the motivation to achieve the results expected of them. In such cases, as Stewart and Stewart (60) suggests: 'Managing poor performers falls into three parts: spotting that there is a problem, understanding the causes of the problem and attempting a remedy.'

Poor performance can result from poor leadership. It is the manager's responsibility to specify the results expected and the levels of skill and competence required.

Performance also depends on the system of work. The quality guru William Deming (13) states unequivocally that differences in performance are largely due to systems variations. It is not necessary to accept that statement in its entirety, but it is essential to analyse the causes of poor performance in terms of influences beyond the individual's control.

THE STEPS REQUIRED TO MANAGE UNDER-PERFORMANCE

Given that the performance failure cannot be attributed to poor leadership or the system of work, the five steps required to manage under-performance are as follows:

1. *Identify and agree the problem.* Analyse the feedback and, as far as possible, obtain agreement from the individual on what the shortfall has been. Feedback may be provided by managers, but it can in a sense be built into the job. This takes place when individuals are aware of their targets and standards, know what performance measures will be used and either receive feedback/control information automatically or have easy access to it. They will then be in a position to measure and assess their own performance and, if they are well motivated and well trained, take their own corrective actions. In other words, a self-regulating feedback mechanism exists. This is a situation which managers should endeavour to create on the grounds that prevention is better than cure.

2. *Establish the reason(s) for the shortfall.* When seeking the reasons for any shortfalls, the manager should not crudely be trying to attach blame. The aim should be for the manager and the individual jointly to identify the facts that have contributed to the problem. It is on the basis of this factual analysis that decisions can be made on what to do about it by the individual, the manager or the two of them working together.

   It is necessary first to identify any causes which are outside the control of the individual. These will include external pressures, changes in requirements, systems faults, inadequate resources (time, finance, equipment), jobs or tasks allocated to people who do not have the necessary experience or attributes, inadequate induction and continuation training, and poor leadership, guidance or support from the manager, team leader or colleagues. Any factors which are within the control of the individual and/or the manager can then be considered. What needs to be determined is the extent to which the reason for the problem is because the individual:

   - did not receive adequate support or guidance from their manager;
   - did not fully understand what they were expected to do;

- could not do it – ability;
- did not know how to do it – skill;
- would not do it – attitude.

3. *Decide and agree on the action required.*   Action may be taken by the individual, the manager or both parties. This could include:

- taking steps to improve skills – joint;
- changing behaviour – this is up to individuals as long as they accept that their behaviour needs to be changed. The challenge for managers is that people will not change their behaviour simply because they are told to do so. They can only be helped to understand that certain changes to their behaviour could be beneficial not only to the organization but also to themselves;
- changing attitudes – changing behaviour is easier than changing attitudes, which may be deep-rooted; the sequence is therefore to change behaviour first, so far as this is possible, and encourage attitude changes later;
- providing more support or guidance from the manager;
- jointly clarifying expectations;
- jointly developing abilities and skills in the sense that individuals may be expected to take steps to develop themselves but managers may provide help in the form of coaching, additional experience or training;
- redesigning the job.

Whatever action is agreed, both parties must understand how they will know that it has succeeded. Feedback arrangements can be made but individuals should be encouraged to monitor their own performance and take further action as required.

4. *Resource the action.*   Provide the coaching, training, guidance, experience or facilities required to enable agreed actions to happen.

5. *Monitor and provide feedback.*   Both managers and individuals monitor performance, ensure that feedback is provided or obtained and analysed, and agree on any further actions that may be necessary.

HANDLING DISCIPLINARY INTERVIEWS

If poor performance persists, it may be necessary to invoke a disciplinary procedure. Make sure that you have got all the facts and then use the following approach:

1. Give employees notice that the interview is going to take place so that they can be prepared and can get a representative to accompany them.
2. Arrange for a colleague to be present to help conduct the interview and to take notes.
3. State the complaint to the employee, giving chapter and verse and giving supporting statements from other people involved where appropriate.
4. Allow employees to give their side of the story and call any supporting witnesses.
5. Question employees and their witnesses and allow them to do the same.
6. Allow time for a general discussion on the issues raised and any other relevant issues.
7. Give employees an opportunity to have a final say and mention any mitigating circumstances.
8. Sum up the points emerging from the meeting as you see them, but allow employees to comment on them and be prepared to amend your summary.
9. Adjourn the meeting so that you can consider your decision on the basis of what came out in the interview. It is best not to announce the decision during the initial meeting. The adjournment may be only half an hour or so in a straightforward case. It could be longer in a more complex case.
10. Reconvene the meeting and announce your decision.
11. Confirm your decision in writing.

A SEVEN-STEP APPROACH TO MANAGING UNDER-PERFORMANCE

1. Identify the areas of under-performance – be specific.
2. Establish the causes of poor performance – the individual, the manager, the system of work or any combination of these three.
3. Adopt a problem-solving approach to dealing with the situation – obtain agreement on the actions required by the individual and/or by the manager.
4. Ensure that the necessary support (coaching, training, extra resources, etc) are provided to enable the problem to be overcome.
5. Monitor progress and provide feedback.

6. Provide additional guidance as required.
7. As a last resort, invoke the capability or disciplinary procedure, starting with an informal warning.

DISMISSING PEOPLE

You should always try to help someone to improve, and if there are performance problems you should go conscientiously through each stage of the capability or disciplinary procedure. Unfortunately, however, you may still find yourself unable to avoid having to dismiss a person because of a continuing failure to meet an acceptable standard. The following are the points to bear in mind if this happens:

1. Come straight to the point. Tell the person within 30 seconds of starting the interview that he or she has to go.
2. Be clear about shortcomings, quoting chapter and verse, but avoid 'badmouthing' the individual.
3. Don't apologize. If you are certain that this is the right course of action, you have nothing to apologize for.
4. Make it plain that as far as you are concerned, the decision is irrevocable but that the employee has the right to appeal.
5. Ensure that you have a witness in case there is an appeal or legal action.
6. Carry out the dismissal on a Friday.
7. Take steps to ensure that the individual does not have access to a computer or confidential information after dismissal. But do not arrange for him or her to be 'marched off the premises' as sometimes happens.
8. Be aware of the legal issues, ie the possibility of a claim for unfair dismissal if you have not followed the disciplinary procedure or do not have just cause for your action.

30

Managing your boss

If you want to achieve results, innovate and get on, you have to learn how to manage your boss. The word 'manage' is defined in the *Oxford English Dictionary* as:

- to conduct affairs;
- to control; cause to submit to one's rule;
- to bring (a person) to consent to one's wishes by artifice, flattery, or judicious suggestion of motives;
- to operate upon, manipulate for a purpose;
- to bring to pass by contrivance; to succeed in accomplishing;
- to deal with or treat carefully.

Although such concepts as artifice, flattery and manipulation would not normally play any part, all these definitions provide clues as to the various aspects of managing one's boss.

If you really believe that something needs to be done and you cannot do it without the consent of your boss, you have to work out how you are going to manage him. And it is worth careful and continuous thought. It is too easy to neglect this essential part of the art of management.

To manage your boss you need to know how to:

● Get agreement from him on what you want to do.
● Deal with him over problems.
● Impress him, so that he is more likely to accept your proposals and to place his trust in you.

GETTING AGREEMENT

Getting agreement from your boss is in many ways like getting agreement from anyone else. You need to be good at case presentation and at persuasion. More specifically you need to do the following things:

1. Find out what he expects.
2. Learn about his likes and dislikes, his quirks and his prejudices.
3. Establish how he likes things presented to him. Does he like long, carefully worked out, written reports? Or does he prefer a succinct proposal on one side of one sheet of paper? Perhaps he is more likely to be persuaded if he is introduced gradually to a proposal – a softening-up process, as it were. It is often advisable to test the water before plunging straight in. Some people prefer to start by talking all the way round a problem before getting down to its essential elements. They don't like surprises.
4. Get to know how he likes things done – by observation and by asking other people. If something goes wrong, choose the right moment and ask his advice on how to do it better next time (most people love being asked for their advice).
5. Find out the right time to approach him. Some people are at their best first thing. Others take time to warm up. It is obviously inadvisable to spring surprises if he is at the end of a long hard day. Check on his mood in advance. His secretary can help. And it is always worthwhile having her on your side. Secretaries can be good friends but bad enemies.
6. Work out the best circumstances in which to tackle him. Alone in his office, or over lunch, or driving him at speed along a motorway (there is a lot to be said for making him a captive audience). Getting away from the office may be an advantage:

there will be no interruptions and your boss is less likely to call in his henchman, and you will not then have to persuade two people at once. (Picking them off one at a time is much more likely to be successful.) Beware of the 'abominable no-man'. Most organizations have at least one – often the head of finance. He no doubt performs a useful role but keep him out of your way if you can.

7. Decide whether you want support. You may be able to make a better case on a one-to-one basis. There is a lot to be said for standing firmly on your own two feet.

8. Don't go in for open confrontation if you cannot get your own way at first. Get your boss to agree with what he is prepared to agree and then turn to the problem areas. Impress upon him that you want the two of you to cover every possible angle. Emphasize joint responsibility.

9. Leave him an escape route – a way open to consent without his having to climb down. Don't beat him into the ground – you might win this one but what about the next time?

10. Don't overwhelm him with your ideas. Don't expect to achieve everything at once. Tackle one important thing at a time. Keep it simple. If you come up against a strong objection don't fight it for too long. Survive to fight another day. This does not mean that you should not argue your case strongly, but that you should avoid giving the impression of being pig-headed.

11. Keep in reserve alternative proposals or modifications to your original idea to use if you are getting nowhere.

12. If your boss comes up with a better idea than yours, recognize and accept it. Everybody likes recognition. There is no need to flatter him. You are only reacting to him the way you would like him to react to you.

13. If you can't convince him first time remember that he's the boss. He makes the ultimate decisions. If he says 'that's the way it's going to be' you *may* have to accept it. In the end he could say to you 'we're in a two-horse race and only one can win and that's going to be me'. But you don't have to give up completely. Watch for any signs that he might be prepared to change his mind – given time and a revision to your argument or proposal. Don't nag. If you press too hard he will become stubborn and begin to think that you are challenging his authority and his position. Retire in good order and re-open your campaign at the right moment.

DEALING WITH PROBLEMS

Things are going wrong. You've made a mistake. You need your boss's help in sorting out a problem. How do you tackle him? You should adopt the following approach:

1. Keep him informed. Never let him be taken by surprise. Prepare him in advance for the bad news. If 'troubles come not in single spies but in battalions', don't let him have it all at once. Let him down as gently as possible. Don't use the 'first the good news then the bad news' line too crudely, but don't be too gloomy. Give him hope.
2. If something has gone wrong, explain what has happened, why it has happened (no excuses) and what you would like to do about it. Don't dump the problem in his lap in a 'take it or leave it' spirit.
3. Emphasize that you are seeking his views on what you propose, as well as his agreement.
4. If you think he is to blame, never say 'I told you so'. If you do, you will make an enemy for life.
5. If you admit responsibility, try to stop your boss keeping on at you. Steer him away from recriminations into a positive attitude on what you can *jointly* do to solve the problem.

IMPRESSING YOUR BOSS

Your purpose as a manager is not solely to impress your boss. Nor is it to make him like you. But you will get more done and get on better if you impress him. And why make an enemy of your boss when you can have him as a friend?

Your boss needs to trust you, to rely upon you and to believe in your capacity to come up with good ideas and to make things happen. He doesn't want to wet-nurse you or to spend his time correcting your mistakes or covering up.

To succeed in impressing your boss without really trying – it's fatal to push too much – you should:

1. Always be frank and open. Admit mistakes. Never lie or even shade the truth. If there is the faintest suspicion that you are not perfectly straightforward, your boss will never trust you again.

2. Aim to help your boss to be right. This does not mean being subservient or time-serving. Recognize, however, that you exist to give him support – in the right direction.
3. Respond fast to his requests on a can do/will do basis.
4. Don't trouble him unnecessarily with your problems.
5. Provide him with protection where required. Loyalty is an old-fashioned virtue, but you owe it to your boss. If you cannot be loyal to him then you should get out from under as quick as you can.
6. Provide your boss with what the army calls 'completed staff work'. This means that if you are asked to do something you should do it thoroughly. Come up with solutions, not problems. Test your ideas in draft form if you like but, having done so, present a complete proposal with whatever supporting arguments or evidence you need. Avoid half-baked suggestions. Your boss wants answers not questions. When you have finished your report and studied your conclusions and recommendations, ask yourself the question: 'If I were my boss would I stake my reputation on this piece of work and put my name to it?' If the answer is 'No', tear up your report and do it again. It's not completed staff work.

31

Meetings

DOWN WITH MEETINGS

Meetings bloody meetings, the title of a well-known training film, strikes a familiar chord with us all. When you think how many committees exist and how many meetings are held in any organization, it is remarkable how hard it is to find anyone who has a good word to say about them.

It has been said that committees are made up of the unfit appointed by the incompetent to do the unnecessary, and, again, that a camel is a horse designed by a committee. Experience of badly organized and pointless meetings is so widespread that, for many people, these cynical comments come very close to the truth.

WHAT'S WRONG WITH MEETINGS?

Meetings are criticized because they:

● Waste time – too many people talk too much.

- Fail to produce decisions and can be slow, exasperating and frustrating – they legitimize procrastination and indecisiveness.
- Tend to be dominated by a few people with strong personalities.
- Make lowest common denominator recommendations.
- Encourage political decisions where vested interests can prevail by means of lobbying and pressure.
- Dilute responsibility.
- Are costly in time and money.
- Concentrate on trivialities they can grasp rather than big issues beyond their scope. Northcote Parkinson cited as an example of this a committee which approved a £1 million capital development project (which it couldn't properly understand) in 10 minutes flat yet spent two hours arguing about a new cycle shed costing £800.

WHAT'S RIGHT WITH MEETINGS?

Meetings tend to incite such criticism because they are not properly organized. Many of the criticisms levelled at meetings are really criticisms of their misuse, not their proper use. A well-organized meeting held at the right time for the right reasons can bring a number of benefits. It can:

- Ensure that important matters receive proper consideration from all involved.
- Clarify thinking in that members have to justify their positions before the others present.
- Ensure that different viewpoints are aired.
- Act as a medium for the exchange of information.
- Save time by getting a number of people together.
- Promote co-ordination.
- Create something as a group which the individuals could not have achieved working separately – this is the process of synergy, where the whole is greater than the parts.

To make meetings work there are three things that must happen:

- They should be set up properly.
- There should be a good chairman.
- The members should be able to participate effectively.

DOS AND DON'TS OF MEETINGS

DO

Use a meeting if the information or the judgement is too great for one person.

Set up committees only when it is essential to assemble people with different viewpoints in one place at one time.

Appoint a chairman who is going to be able to control the meeting and get the best out of it.

Put people with different backgrounds who can contribute ideas on the committee.

Tell committees what they are to do and what their authority is.

Be explicit about when you want the meeting to report back.

Use meetings where they work best – reviewing or developing policies, co-ordinating decisions, ensuring that all concerned with a programme are consulted and kept informed.

Wind up committees as soon as they have served their purpose.

DON'T

Use a meeting if one person can do the job better.

Set up a committee if you want sharp, clear responsibility.

Use a committee to administrate anything.

Use a meeting or committee if you need speedy action.

Appoint a bigger committee than you need – over 10 people can become unwieldy.

Hold unnecessary meetings – it may be good to meet regularly on the first Friday of every month but it may be even better to meet only when you have something to discuss.

CHAIRING MEETINGS

The success or failure of a meeting largely depends on the chairman. If you are chairing a meeting this is what you must do.

Prior to the meeting

Before the meeting starts ensure that it has proper terms of reference and that the members are briefed on what to expect and what they should be prepared to contribute. Plan the agenda to provide for a structured meeting, covering all the issues in a logical order. Prepare and issue briefing papers which will structure the meeting and spell out the background, thus saving time going into detail or reviewing purely factual information during the meeting.

During the meeting

1. Start by clearly defining the objective of the meeting, setting a time-scale which you intend to keep.
2. Go through each item of the agenda in turn ensuring that a firm conclusion is reached and recorded.
3. Initiate the discussion on each item by setting the scene very briefly and asking for contributions – ask for answers to specific questions (which you should have prepared in advance) or you may refer the matter first to a member of the meeting who can make the best initial contribution (ideally, you should have briefed that individual in advance).
4. Invite contributions from other members of the meeting, taking care not to allow anyone to dominate the discussions.
5. Bring people back to order if they drift from the point.
6. If there is too much talk, remind members that they are there to make progress.
7. Encourage the expression of different points of view and avoid crushing anyone too obviously if he or she has not made a sensible comment.
8. Allow disagreement between members of the meeting but step in smartly if the atmosphere becomes too contentious.
9. Chip in with questions or brief comments from time to time, but do not dominate the discussion.
10. At appropriate moments during the meeting summarize the discussion, express views on where the committee has got to and outline your perception of the interim or final decision that has been made. Then check that the meeting agrees, amending the conclusion as necessary, and ensure that the decision is recorded exactly as made.
11. Summarize what has been achieved at the end of the meeting, indicating who has to do what by when.

12. If a further meeting is needed, agree the purpose of the meeting and what has to be done by those present before it takes place.

Remember that meetings can run in phases. For example, they start with an explanation, continue with a discussion of pros and cons, run into a side track and have to be brought into line, generate some heat because of contending points of view and eventually reach a point where you realize a decision has to be taken.

If you are chairing a meeting you may have to change your style accordingly. You may have to be decisive in bringing people to the point or business to a close, relaxed if you want to allow the discussion to keep going, or persuasive in order to draw people into the discussion.

MEMBERS

If you are a member of a meeting you should:

1. Prepare thoroughly – have all the facts at your fingertips, with any supporting data you need.
2. Make your points clearly, succinctly and positively – try to resist the temptation of talking too much.
3. Remain silent if you have nothing to say.
4. Keep your powder dry if you are not leading the discussion or if it is a subject you are not knowledgeable about. Listen, observe and save your arguments until you can make a really telling point. Don't plunge in too quickly or comprehensively – there may be other compelling arguments.
5. If you are not too sure of your ground, avoid making statements such as 'I think we must do this'. Instead, pose a question to the chairman or other member of the meeting such as, 'Do you think there is a case for doing this?'
6. Be prepared to argue your case firmly, but don't persist in fighting for a lost cause. Don't retire in a sulk because you cannot get your own way; accept defeat gracefully.
7. Remember that if you are defeated in committee, there may still be a chance for you to fight another day in a different setting.

32

Motivating people

Motivating people is the process of getting people to move in the direction you want them to.

The organization as a whole can provide the context within which high levels of motivation can be achieved through reward systems and the provision of opportunities for learning and development. But individual managers still have a major part to play in deploying their own motivating skills to get individual members of their team to give of their best, and to make good use of the motivational systems and processes provided by the company.

To do this it is necessary to understand:

- The process of motivation.
- The different types of motivation.
- The basic concepts of motivation.
- The implications of motivation theory.
- Approaches to motivation.
- The role of financial and non-financial rewards as motivators.

THE PROCESS OF MOTIVATION

Motivation is concerned with goal-directed behaviour. People are motivated to do something if they think it will be worth their while.

The process of motivation is initiated by someone recognizing an unsatisfied need. A goal is then established which, it is thought, will satisfy that need, and a course of action is determined which is expected to lead towards the attainment of that goal.

Basically, therefore, management and managers motivate people by providing means for them to satisfy their unsatisfied needs. This can be done by offering incentives and rewards for achievement and effort. But the needs of individuals and the goals associated with them vary so widely that it is difficult, if not impossible, to predict precisely how a particular incentive or reward will affect individual behaviour.

TYPES OF MOTIVATION

Motivation at work can take place in two ways. First, people can motivate themselves by seeking, finding and carrying out work which satisfies their needs or at least leads them to expect that their goals will be achieved. Second, people can be motivated by management through such methods as pay, promotion, praise, etc.

These two types of motivation are described as:

● *Intrinsic motivation* – the self-generated factors which influence people to behave in a particular way or to move in a particular direction. These factors include responsibility (feeling the work is important and having control over one's own resources), freedom to act, scope to use and develop skills and abilities, interesting and challenging work and opportunities for advancement.

● *Extrinsic motivation* – what is done to or for people to motivate them. This includes rewards such as increased pay, praise or promotion; and punishments, such as disciplinary action, withholding pay or criticism.

The extrinsic motivators can have an immediate and powerful effect, but this will not necessarily last for long. The intrinsic motivators, which are concerned with the quality of working life, are likely to have a deeper and longer-term effect because they are inherent in individuals and not imposed from outside.

BASIC CONCEPTS OF MOTIVATION

The basic concepts of motivation are concerned with needs, goals, reinforcement and expectations (expectancy theory).

Needs

Needs theory states that behaviour is motivated by unsatisfied needs. The key needs associated with work are those for achievement, recognition, responsibility, influence and personal growth.

Goals

Goal theory states that motivation will be increased if goal-setting techniques are used with the following characteristics:

● The goals should be specific.
● They should be challenging but reachable.
● They should be seen as fair and reasonable.
● Individuals should participate fully in goal-setting.
● Feedback ensures that people feel pride and satisfaction from the experience of achieving a challenging but fair goal.
● Feedback is used to gain commitment to even higher goals.

Reinforcement

Reinforcement theory suggests that success in achieving goals and rewards act as positive incentives and reinforce the successful behaviour, which is repeated the next time a similar need arises.

Expectancy theory

Expectancy theory states that motivation only happens when individuals:

● feel able to change their behaviour;

- feel confident that a change in their behaviour will produce a reward;
- value the reward sufficiently to justify the change in behaviour.

The theory indicates that motivation is only likely when a clearly perceived and usable relationship exists between performance and outcome and the outcome is seen as a means of satisfying needs. This applies just as much to non-financial as to financial rewards. For example, if people want personal growth they will only be motivated by the opportunities available to them if they know what they are, if they know what they need to do to benefit from them (and can do it) and if the opportunities are worth striving for.

Expectancy theory explains why extrinsic motivation – for example, an incentive or bonus scheme – works only if the link between effort and reward is clear and the value of the reward is worth the effort. It also explains why intrinsic motivation arising from the work itself can sometimes be more powerful than extrinsic motivation. Intrinsic motivation outcomes are more under the control of individuals, who can place greater reliance on their past experiences to indicate the extent to which positive and advantageous results are likely to be obtained by their behaviour.

IMPLICATIONS OF MOTIVATION THEORY

Motivation theory conveys two important messages. First, there are no simplistic solutions to increasing motivation. No single lever such as performance-related pay exists which is guaranteed to act as an effective motivator. This is because motivation is a complex process. It depends on:

- *Individual needs and aspirations* which are almost infinitely variable.
- Both *intrinsic and extrinsic motivating factors*, and it is impossible to generalize on what the best mix of these is likely to be.
- *Expectations* about rewards which will vary greatly among individuals according to their previous experiences and perceptions of the reward system.
- *The social context* where the influences of the organization culture, managers and co-workers can produce a wide variety of motivational forces which are difficult to predict and therefore to manage.

The second key message provided by motivation theory is the significance of expectations, goal-setting, feedback and reinforcement as motivating factors.

The implications of these messages are considered below.

APPROACHES TO MOTIVATION

Creating the right climate

It is necessary, in general, to create a climate which will enable high motivation to flourish. This is a matter of managing the culture. The aims would be, first, to reinforce values concerning performance and competence; second, to emphasize norms (accepted ways of behaviour) relating to the ways in which people are managed and rewarded; and third, to demonstrate the organization's belief in empowerment – providing people with the scope and 'space' to exercise responsibility and use their abilities to the full (see also Chapter 29). Without the right climate, quick fixes designed to improve motivation, such as performance-related pay, are unlikely to have much of an impact on overall organizational effectiveness, although they may work with some individuals.

Goal-setting, feedback and reinforcement

Goal-setting, feedback and reinforcement can all contribute to high motivation and they are all within your control.

Managing expectations

It is necessary to manage expectations. No reward offered through an incentive, bonus or performance-related pay scheme will be effective as a motivator unless individuals believe it is worth while and can reasonably expect to obtain it through their own efforts. Similarly, people are more likely to be motivated if they know that their achievements will be recognized.

The implications of these approaches as they affect financial and non-financial reward policies and practices are set out below.

FINANCIAL REWARDS

Financial rewards need to be considered from three points of view:

- The effectiveness of money as a motivator.
- The reasons why people are satisfied or dissatisfied with their rewards.
- The criteria which should be used when developing a financial reward system.

Money and motivation

Money is important to people because it is instrumental in satisfying a number of their most pressing needs. It is significant not only because of what they can buy with it but also as a highly tangible method of recognizing their worth, thus improving their self-esteem and gaining the esteem of others.

Pay is the key to attracting people to join an organization, although job interest, career opportunities and the reputation of the organization will also be factors. Satisfaction with pay among existing employees is mainly related to feelings about equity and fairness. External and internal comparisons will form the basis of these feelings, which will influence their desire to stay with the organization.

Pay can motivate. As a tangible means of recognizing achievement, pay can reinforce desirable behaviour. Pay can also deliver messages on what the organization believes to be important. But to be effective, a pay-for-performance system has to meet the following stringent conditions:

- There must be a clear link between performance and reward.
- The methods used to measure performance should be perceived to be fair and consistent.
- The reward should be worth striving for.
- Individuals should expect to receive a worthwhile reward if they behave appropriately.

As a manager you can make sure that the company's reward system is applied in your part of the organization in accordance with these principles.

NON-FINANCIAL REWARDS

Non-financial rewards can be focused on the needs most people have, in varying degrees, for achievement, recognition, responsibility, influence and personal growth. You will be in a position to provide or withhold these rewards for those of your staff who are doing well or badly.

Achievement

The need for achievement is defined as the need for competitive success measured against a personal standard of excellence.

Achievement motivation can take place by providing people with the opportunity to perform and the scope in their jobs to use their skills and abilities.

Recognition

Recognition is one of the most powerful motivators. People need to know not only how well they have achieved their objectives or carried out their work but also that their achievements are appreciated.

Praise, however, should be given judiciously – it must be related to real achievements. And it is not the only form of recognition. Financial rewards, especially achievement bonuses awarded immediately after the event, are clear symbols of recognition to which tangible benefits are attached, and this is an important way in which mutually reinforcing processes of financial and non-financial rewards can operate. There are other forms of recognition such as long service awards, status symbols of one kind or another, sabbaticals and trips abroad, all of which can be part of the total reward process.

Recognition is also provided by managers who listen to and act upon the suggestions of their team members and, importantly, acknowledge their contribution. Other actions which provide recognition include promotion, allocation to a high-profile project, enlargement of the job to provide scope for more interesting and rewarding work, and various forms of status or esteem symbols.

Responsibility

People can be motivated by being given more responsibility for their own work. This is essentially what empowerment is about and is in line with the concept of intrinsic motivation based on the content of the job. It is also related to the fundamental concept that individuals are motivated when they are provided with the means to achieve their goals.

The characteristics required in jobs if they are to be intrinsically motivating are that first, individuals must receive meaningful feedback about their performance, preferably by evaluating their own performance and defining the feedback they require; second, the job must be perceived by individuals as requiring them to use abilities they value in order to perform the job effectively; and third, individuals must feel that they have a high degree of self-control over setting their own goals and defining the paths to these goals.

Influence

People can be motivated by the drive to exert influence or to exercise power. David McClelland's (38) research established that alongside the need for achievement, the need for power was a prime motivating force for managers, although the need for 'affiliation', ie warm, friendly relationships with others was always present. The organization, through its policies for involvement, can provide motivation by putting people into situations where their views can be expressed, listened to and acted upon. This is another aspect of empowerment.

Personal growth

In Maslow's (37) hierarchy of needs, self-fulfilment or self-actualization is the highest need of all and is therefore the ultimate motivator. He defines self-fulfilment as 'the need to develop potentialities and skills, to become what one believes one is capable of becoming'.

Ambitious and determined people will seek and find these opportunities for themselves, although the organization needs to clarify the scope for growth and development it can provide (if it does not, they will go away and grow elsewhere).

Increasingly, however, individuals at all levels in organizations, whether or not they are eaten up by ambition, recognize the importance of continually upgrading their skills and of progressively developing their careers. Many people now regard access to training as a key element in the overall reward package. The availability of learning opportunities, the selection of individuals for high-prestige training courses and programmes, and the emphasis placed by the organization on the acquisition of new skills as well as the enhancement of existing ones, can all act as powerful motivators.

ACHIEVING HIGH LEVELS OF MOTIVATION

The following steps need to be taken if you wish to achieve higher levels of motivation:

1. Set and agree demanding but achievable goals.
2. Provide feedback on performance.
3. Create expectations that certain behaviours and outputs will produce worthwhile rewards when people succeed but will result in penalties if they fail.
4. Design jobs which enable people to feel a sense of accomplishment, to express and use their abilities and to exercise their own decision-making powers.
5. Provide appropriate financial incentives and rewards for achievement (pay-for-performance).
6. Provide appropriate non-financial rewards such as recognition and praise for work well done.
7. Communicate to individuals and publicize generally the link between performance and reward – thus enhancing expectations.
8. Select and train team leaders who will exercise effective leadership and have the required motivating skills.
9. Give people guidance and training which will develop the knowledge, skills and competencies they need to improve their performance.
10. Show individuals what they have to do to develop their careers.

33

Negotiating

Negotiation is the process of coming to terms and, in so doing, getting the best deal possible for your firm, your union or yourself.

Negotiations involve a conflict of interest. Sellers prefer a high price to a low one and buyers prefer a low price to a high one. Unions want the highest settlement they can get, management wants the lowest. What one side gains the other loses. No one likes to lose, so there is conflict, which has to be managed if an amicable agreement is to be achieved. And negotiators do, or should, try to end up on friendly terms, whatever differences of opinion have occurred on the way. After all, they may well meet again.

Another important feature of negotiations is that they take place in an atmosphere of uncertainty. Neither side necessarily knows what the other wants or will give.

There are two main types of negotiation – commercial and trade union.

COMMERCIAL NEGOTIATIONS

Commercial negotiations are mainly about the price and the terms for supplying goods or services.

In their simplest form they are no more than a haggle between buyer and seller, much the same as what happens when you trade in your car for a new one. At their more complex they concern a package in which a number of extras are on offer along with the basic product. Sellers can usually offer a range of prices to suit the needs of the buyer: an 'ex-works' price, a delivered price, an installed price and a price which includes service. Various methods of staging payments or providing credit may also be offered.

Negotiations of this type usually start with the buyer producing a specification. The seller then produces a proposal and negotiation starts. The seller will have included a negotiating margin in the proposal and will be prepared to vary the price according to the package required.

Commercial negotiations are usually conducted in a friendly manner, and that's your major problem. You can too easily be seduced into accepting a less than satisfactory deal by the blandishments of the negotiator.

TRADE UNION NEGOTIATIONS

Trade union negotiations can be much tougher. They may involve a simple pay settlement, but usually they involve a package. Extra benefits will be at issue, which can be traded for concessions if need be.

In this type of negotiation, both parties are probably quite clear as to the maximum they will give or the minimum they will accept. They will have predetermined their opening demands and offers and their shopping list of extras will have been analysed to determine which points can be conceded in return for some benefit.

There are a number of bargaining conventions used in union negotiations, of which the following are the most generally accepted:

● Whatever happens during the bargaining, both parties hope to come to a settlement.

- Attacks, hard words, threats and (controlled) losses of temper are treated by both sides as legitimate tactics and should not be allowed to shake either party's belief in the other's integrity, or their desire to settle without taking drastic action.
- Off-the-record discussions (beneficial as a means of probing attitudes and intentions) should not be referred to specifically in formal bargaining sessions, unless both sides agree in advance.
- Each side should be prepared to move from its original position.
- It is normal, although not inevitable, for the negotiation to proceed by a series of offers and counter-offers which lead steadily towards a settlement.
- Concessions, once made, cannot be withdrawn.
- Firm offers must not be withdrawn, although it is legitimate to make and withdraw conditional offers.
- A third party should not be brought in until both parties are agreed that no further progress would be made without one.
- The final agreement should mean exactly what it says. There should be no trickery and the terms agreed should be implemented without amendment.
- If possible, the final settlement should be framed so that both sides can save face and credibility.

THE PROCESS OF NEGOTIATION

In both cases the process is much the same. Here each stage is illustrated by a summary of what took place in an actual trade union negotiation.

Stage 1: Preparation – Setting objectives (or drawing up specifications), assembling data, and deciding on negotiating strategy
The union's aim was to achieve a settlement at, or above, the current rate of inflation (8 per cent). Its strategy was to force management on to the defensive by asking them to make an offer without divulging what the union wanted. In addition, the union asked for a reduction of one hour in the working week, an extra three days' holiday and a Christmas bonus of one week's pay.

The management's objective was to settle at no more than the rate of inflation, and to concede nothing that would raise the total cost of the package above 8 per cent. There was some debate within the management team about strategy. One hawk wanted to pre-empt the union claim by starting with the final offer, allowing no room for bargaining. He was overruled on the grounds that this would cause a confrontation and hence long-term damage to relations with the union. The next question was how much room for manoeuvre should be allowed between the opening and closing offer. Some wanted to start as low as possible, say 3 per cent, so as to close well below the 15 per cent claim expected from the union. The prevailing view, however, was that too low an offer would prolong the negotiations unnecessarily. It was thought better to start at 5 per cent, so that, if it had to, the firm could take two steps of 1½ per cent before reaching its maximum of 8 per cent.

Stage 2: Opening – Negotiators reveal their initial bargaining positions to their opposite numbers
The union started by stating its case. It wanted a substantial increase to protect its members from inflation and to restore the differentials lost over the previous three years. The extras (reduced working week, etc) were thrown in almost as make-weights, giving management the clue that there might be scope for some trading later on.

Management stated that no 'substantial offer' could be expected. It emphasized the poor trading results of the firm and the fact that, overall, the pay of the union's members compared favourably with other workers. The point was also made (it was to be repeated many times in ensuing meetings) that the firm could not guarantee that pay increases would match inflation. Having set out their opening positions and their main arguments the two parties agreed to adjourn the meeting.

Stage 3: Bargaining – At this stage both parties have the same aims. As a negotiator you will be trying: (a) to probe the weaknesses in the other side's case, and (b) to convince the other side that they must abandon their position and move closer to your own. You will also be checking to see if your own position holds good in the light of information received from your opponents and their reactions to your case. Your original judgement may be confirmed or you may have to adjust it now. You may also decide to apply pressure or give concessions now in order to move towards a satisfactory conclusion.
In the bargaining stage three meetings were held. At each of them the arguments of both management and union teams were the same as in the opening phase.

Each party aimed to discover how strongly the other believed in their arguments and to what extent they were prepared to shift position. Every phrase was analysed to discover just what was behind it, both sides seeking hints as to how much support the other was getting – from the shop floor and top management respectively.

Management opened with a 5 per cent offer and got the usual reaction: it was 'derisory', 'insulting', and so on. The union refused to state exactly what it wanted, hoping to mystify and wrong-foot the management.

Between the second and third meetings the management team were agreed in the belief that the union was hoping to get 10 per cent but, if pushed, might settle for 8. It was decided that an offer to reduce the working week by 30 minutes might be made, but only as a last-minute trade-off if a reasonable settlement seemed unlikely.

At the third meeting, management increased its offer to 7 per cent, saying that this was as far as it could go. When pressed to state whether this was, or was not, their final offer, the management team refused to elucidate. The union rightly interpreted this to mean that there was more in the kitty and that top management would release it if pressed hard enough. The union demanded 10 per cent *and* the other concessions.

Stage 4: Closing – Each party judges whether the other side is determined to stick to its position or will settle for a compromise. The final moves are made. It is during this stage that final 'trade-offs' may lead to a settlement.

The final meeting lasted all day and into the night. Management stuck to its 7 per cent offer and made no other concessions. The union tried several tactics. Pleading, controlled loss of temper and threats of industrial action were all used. The management team finally judged that the only way to get a settlement was to attempt a trade-off. They offered 7 per cent plus one hour off the working week, in return for an agreement to abolish the customary five minutes 'wash-up' time (a practice that had been consistently abused).

Management reiterated that this was the final offer and was as much as the firm could afford and managed to convince the union by sheer force of argument that it meant what it said. The union accepted the offer after balloting its members.

NEGOTIATING TACTICS

(a) Preparation

1. Define your bargaining objectives as follows:

   - *Ideal* – the best you can hope to achieve.
   - *Minimum* – the least you would be prepared to settle for.
   - *Target* – what you are going to try for and believe, realistically, you have a good chance of achieving.

2. Consider how you might build up a package which would allow concessions to be exchanged. For example, could you accept a higher price for a concession on payment terms, or increase a pay offer if the union agrees to remove a restrictive practice?

3. Assess what the other party wants or is prepared to offer. For example, if you are a manufacturer negotiating terms with a store it pays to know, say, that the buyer is constrained by company policy which insists on a three times mark-up. Knowing the retail price that the store will want to charge you will have a good idea of the maximum the buyer will pay. You can then judge whether you should press for a larger order to justify a lower selling price than you would normally accept.

   In a typical wage negotiation the union or representative body making the claim will come to the table with a predetermined target, minimum and opening claims. Similarly, you, as the employer, will have your own target, maximum and opening offer.

   The difference between their claim and your offer is the negotiating range. If your maximum exceeds their minimum this will indicate the settlement zone. This is demonstrated in Figure 33.1. In this example the chance of settlement without too much trouble is fairly high. It is when your maximum is less than their minimum, as in Figure 33.2, that the trouble starts.

4. Decide on your strategy and tactics – your opening offer, the steps you are going to take, the concessions you are prepared to offer and the arguments you are going to use.

5. Collect the facts needed to support your case.

6. Assemble any documents you need, such as standard contract terms.

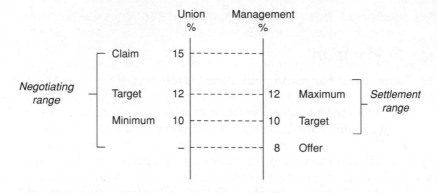

Figure 33.1 *Negotiating range with a settlement zone*

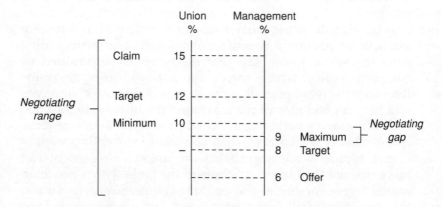

Figure 33.2 *Negotiating range without a settlement zone*

7. In a trade union negotiation:

- Select the negotiating team. This should never have fewer than two members, and for major negotiations should have three or more: one to take the lead, one to take notes and feed the negotiator with any supporting information needed, and the others to observe their opposite numbers and play a specific part in negotiations in accordance with their brief.
- Brief the members of the negotiating team on their roles and the negotiating strategy and tactics that are to be

adopted. If appropriate, prepared statements or arguments should be issued at this stage to be used as required by the strategic plan.

● Rehearse the members of the team in their roles. They can be asked to repeat their points to other members and deal with responses from them; or someone can act as devil's advocate and force the leader or other members of the team to handle awkward points or negotiating ploys.

At this stage it may be possible to meet your opponents informally to sound out their position, while they sound out yours. You can use such a session as an 'early warning' system to get your opponents to modify their initial demands by convincing them of the strength of your own position or your determination to resist.

In a recent trade union negotiation these 'corridor tactics' met with success. The union concerned had asked management to introduce a new technology agreement with the usual clauses about consultation, job protection and health precautions.

During the first two meetings management stuck firmly to its view that all these requirements were catered for by existing agreements and published policies. But the union insisted that this was not so. The negotiation seemed to have reached an impasse. Whatever the union leader felt, he could not weaken too obviously during the actual meetings. Neither could the general manager who was heading the management team.

To break the impasse the general manager asked his industrial relations manager to hold an off-the-record meeting with the trade union leader. At this meeting it was made clear that the company would not agree to a separate new technology agreement in any circumstances. But the industrial relations manager suggested that the company would be prepared to add a stronger prior consultation clause to the existing agreement.

From previous experience, the union leader knew this man meant what he said. He saw no point in having a major confrontation on this issue and knew he would get little support from his members, who did not see new technology as a real issue. But he felt that if he had to give a concession he should get something back. In other words, he wanted a trade-off.

He therefore agreed to go along with the idea, so long as the company let the union monitor the introduction of any major new technology schemes over the next six months. This was accepted by the industrial relations manager. Both parties understood the convention that there was no commitment and that no reference would be made to their discussion in future formal meetings. They then cleared the informal understanding with their respective committees and, at the subsequent formal meeting, the terms were agreed without any difficulty. What looked like being a major problem had been solved by corridor negotiations.

(b) Opening

Your tactics when opening the negotiation should be to:

● Open realistically and move moderately.
● Challenge your opponents' position as it stands, but on no account limit their ability to move.
● Explore attitudes, ask questions, observe behaviour and, above all, listen; assess your opponents' strengths and weaknesses, their tactics and the extent to which they may be bluffing.
● Make no concessions of any kind at this stage.
● Be non-committal about proposals and explanations (do not talk too much).

(c) Bargaining

Your aim is to narrow the gap between the two initial positions and to persuade your opponents that your case is so strong that they must accept less than they had planned. You should:

● Always make conditional proposals: 'If you will do this I will consider doing that'.
● Never make one-sided concessions: always trade-off against a concession from the other party: 'If I concede x then I expect you to concede y'.
● Negotiate on the whole package: never allow your opponents to pick you off item by item; keep all the issues open so as to extract the maximum benefit from potential trade-offs.

Reading the signals

During the bargaining stage you must be sensitive to any signals made by the other party. Every time they make a conditional statement it shows that they are prepared to move. Explore the possibilities with questions. Try to get behind what people *say* and understand what they really *mean*. For example:

What they say	*What they mean*
That's as far as I can go.	I might be able to persuade my boss to go further.
We don't usually give more than 5 per cent discount.	We're prepared to give more if you give us something in return.
Let's think about that point.	I'm prepared to negotiate.
I need notice of that question.	It's difficult, but not impossible. Try again.
It will be very difficult for us to meet that requirement.	It's not impossible but we'll want a trade-off.
I shall certainly consider your offer.	I am going to accept it but I don't want to appear to be too easy a touch.
This is our standard contract.	We're prepared to negotiate on the terms.
We're prepared to offer you £x per 1,000 units.	The price is negotiable.
That's my final offer.	My boss *might* go further if pushed (or if it is made worth his while).
We couldn't meet your delivery requirements at that price.	I will negotiate on delivery or price.

Arguing

During the bargaining stage much of your time will be spent in arguing. Clear thinking (see Chapter 4) will help you to present your case and expose the fallacies in your opponent's arguments.

You should also consider the *manner* in which you argue. You are not there to beat your opponent into the ground. In fact, in the interests of future good relationships (which will benefit *you* as well as your opponent) it is wise to leave an escape route. As a leading trade unionist said: 'Always leave the other fellow the price of his bus ticket home.'

Avoid brow-beating your opponent. Disagree firmly, but don't shoot him down. Don't try to make your opponent look small. Score points, if you must, to discredit arguments or expose fallacious reasoning but never in order to discredit him as a person. If you indulge in personal attacks or abuse, your opponents will close ranks.

To argue effectively you must be prepared to listen both to the stated, and to the implied, points made by your opponent. Don't talk too much yourself; it will prevent you reading signals, and you may give too much away. Wherever you can, challenge your opponent to justify the case on an item-by-item basis. Put the onus on him by questioning for clarification. Answer a question with another question if you want time to consider.

Argue calmly and without emotion, but emphasize the points you really want to ram home either by raising your voice slightly and slowing down to highlight your argument, or by repetition.

Control your anger. Express yourself strongly, by all means, but you will lose everything if you lose your temper.

Always remember that you are *not* trying to win at all costs. If your opponent wants something which you cannot give, don't just say no. Offer an alternative package. If your opponent is asking for a higher specification than you normally provide for the price and wants a delivery date which you cannot meet without incurring extra overtime costs, say that you can meet the specifications and the delivery deadline as long as he is prepared to cover the costs.

Gambits

There are a number of standard bargaining gambits. Here are a few of the more common ones:

- *Uttering threats* – 'Agree to what I want or I'll call out the lads'; or '… I'll take my custom elsewhere'. Never react to such threats and never utter empty ones.
- *No negotiation under duress* – 'We refuse to discuss your claim unless and until you cancel your overtime ban.' An excellent approach, if you can get away with it.
- *It will reflect badly on you* – 'Do you really want to get the reputation of being a heartless employer?' This is an emotional appeal and, as such, should be discounted.
- *The bluff direct* – 'I have two or three quotations lower than yours.' The answer to this gambit is to call your opponent's bluff – 'What are they offering for the price?' 'OK, why not accept them, why bother talking to me?'
- *The leading question* – 'Do you think it is a good idea to reward people according to merit?' 'Yes.' 'Then why do you insist on

retaining this fixed incremental scheme which benefits everybody irrespective of how well they've done?' Never fall for a leading question.

● *The piecemeal or 'salami' technique* – In this your opponent will try to pick off the items one by one. 'That's the price agreed, now we can deliver in three months, OK?' 'Right, we've agreed the delivery terms, now this is how we charge for maintenance.' Always negotiate the whole package. Don't allow yourself to be railroaded into a piecemeal approach.

● *The yes, but… approach* – 'Yes, we agree to accept an increase of 8 per cent but before we can agree to everything there is this other problem of compensation for redundancy we must tackle.' To avoid being caught in a yes/but trap, always make offers on one part of a package conditional on accepting another part: 'We are prepared to consider an 8 per cent offer but only if you agree to drop your claim for enhanced redundancy pay.'

(d) Closing

When and how you close depends on your assessment of the strength of your opponent's case and his or her determination to see it through. You may close by:

1. Making a concession, preferably a minor one, and trading it off against an agreement to settle. The concession can be offered more positively than at the bargaining stage: 'If you will agree to settle at x, I will concede y.'
2. Doing a deal: You might split the difference, or bring in something new – such as extending the settlement time-scale, agreeing to back payments, phasing increases, making a joint declaration of intent to do something in the future (for example to introduce a productivity plan), or offering an incentive discount.
3. Summarizing what has happened to date, emphasizing the concessions that have been made and the extent to which you have moved, and stating that you have reached your final position.
4. Applying pressure through a threat of the consequences which will follow if your offer is not accepted.
5. Giving your opponent a choice between two courses of action.

Do not make a final offer unless you mean it. If it is not really your final offer and your opponent calls your bluff, you will have to make further concessions and your credibility will be undermined. He or she will, of course, attempt to force you into revealing how close you are to your final position. Do not allow yourself to be hurried into this. If you want to avoid committing yourself and thus devaluing the word 'final', state as positively as you can that this is as far as *you* are prepared to go.

34

Objective setting

One of your most important tasks as a manager is to make sure that the members of your team understand what is expected of them. Each individual and the team as a whole must know what they have to do and achieve. This is the management of expectations aspect of your role.

Your task is to ensure that performance requirements expressed as objectives are defined and agreed. You will then be in a position to review achievements in relation to agreed objectives. This is done through agreed performance measures and indicators.

WHAT ARE OBJECTIVES?

An objective describes something which has to be accomplished – a point to be aimed at. Objectives or goals (the terms are interchangeable) define what organizations, functions, departments, teams and individuals are expected to achieve.

There are two main types of objective: work and personal.

Work objectives

Work or operational objectives refer to the results to be achieved or the contribution to be made to the accomplishment of team, departmental and corporate objectives. At *corporate level* they are related to the organization's mission, core values and strategic plans.

At *departmental or functional level* they are related to corporate objectives, spelling out the specific mission, targets and purposes to be achieved by a function or department.

At *team level* they will again be related specifically to the purpose of the team and the contribution it is expected to make to achieving departmental and corporate goals.

At *individual level* they are job-related, referring to the principal accountabilities, main activity areas or key tasks which constitute the individual's job. They focus on the results individuals are expected to achieve and how they contribute to the attainment of team, departmental and corporate goals and to upholding the organization's core values.

Personal objectives

Personal or learning objectives are concerned with what individuals should do and learn to improve their performance (performance improvement plans) and/or their knowledge, skills and overall level of competence (training and personal development plans).

HOW ARE INDIVIDUAL WORK OBJECTIVES EXPRESSED?

Individual objectives define the results to be achieved and the basis upon which performance in attaining these results can be measured. They can take the form of target- or project-related objectives or standing objectives.

Target- or project-related objectives

Individual objectives can be expressed as quantified output or improvement targets (open 24 new accounts by 31 December, reduce cost per unit of output by 2.5 per cent by 30 June) or in terms of projects to be completed (open distribution depot in Northampton by 31 October). Targets may be reset regularly, say once a year or every six months, or be subject to frequent amendments to meet new requirements or changed circumstances.

Standing objectives

Objectives for some aspects of a job (or for all aspects of some jobs) can be what might be described as 'standing objectives'. These are concerned with the permanent or continuing features of a job. They incorporate or lead to defined standards of performance which may be expressed in quantified terms such as the requirement to ensure that all deliveries are made within three days of receiving an order. Alternatively, they may have to be defined as qualitative standards such as:

> Performance will be up to standard if requests for information are dealt with promptly and helpfully on a can do/will do basis and are delivered in the form required by the user.

Qualitative standing objectives may also be defined for behaviour which will contribute to upholding the core values of the organization. For example, if one of the core values relates to the development of the skills and competences of employees, a performance standard for employee development could be one of the objectives agreed for all managers and team leaders.

WHAT IS A GOOD WORK OBJECTIVE?

Good work or operational objectives are:

- *Consistent* with the values of the organization and departmental and organizational objectives.
- *Precise:* clear and well defined, using positive words.
- *Challenging:* to stimulate high standards of performance and to encourage progress.
- *Measurable:* they can be related to quantified or qualitative performance measures.
- *Achievable:* within the capabilities of the individual. Account should be taken of any constraints which might affect the

individual's capacity to achieve the objectives; these could include lack of resources (money, time, equipment, support from other people), lack of experience or training, external factors beyond the individual's control, etc.

- *Agreed* by the manager and the individual concerned. The aim is to provide for the ownership, not the imposition, of objectives, although there may be situations where individuals have to be persuaded to accept a higher standard than they believe themselves capable of attaining.
- *Time-related* – achievable within a defined time-scale (this would not be applicable to a standing objective).
- *Teamwork orientated* – emphasize teamwork as well as individual achievement.

Some organizations use the acronym SMART to define a good objective:

S = stretching
M = measurable
A = agreed
R = realistic
T = time-related.

DEFINING WORK OBJECTIVES

The process of agreeing objectives need not be unduly complicated. It must start from an agreed list of the principal accountabilities or main tasks of the job. It is then simply a matter of jointly examining each area and agreeing targets and standards of performance as appropriate. Agreement can also be reached on any projects to be undertaken which might be linked to a specific accountability, or maybe more general projects which fall broadly within the remit of the jobholder.

Define targets

The first step is to identify the key result areas of the job from the list of accountabilities or main tasks to which targets can be attached.

Targets are quantified and time based – they always define specific and measurable outputs and when they have to be reached.

The target may be to achieve a specified level of output or to improve performance in some way. Targets may be expressed in financial terms such as profits to be made, income to be generated, costs to be reduced or budgets to be worked within. Or they may be expressed in numerical terms as a specified number of units to be processed, responses to be obtained or clients or customers to be contacted over a period of time.

Output targets are expressed in financial or unitary terms, for example:

- Achieve sales of £1.6 million by 30 June.
- Maintain inventory levels at no more than £12 million.
- Maintain throughput at the rate of 800 units a day.

Performance improvement targets may be expressed in terms such as:

- Increase sales turnover for the year by 8 per cent in real terms.
- Reduce the overhead to sales ratio from 22.6 to 20 per cent over the next 12 months.
- Increase the ratio of successful conversions (enquiry to sales) from 40 to 50 per cent.

Define performance standards

The next stage is to define performance standards for any area (accountability or main task) to which specific, time-based targets cannot be attached. These are sometimes described as standing or continuing objectives because, as explained earlier in this chapter, their essential nature may not change significantly from one review period to the next if the key task remains unaltered, although they may be modified if new circumstances arise.

Performance standards should have been broadly defined in outcome terms in the why part of the accountability/task definition. But the broad definition should be expanded and, as far as possible, particularized. They should preferably be quantified in terms, for example, of level of service or speed of response. Where the standard cannot be quantified, a more qualitative approach may have to be adopted, in which case the standard of performance definition would in effect state: 'this job or task will have been well done if... (the following things happen)'. Junior or more routine jobs are likely to have a higher proportion of standing objectives to which performance standards are attached than senior and more flexible or output-orientated jobs.

The following are some examples of performance standards which spell out the end results required in quantitative terms:

- Prepare and distribute management accounts to managers within three working days of the end of the accounting period.
- Deal with 90 per cent of customer complaints within 24 hours – the remainder to be acknowledged the same day and answered within five working days.
- Hear job evaluation appeals within five working days.

It may not always be possible to quantify performance standards as in the examples given above. The end results required may have to be defined in qualitative terms.

It is often assumed that qualitative performance standards are difficult to define. But all managers make judgements about the standards of performance they expect and obtain from their staff, and most people have some idea of whether or not they are doing a good job. The problem is that these views are often subjective and are seldom articulated. Even if, as often happens, the final definition of a performance standard is somewhat bland and unspecific, the discipline of working through the requirements in itself will lead to greater mutual understanding of performance expectations.

A performance standard definition should take the form of a statement that performance will be up to standard if a desirable, specified and observable result happens.

The following are some examples of qualitative performance standards:

- Performance will be up to standard if line managers receive guidance on the interpretation and implementation of inventory policies which is acted upon and makes a significant contribution to the achievement of inventory targets.
- Performance will be up to standard when callers are dealt with courteously at all times, even when they are being difficult.
- Performance will be up to standard if proposals for new product development are fully supported by data provided from properly conducted product research, market research and product testing programmes, and are justified by meeting return on investment criteria policies.

Define projects

Projects may already have been defined as part of a team, departmental or functional plan, and when setting individual objectives it is simply necessary to agree on the part that the individual will play and the contribution he or she is expected to make. Alternatively, projects may be linked to one or more specific accountabilities or they may be related generally to the overall purpose of the job.

Objective setting for projects will specify the required outcome of the project (results to be achieved), its budget and its time-scale.

When a number of projects have to be undertaken by the jobholder, agreement should be reached on priorities.

Project or task achievement objectives may be expressed in terms such as:

- Introduce new stock control system by 30 November.
- All employees to have received training on the implementation of equal opportunities policies by 1 June.
- New distribution centre to be operational by 1 March.
- Reorganization of finance department to be completed by 1 October.

For each project or task it would also be necessary to set out the success criteria, for example:

> Introduce a new stock control system by 30 November to provide more accurate, comprehensive and immediate information on stock and thus enable inventory targets to be achieved without prejudicing production flows or customer service levels.

PERFORMANCE MEASURES

Measurement is a key aspect of managing performance on the grounds that 'if you can't measure it you can't improve it'. It is pointless to define objectives or performance standards unless there is agreement and understanding on how performance in achieving these objectives or standards will be measured.

Performance measures should provide evidence of whether or not the intended result has been achieved and the extent to which the jobholder has produced that result. This will be the basis for generating feedback information for use not only by you but also by individuals to monitor their own performance.

Types of measure

Performance measures may refer to such matters as income generation, sales, output, units processed, productivity, costs, delivery-to-time, 'take up' of a service, speed of reaction or turnround, achievement of quality standards or customer/client reactions.

Measures or metrics can be classified under the following headings:

- *finance* – income, shareholder value, added value, rates of return, costs.
- *output* – units produced or processed, throughput, new accounts.
- *impact* – attainment of a standard (quality, level of service, etc) changes in behaviour (internal and external customers), completion of work/project, level of take-up of a service, innovation.
- *reaction* – judgement by others, colleagues, internal and external customers.
- *time* – speed of response or turnround, achievements compared with timetables, amount of backlog, time to market, delivery times.

Defining performance measures

It is important to agree performance measures at the same time as objectives are defined. This is the only way in which a fair assessment of progress and achievements can be made, and the successful definition of performance measures will provide the best basis for feedback.

Performance measures should:

- be related to the strategic goals and measures which are organizationally significant and drive business performance;
- be relevant to the objectives and accountabilities of the teams and individuals concerned – they are only effective if they are derived from statements of accountabilities and/or are based on well-researched competence frameworks;

- focus on measurable outputs and accomplishments;
- indicate the data or evidence that will be available as the basis for measurement;
- be verifiable – provide information which will confirm the extent to which expectations have been met;
- be as precise as possible in accordance with the purpose of the measurement and the availability of data;
- provide a sound basis for feedback and action;
- be comprehensive, covering all the key aspects of performance so that a family of measures is available.

35

Organizing

An effective enterprise ensures that collective effort is organized to achieve specific ends. Organizing involves dividing the overall management task into a variety of processes and activities and then establishing means of ensuring that these processes are carried out effectively and that the activities are co-ordinated. It is about differentiating activities in times of uncertainty and change, integrating them – grouping them together to achieve the organization's overall purpose – and ensuring that effective information flows and channels of communication are maintained.

ORGANIZATION DESIGN

Organization design is based on the analysis of activities, processes, decisions, information flows and roles. It produces a structure which consists of positions and units between which there are relationships involving co-operation, the exercise of authority and the exchange of information.

Within the structure there will be line managers who are responsible for achieving results in the organization's key areas of activity by managing teams and individuals, and specialists who provide support, guidance and advice to the line. The structure must be appropriate to the organization's purpose, technology and the environment in which it exists. It must be flexible enough to adapt itself easily to new circumstances – organization design is a continuous process of modification and change, it is never a one-off event. It must also be recognized that, although the formal organization structure may define who is responsible for what and the ostensible lines of communication and control, the way in which it actually operates will depend on informal networks and other relationships which have not been defined in the design process and arise from people's daily interaction.

THE APPROACH TO ORGANIZATION DESIGN

Organization design aims to clarify roles and relationships so far as this is possible in fluid conditions. It is also concerned with giving people the scope and opportunity to use their skills and abilities to better effect – this is the process of empowerment which is examined in Chapter 20. Jobs should be designed to satisfy the requirements of the organization for productivity, operational efficiency and quality of product or service. But they must also meet the needs of individuals for interest, challenge and accomplishment. These aims are interrelated and an important aim of organization and job design is to integrate the needs of the individual with those of the organization.

When it comes to designing or modifying the structure a pragmatic approach is necessary. It is first necessary to understand the environment, the technology and the existing systems of social relationships. An organization can then be designed which is *contingent* upon the circumstances. There is always some choice, but designers should try to achieve the best fit they can. And in making their choice, they should be aware of the structural, human, process and system factors which will influence the design, and of the context within which the organization operates.

Organization design is ultimately a matter of ensuring that the structure, processes and methods of operation fit the strategic requirements of the business and its technology within its environment. Disruption occurs if internal and external coherence and consistency are not achieved. And, as Mintzberg (41) suggests: 'Organizations, like individuals, can avoid identity crises by deciding what they wish to be and then pursuing it with a healthy obsession.'

Organization design is always an empirical and evolutionary process for which absolute principles cannot be laid down. But there are a number of broad guidelines which should be taken into account even if they are not followed slavishly.

ORGANIZATION GUIDELINES
Allocation of work

Related activities should be grouped logically together into functions and departments. Unnecessary overlap and duplication of work, either horizontally or vertically within a hierarchy, should be avoided.

A matrix organization may be developed in which multi-disciplinary project teams are created specially to accomplish a specified task but the members of those teams are responsible on a continuing basis to a functional leader who allocates them to projects, assesses their performance, provides rewards and deals with training and career development needs.

Close attention should be given to the processes within the business. These are the interconnected sequence of activities which convert inputs into outputs. Thus, 'order fulfilment' is a process which starts with an order as its input and results in an 'output', ie the delivery of the ordered goods. The organization design should ensure that the flow of such processes can proceed smoothly, efficiently and effectively.

Business process re-engineering, as described in Chapter 24, can help to achieve this by subjecting the processes that link key organizational functions together from initiation to completion to critical examination and, as necessary, redesign. It is sometimes better to organize these processes properly before becoming over-involved in the design of rigid structures which can inhibit the flow of work.

The work that needs to be done and accountabilities for results should be defined and agreed with teams and individual jobholders.

Matters requiring a decision should be dealt with as near to the point of action as possible by individuals or self-managing teams (see Chapter 48). Managers should not try to do too much themselves, nor should they supervise too closely.

Levels in the structure

Too many levels of management and supervision inhibit communication and teamwork and create extra work (and unnecessary jobs). The aim should be to reduce the number of levels to a minimum. However, the elimination of middle managers and wider spans of control mean that more attention has to be paid to improving teamwork, delegation and methods of integrating activities.

Span of control

There are limits to the number of people anyone can manage or supervise well, but these vary considerably between different jobs. Most people can work with a far greater span of control than they imagine, as long as they are prepared to delegate more effectively, to avoid becoming involved in too much detail, and to develop good teamwork among the individuals reporting to them. In fact, wide spans of control are beneficial in that they can enforce delegation and better teamwork and free the higher-level manager to spend more time on policy-making and planning.

Limited spans of control encourage managers to interfere too much with the work going on beneath them and therefore constrain the scope that should be given to their subordinates to grow with their jobs.

One person, one boss

Generally speaking, individuals should be accountable only to one boss for the results they achieve, to avoid confusion on operational matters. But in a project-based or matrix organization individuals might be responsible to their project leader for contributing to the outcome of the project while also being responsible to their departmental manager or the head of their discipline for the continuing requirements of their role and for achieving agreed standards of overall performance.

Individuals in functional roles such as finance or personnel may be directly responsible to a line manager but may also have a 'dotted line' relationship of responsibility to the head of their function on matters of corporate policy.

Decentralization

Authority to make decisions should be delegated as close to the action as possible.

Optimize the structure

Develop an ideal organization by all means, but also remember that it may have to be modified to fit in the particular skills and abilities of key individuals.

Relevance to organizational needs

The organization has to be developed to meet the needs of its situation. In today's conditions of turbulence and change this inevitably means a tendency towards more decentralized and flexible structures, with greater responsibility given to individuals and an extension of the use of task forces and project teams to deal with opportunities or threats. This implies an informal, non-bureaucratic, organic approach to organization design – the form of the organization will follow its function, not the other way around.

The organization may be largely based on multi-disciplinary project teams, as in a matrix organization, or greater emphasis will be placed on ensuring that flows of work involved in the key business processes are properly catered for rather than the creation of a traditional formal and hierarchical structure.

THE BASIC APPROACH TO ORGANIZATION DESIGN

The basic approach to organization design is to:

● Define what the organization exists to do – its purpose and objectives.
● Analyse and identify the processes, activities or tasks required to do it and, as appropriate, the flow of decision-making and work throughout the organization.

- Allocate related activities to teams and individual jobholders as appropriate.
- Group related activities carried out by teams and individual jobholders logically into organizational units while ensuring that the flow of work across organizational boundaries is not inhibited.
- Provide for the management and co-ordination of the processes and activities at each level of responsibility.
- Ensure that attention is given to developing the processes of teamwork and communication.
- Establish reporting and communicating relationships.
- Recognize the importance of informal networks as means of communicating information and joint decision-making.
- Provide, as far as possible, for organizational processes to adapt to change.

DEFINING STRUCTURES

Structures are usually defined by means of organization charts. Such charts have their uses in planning and reviewing organizations. They can indicate how work is allocated and how activities are grouped together. They show who is responsible to whom, and they illustrate lines of authority. Drawing up a chart can be a good way of clarifying what is currently happening: the mere process of putting the organization down on paper will highlight any problems. And when it comes to considering changes, charts are the best way of illustrating alternatives.

The danger with organization charts is that they can be mistaken for the organization itself. They are no more than a snapshot of what is supposed to be happening at a given moment. They are out of date as soon as they are drawn, and they leave out the informal organization and its networks. If you use little boxes to represent people, they may behave as if they were indeed little boxes, sticking too closely to the rule book.

Charts can make people very conscious of their superiority or inferiority in relation to others. They can make it harder to change things, they can freeze relationships, and they can show relationships as they are supposed to be, not as they are. Robert Townsend (62) said of organization charts: 'Never formalize, print and circulate them. Good organizations are living bodies that grow new muscles to meet challenges.'

DEFINING ROLES

Role definitions describe the part to be played by individuals in fulfilling their job requirements. Roles therefore indicate the behaviour required to carry out a particular task or the group of tasks contained in a job – they will set out the context within which individuals work as part of a team as well as the tasks they are expected to carry out.

The traditional form for defining roles is the job description but, like organization charts, job descriptions can be too rigid and stifle initiative. It is better to use a role definition format along the following lines:

- Job title.
- Reporting relationships.
- Main purpose of the role – a brief description of why the role exists.
- Main areas of responsibility – these are defined in terms of the results expected; no attempt should be made to go into any detail of how the work is done.
- Context – how the job fits in with others, flexibility requirements, decision-making authority, any particular requirements or pressures.

A role definition emphasizes the dynamic aspects of a job in terms of output, relationships and flexibility. It should focus on performance and delivery, not on tasks and duties.

IMPLEMENTING STRUCTURES

At the implementation stage it is necessary to ensure that everyone concerned:

- knows how they will be affected by the change;
- understands how their relationships with other people will change;
- accepts the reasons for the change and will not be reluctant to participate in its implementation.

It is easy to tell people what they are expected to do; it is much harder to get them to understand and accept how and why they should do it. The implementation plan should therefore cover not only the information to be given but also how it should be presented. The presentation will be easier if, in the analysis and design stage, full consultation has taken place with the individuals and groups who will be affected by the change. Too many organizational changes have failed because they have been imposed from above or from outside without proper consideration for the views and feelings of those most intimately concerned.

Implementation is often attempted by purely formal means – issuing edicts, distributing organization manuals or handing out job descriptions. These may be useful as far as they go, but while they provide information, they do not necessarily promote understanding and ownership. This can only be achieved on an informal but direct basis. Individuals must be given the opportunity to talk about what the proposed changes in their responsibilities will involve – they should already have been given the chance to contribute to the thinking behind the change, so discussions on the implications of the proposals should follow quite naturally. There is no guarantee that individuals who feel threatened by change will accept it, however much they have been consulted. But the attempt should be made. Departmental, team and interfunctional meetings can help to increase understanding. Change management is discussed in more detail in Chapter 3.

The implementation plan may have to cater for the likelihood that all the organizational changes cannot be implemented at once. Implementation may have to be phased to allow changes to be introduced progressively, to enable people to absorb what they will be expected to do and to allow for any necessary training. Changes may in any case be delayed until suitable people for new positions are available.

36

Performance management

Performance management is a systematic approach to improving individual and team performance. It is based on two simple propositions:

1. People are most likely to perform well when they know and understand what is expected of them and have taken part in defining these expectations.
2. The ability to meet these expectations depends on the level of competence and motivation of individuals and the leadership and support they receive from their managers.

HOW PERFORMANCE MANAGEMENT WORKS

Performance management takes the form of a continuous cycle as shown in Figure 36.1.

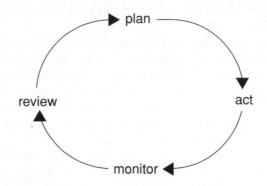

Figure 36.1 *The performance management cycle*

This is, in fact, the normal cycle of management as defined by William Deming and others. Performance management is therefore a natural process of management – it is not an appraisal system imposed on line managers by the personnel function.

As a natural process of management, performance management involves:

1. *Planning* – reaching agreement on objectives and standards to be achieved and the level of competence to be attained; discussing and agreeing performance improvement and personal development plans.
2. *Action* – taking action to implement plans and to achieve the required standards of day-to-day work. This action is carried out by individuals with the guidance and support of their managers.
3. *Monitoring* – actions and outcomes are monitored continuously by individuals and, as necessary, by their manager (the more this can be left to individuals so that they are in effect managing their own performance, the better).
4. *Reviews* – these can take place at any appropriate time during the year. Performance management is an all-the-year process, not an annual event. The reviews can be quite informal with feedback from the manager or, preferably, generated by the individual from feedback information available directly to him or her. A more formal review may take place periodically, say once or twice a year.

251

FORMAL REVIEW AND FEEDBACK

Formal review meetings provide an occasion for structured feedback and reflection. The feedback will summarize and draw conclusions from what has been happening since the last review but it will be based on events and observations rather than opinion. These should have been raised at the time – there should not be any surprises during the formal discussion. But the conversation – and that is what it should be – will concentrate on analysis and review of the significant points emerging from the period under consideration. It will recognize successes and identify things that have not gone according to plan in order to learn lessons for the future. It should be a joint affair – both parties are involved, so there may well be an element of self-assessment by the individuals. (Techniques of providing feedback are described in Chapter 41.)

The review should be rooted in the reality of what the individual has been doing. It is concrete, not abstract, and it allows managers and individuals together to take a positive look at how performance can become even better in the future and how any problems in achieving objectives or meeting standards can be resolved by the individual alone or jointly by the individual and the manager – for example, by coaching or arranging training. The points which can be covered in a review include:

- the achievement of objectives, including an analysis of why they have or have not been achieved;
- the level of competency achieved under each competency heading;
- the contribution made by the person to upholding core values;
- achievements in implementing the personal development plan;
- areas for future consideration – development of strengths, aspects of performance which need to be improved, training needs;
- feelings about the work – nature, scope, demand, opportunity to use abilities and develop skills, etc;
- aspirations – different types of work, career;
- comments from the individual about the support given by his or her manager.

In a sense the review is partly a stocktaking exercise answering the questions 'where have we got to?' and 'how did we get here?' But there is much more to it than that. It is not just an historical exercise, dwelling on the past and conducting post mortems. The true purpose of the review is to look forward to what needs to be done by people to achieve the overall purpose of their jobs, to meet new challenges, to make even better use of their skills, knowledge and abilities, and to develop their skills and competencies to further their career and increase their employability, within and outside the organization.

CONDUCTING A CONSTRUCTIVE PERFORMANCE REVIEW MEETING

A constructive review meeting is most likely to take place if reviewers:

● encourage reviewees to do most of the talking;
● listen actively to what they say;
● allow scope for reflection and analysis;
● analyse performance, not personality – concentrate on what reviewees have done, not the sort of people they are;
● keep the whole period under review, not concentrating on isolated or recent events.
● adopt a 'no surprises' approach – performance problems should have been identified and dealt with at the time they occurred.
● recognize achievements and reinforce strengths;
● end the meeting positively with agreed action plans and an understanding of how progress in implementing them will be reviewed.

PERFORMANCE REVIEW SKILLS

The main skills applied to performance reviews are asking the right questions and listening actively, as discussed below, and providing feedback, as covered in Chapter 41. Performance review meetings also provide opportunities for coaching and counselling, as described in Chapters 5 and 12 respectively.

Asking the right questions

The aim of a performance and development review meeting it to obtain effective interaction. This can be promoted by asking the right questions, allowing thinking time for response, listening carefully (see below) and maintaining a friendly atmosphere. Only one question should be asked at a time, and, if necessary, unclear responses should be played back to check understanding.

The two main approaches to use are open and probe questions.

Open questions

These are general not specific. They provide room for people to decide how they should be answered and encourage them to talk freely. They set the scene for the more detailed analysis of performance that will follow later and can be introduced at any point to open up a discussion on a new topic. Open questions help to create an atmosphere of calm and friendly enquiry and can be expressed quite informally, for example:

● How do you think things have been going?
● How can we build on that in the future?
● What can we learn from that?

Open questions can be put in a 'tell me' form such as:

● Tell me, why do you think that happened?
● Tell me, how did you handle that situation?
● Tell me, how is this project going?
● Tell me, what do you think your key objectives are going to be next year?

Probe questions

Probe questions seek specific information on what has happened and why. They can:

● show interest and encouragement by making supportive statements followed by questions: 'I see, and then what?'
● seek further information by asking 'Why?' or 'Why not?' or 'What do you mean?'
● explore attitudes: 'To what extent do you believe that…?'
● reflect views: 'Have I got the right impression, do you feel that…?'

Listening

In a review meeting it is necessary to listen carefully. Good listeners:

- concentrate on the speaker; they are alert at all times to the nuances of what is being said;
- respond quickly when appropriate but do not interrupt unnecessarily;
- ask questions to clarify meaning;
- comment as necessary on the points made to demonstrate understanding but not at length.

37

Planning and prioritizing

PLANNING

Planning is the process of deciding on a course of action, ensuring that the resources required to implement the action will be available and scheduling the programme of work required to achieve a defined end result. It also involves prioritizing work – deciding the order in which to do things.

As a manager you will normally plan ahead over a relatively short period of time – up to one or, at most, two years. And your objectives, targets and budgets will probably have been fixed by the corporate plan or company budget.

You plan to complete tasks on time without using more resources than you were allowed. Your aim should be to avoid crises and the high costs that they cause; to have fewer 'drop everything and rush this' problems. Planning warns you about possible crises and gives you a chance to avoid them. Contingency or fall-back plans should be prepared if you have any reason to believe that your initial plan may fail for reasons beyond your control.

When you plan, you choose certain courses of action and rule out others; that is to say, you lose flexibility. This will be a disadvantage if the future turns out differently from what you expected – which is only too likely. Try to make plans that you can change at reasonable cost if you have to. It is a bad plan that admits no change.

PLANNING ACTIVITIES

As a manager, there are eight planning activities you need to carry out:

- *Forecasting*
    - What sort of work has to be done, how much and by when.
    - How the workload might change.
    - The likelihood of the department being called on to undertake specialized or rush jobs.
    - Possible changes within or outside the department which might affect priorities, the activities carried out, or the workload.

- *Programming* – deciding the sequence and time-scale of operations and events required to produce results on time.
- *Staffing* – deciding how many and what type of staff are needed and considering the feasibility of absorbing peak loads by means of overtime or temporary staff.
- *Setting standards and targets* – for output, sales, times, quality, costs or for any other aspect of the work where performance should be planned, measured and controlled.
- *Procedure planning* – deciding how the work should be done and planning the actual operations by defining the systems and procedures required.
- *Materials planning* – deciding what materials, bought-in parts or subcontracted work are required and ensuring that they are made available in the right quantity at the right time.
- *Facilities planning* – deciding on the plant, equipment, tools and space required.
- *Budgeting*.

PLANNING TECHNIQUES

Most of the planning you do as a manager is simply a matter of thinking systematically and using your common sense. Every plan contains three key ingredients:

- Objective – the innovation or improvement to be achieved.
- Action programme – the specific steps required to achieve the right objective.
- Financial impact – the effect of the action on sales, turnover, costs and, ultimately, profit.

Figure 37.1 is an example of how a manufacturing plan could be set out.

Action Programme

Steps	Responsibility	Completion by
1. Ensure recognition by supplier of problem with 'hard spots' in castings.	Purchasing Manager Production Manager	15 January
2. Negotiate price concession on all castings received during weeks when we return more than 10 bad castings.	Purchasing Manager	31 January
3. Set up storage area to accumulate ruined castings.	Facilities Manager	15 February
4. Establish procedures to record machine downtime and cutter breakage with individual castings.	Production Controller	1 March
5. Ensure XYZ Company agrees new arrangements.	Purchasing Manager	15 March

Profit Impact

		£ 19.. *Profit Increase (Decrease)*
Price concessions		7,000
Effect of improved quality	Scrap	8,500
	Overtime	3,500
	Expense tools	9,000
	Lost production	20,000
	Other	12,000
Modifications in storage area		(2,000)
Recording procedures		(1,000)
Other costs		(3,000)
	Total profit impact	£54,000

Figure 37.1 *Example of a manufacturing plan*

Step (detailed in action programme)	Responsibility	January	February	March
1. Get XYZ Company to recognize problem.	Purchasing Manager	▭		
2. Negotiate price concession.	Purchasing Manager	▭		
3. Set up storage area.	Facilities Manager	▭		
4. Establish downtime recording procedures.	Production Controller		▭	
5. Get XYZ Company to agree new arrangements.	Purchasing Manager			▭

Figure 37.2 *A Gantt chart*

Bar charts should be used to express plans more graphically wherever there is more than one activity and care has to be taken to sequence them correctly. The manufacturing plan illustrated in Figure 37.1 could be expressed as a Gantt chart (see Figure 37.2).

A more refined method of planning activities in a complex programme, where many interdependent events have to take place, is network planning. This requires the recording of the component parts and their representation in a diagram as a network of interrelated activities. Events are represented by circles, activities by arrows, and the time taken by activities by the length of the arrows. There can also be dotted arrows for dummy activities between events that have a time rather than an activity relationship. A critical path can be derived which highlights those operations or activities which are essential for the completion of the project within the allocated time-scale. All illustration of part of a basic network is given in Figure 37.3.

There may be occasions when even more sophisticated planning techniques, using computer models, can be made available to help the manager, especially when large quantities of information have to be processed against a number of fixed assumptions or parameters, or where alternative assumptions have to be assessed. In Book Club Associates, for example, the loading required in the warehouse in terms of machine time and work hours can be projected two years ahead by feeding parameters for projected activity levels

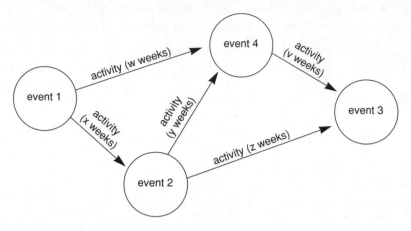

Figure 37.3 *Part of a basic network*

into the programme. Plans can then be made to ensure that workers and machine capacity are available to deal with forecast work levels.

PRIORITIZING

The prioritization of work involves deciding on the relative importance of a range of demands or tasks so that the order in which they are undertaken can be determined. The fragmented nature of managerial work as described in Chapter 1 and the sudden and often conflicting demands made on managers' time means that they are constantly faced with decisions on when to do things. They may often be in a situation where they have to cope with conflicting priorities. This can be stressful unless they adopt a systematic approach to prioritization.

Prioritization can be carried out in the following stages:

1. List all the things you have to do. These can be classified into three groups:

    ● regular duties such as submitting a report, calling on customers, carrying out a performance review;
    ● special requests from managers, colleagues, customers, clients, suppliers, etc delivered orally, by telephone, letter, fax or e-mail;

- self-generated work such as preparing proposals on an innovation.

2. Classify each item on the list according to:

   - the significance of the task to be done in terms of its impact on your work (and reputation) and on the results achieved by the organization, your team or anyone else involved;
   - the importance of the person requesting the work or expecting you to deliver something – less significant tasks may well be put higher on the priority list if they are set by the chief executive or a key client;
   - the urgency of the tasks – deadlines, what will happen if they are not completed on time;
   - any scope there may be for extending deadlines – altering start and finish times and dates;
   - how long each task will take to complete – noting any required or imposed starting and completion times which cannot be changed.

3. Assess how much time you have available to complete the tasks, apart from the routine work which you must get done. Also assess what resources, such as your own staff, are available to get the work done.

4. Draw up a provisional list of priorities by reference to the criteria of significance, importance and urgency listed at (2) above.

5. Assess the possibility of fitting this prioritized schedule of work into the time available. If this proves difficult, put self-imposed priorities on a back-burner and concentrate on the significant tasks. Negotiate delayed completion or delivery times where you believe this is possible and, if successful, move the task down the priority list.

6. Finalize the list of priorities and schedule the work you have to do (or you have to get others to do) accordingly.

Set out step by step like this, prioritization looks like a formidable task. But experienced managers go through all these stages almost unconsciously, although systematically, whenever they are confronted with a large workload or conflicting priorities. What many people do is simply write out a 'things to do' list at the beginning of the week or, in their minds, quickly run through all the considerations described in the above six-stage sequence and make notes on a piece of paper.

38

Power and politics

Power and politics in an organization go together. You may feel, like Nietzsche, that 'power has crooked legs'. But things don't get done without the exercise of authority, and authority requires the use of power. Furthermore, one way of getting authority and power is to indulge in company politics. You may deplore it, and many chief executives deny that it happens in their organizations. It does take place, however, because people seek power and often use political means to attain it.

POWER – GOOD OR BAD?

In his analysis of power in British industry, Anthony Jay (30) commented: 'Power lies in the acceptance of your authority by others, their knowledge that if they try to resist you they will fail and you will succeed. Real power does not lie in documents etc – it lies in what you can achieve.'

And Mary Parker Follett (20) wrote: 'Our task is not to learn where to plan power; it is how to develop power. Genuine power can only be grown, it will slip from every arbitrary hand.'

Power is legitimate if it is used to pursue legitimate ends and is wielded in a responsible way by responsible people. But it can be employed in a harsh way.

David McClelland's (38) studies of power in action involving over 500 managers from 25 different US corporations led him to conclude:

> [Managers] must possess a high need for power, that is, a concern for influencing people. However, this need must be disciplined and controlled so that it is directed towards the benefit of the institution as a whole and not towards the manager's personal aggrandizement... [Managers motivated by a need for power] are able to create a greater sense of responsibility in their divisions and, above all, a greater team spirit.

Here are two cases of power being used effectively.

Case 1: One of the best managers we have in the company has lots of power based on one thing or another over most people. But he seldom if ever just tells or asks someone to do something. He almost always takes a few minutes to try to persuade them. The power he has over people generally induces them to listen carefully and certainly disposes them to be influenced. That, of course, makes the persuasion process go quickly and easily. And he never risks getting the other person upset by making what that person thinks is an unfair request or command.

Case 2: Product manager Stein needed plant manager Billings to 'sign off' on a new product idea (Product X) which Billings thought was terrible. Stein decided there was no way he could logically persuade Billings because Billings just would not listen to him. With time, Stein felt, he could have broken through that barrier. But he did not have that time. Stein also realized that Billings would never, just because of some deal or favour, sign off on a product he did not believe in. Stein also felt it not worth the risk of trying to force Billings to sign off, so here is what he did.

On Monday, Stein got Reynolds, a person Billings respected, to send Billings two market research studies that were very favourable to Product X, with a note attached saying, 'Have you seen this? I found them rather surprising. I am not sure if I entirely believe them, but still...'.

On Tuesday, Stein got a representative of one of the company's biggest customers to mention casually to Billings on the phone that he had heard a rumour about Product X being introduced soon and was 'glad to see you guys are on your toes as usual'.

On Wednesday, Stein had two industrial engineers stand about three feet away from Billings as they were waiting for a meeting to begin and talk about the favourable test results on Product X.

On Thursday, Stein set up a meeting to talk about Product X with Billings and invited only people whom Billings liked or respected and who also felt favourably about Product X.

On Friday, Stein went to see Billings and asked him if he was willing to sign off on Product X. He was.

SOURCES OF POWER

Power is clearly linked to position and rank. But to a certain degree it has to be earned. You can give orders to your subordinates but you are going to get more out of them if you obtain their willing co-operation rather than their grudging submission. Power is bestowed upon you as a manager but you have to justify your use of it.

There are, however, other sources of power, namely:

● *Access to other people with power.* Proximity or a direct line obviously gives you more scope to exert influence, actual or perceived. That is why secretaries are important.
● *Control over information.* 'Knowledge is power' or, alternatively, 'authority goes to the one who knows'. If you are in the know, you are in a better position to control events or, if you want to play politics, to put spokes in other people's wheels.
● *Control over resources.* If you have control over resources such as money, workforce, equipment or services that you or anyone else needs, you have power.
● *Control over rewards and punishments.* You also have power if you can give rewards or punishments or influence others who control them.
● *Expertise.* You gain and keep power if you can convince others that you are the expert.
● *Identification.* You can achieve power over others if you persuade them to identify with what you are doing or with you personally. This is what charismatic leaders do by enthusiasm, dedication, involving people and by sheer force of personality.
● *Sense of obligation.* If you develop a sense of obligation by doing favours for people you can reasonably expect that they will feel an obligation to return those favours.

USING POWER

John Kotter (36) interviewed over 250 managers who were in a position to use power. He found that the successful ones had the following characteristics:

- They use their power openly and legitimately. They are seen as genuine experts in their field and consistently live up to the leadership image they build for themselves.
- They are sensitive to what types of power are most effective with different types of people. For example, experts respect expertise.
- They develop all their sources of power and do not rely too much on any particular technique.
- The seek jobs and tasks which will give them the opportunity to acquire and use power. They constantly seek ways to invest the power they already have to secure an even higher positive return.
- They use their power in a mature and self-controlled way. They seldom if ever use power impulsively or for their own aggrandizement.
- They get satisfaction from influencing others.

POLITICS – GOOD OR BAD?

To be politic, according to the *Oxford English Dictionary*, you can be sagacious, prudent, judicious, expedient, scheming or crafty. So political behaviour in an organization could be desirable or undesirable.

Organizations consist of individuals who, while they are ostensibly there to achieve a common purpose, will, at the same time, be driven by their own needs to achieve their own goals. Effective management is the process of harmonizing individual endeavour and ambition to the common good. Some individuals will genuinely believe that using political means to achieve their goals will benefit the organization as well as themselves. Others will rationalize this belief. Yet others will unashamedly pursue their own ends. They may use all their powers of persuasion to legitimize these ends to their colleagues, but self-interest remains the primary drive. These are the corporate politicians whom the *Oxford*

English Dictionary describes as 'shrewd schemers, crafty plotters or intriguers'. Politicians within organizations can be like this. They manoeuvre behind people's backs, blocking proposals they do not like. They advance their own reputation and career at the expense of other people's. They can be envious and jealous and act accordingly. They are bad news.

But it can also be argued that a political approach to management is inevitable and even desirable in any organization where the clarity of goals is not absolute, where the decision-making process is not clear-cut and where the authority to make decisions is not evenly or appropriately distributed. And there can be few organizations where one or more of these conditions do not apply.

Andrew Kakabadse (31) recognizes this point when he says in *The Politics of Management*: 'Politics is a process, that of influencing individuals and groups of people to your point of view, where you cannot rely on authority.' In this sense, a political approach can be legitimate as long as the ends are justifiable from the viewpoint of the organization.

POLITICAL APPROACHES

Kakabadse identifies seven approaches that organizational politicians adopt:

1. Identify the stakeholders, those who have commitment to act in a particular way.
2. Keep the stakeholders comfortable, concentrating on behaviour, values, attitudes, fears and drives that the individuals will accept, tolerate and manage (comfort zones).
3. Fit the image – work on the comfort zones and align their image to that of the people with power.
4. Use the network – identify the interest groups and people of influence.
5. Enter the network – identify the gatekeepers, adhere to the norms.
6. Make deals – agree to support other people where this is of mutual benefit.
7. Withhold and withdraw – withhold information as appropriate and withdraw judiciously when the going gets rough.

Some of these precepts are more legitimate than others. Organizational life requires managers to identify the key decision-makers when they are involved in developing new approaches and getting things done. Before coming to a final conclusion and launching a fully fledged proposal at a committee or in a memorandum, it makes good sense to test opinion and find out how other people may react. This testing process enables managers to anticipate counter-arguments and modify their proposals either to meet legitimate objections or, when there is no alternative, to accommodate other people's requirements.

Making deals may not appear to be particularly desirable, but it does happen, and managers can always rationalize this type of behaviour by reference to the end result. Withholding information is not legitimate behaviour, but people do indulge in it in recognition of the fact that knowledge is power. Judicious withdrawal may also seem to be questionable, but most managers prefer to live to fight another day rather than launch a doomed crusade.

POLITICAL SENSITIVITY

Organizational politicians exert hidden influence to get their way, and 'politicking' in some form takes place in most organizations. If you want to get on, a degree of political sensitivity is desirable – knowing what is going on so that influence can be exerted. This means:

- knowing how 'things are done around here';
- knowing how decisions are made, including the less obvious factors that are likely to affect decisions;
- knowing where the power base is in the organization – who makes the running; who are the people who count when decisions are taken;
- being aware of what is going on behind the scenes;
- knowing who is a rising star; whose reputation is fading;
- identifying any 'hidden agendas' – trying to understand what people are really getting at, and why, by obtaining answers to the question: 'Where are they coming from?'
- finding out what other people are thinking and seeking;
- networking – as Kakabadse suggests, identifying the interest groups.

DANGERS

The danger of politics, however, is that they can be carried to excess, and they can then seriously harm the effectiveness of an organization. The signs of excessive indulgence in political behaviour include:

- Back-biting.
- Buck-passing.
- Secret meetings and hidden decisions.
- Feuds between people and departments.
- Paper wars between armed camps – arguing by memoranda, always a sign of distrust.
- A multiplicity of snide comments and criticisms.
- Excessive and counter-productive lobbying.
- The formation of cabals – cliques which spend their time intriguing.

DEALING WITH ORGANIZATIONAL POLITICIANS

One way to deal with this sort of behaviour is to find out who is going in for it and openly confront them with the damage they are doing. They will, of course, deny that they are behaving politically (they wouldn't be politicians if they didn't) but the fact that they have been identified might lead them to modify their approach. It could, of course, only serve to drive them further underground, in which case their behaviour will have to be observed even more closely and corrective action taken as necessary.

A more positive approach to keeping politics operating at an acceptable level is for the organization to manage its operations as openly as possible. The aims should be to ensure that issues are debated fully, that differences of opinion are dealt with frankly and that disagreements are de-personalized, so far as this is possible. Political processes can then be seen as a way of maintaining the momentum of the organization as a complex decision-making and problem-solving entity.

USE OF POLITICS

There are occasions when a subtle appeal rather than a direct attack will pay dividends; and sometimes you have to exercise your powers of persuasion indirectly on those whose support you need. The following case study illustrates the legitimate use of politics.

James Hale was the personnel director of a large divisionalized group in the food industry. The rate of growth by expansion and acquisitions had been very rapid. There was a shortage of really good managers and a lack of co-ordination between the divisions in the group and between those divisions and head office. Hale believed that setting up a group management training centre would be a good way of helping to overcome these problems. He knew, however, that he would have to get agreement to this plan not only from the managing director, who would be broadly sympathetic, but also from his co-directors. The MD would not act without the support of a majority on his board.

In any case Hale genuinely felt that there was no point in developing a facility of this sort for people who were not interested in it. He therefore sat back and deliberately worked out a strategy for getting agreement to his proposal. He knew that a frontal attack might fail. Management development was perceived by his colleagues as a somewhat airy-fairy idea which had little relevance to their real concerns as directors. He therefore had to adopt a more subtle approach. He did not call it a political campaign, but that is what it was. He was setting out to influence people indirectly.

The basis of his plan was an individual approach to each of his colleagues, adjusted to their particular interests and concerns. In the case of the marketing director, he got the general sales manager to advocate the need for training in sales management for divisional sales staff. He ran several pilot courses in hotels and invited the marketing director to the winding-up session. He made sure that the marketing director was impressed, not only by what the divisional sales staff had learnt from the course, but also by the new spirit of identification with group aims and policies engendered by the training. Casually, the personnel director let slip the thought that if the group had its own training centre this feeling of commitment could be developed even more strongly.

The same basic technique was used with the production director. In addition he was helped to come to the view that a centre owned by the group could speed up the introduction of new ideas and provide a facility for communicating directly with key staff which was not available at present.

The finance director was a more difficult person to convince. He could easily assess the costs but found it difficult to accept largely subjective views of the potential benefits. In this case James Hale did not try too hard to persuade him against his will. He knew that the majority of the board was now in favour of the plan, including the managing director. Hale felt safe in leaving his financial colleague in an isolated and ultimately untenable position. The qualitative arguments, as absorbed by the other members of the board, including the managing director, had the ring of truth about them which no purely quantitative arguments could overcome.

Hale was content that he had enough support. To clinch the argument he played his last political card by warning the marketing and production directors that there might be some financial opposition. He then got them to agree with the thesis that they wouldn't allow 'Mr Money Bags' to adopt a narrow financial view and thus dictate the destiny of the firm.

James Hale had no difficulty in getting his proposal accepted at the next board meeting.

The non-legitimate use of politics

The following is an example of non-legitimate use of politics. Unfortunately, it is a fairly common one. In most organizations there are people who want to get on, and do not have too many scruples about how they do it. If it involves treading on other people's faces, then so be it.

Two directors of a company both aspired to be the next managing director. Mr Black, the finance director, had the ear of the MD. Mr White, the technical director, was more remote.

Mr White had a number of ideas for introducing new technology and had proved, to his own satisfaction at least, that the pay-off was considerable. Unfortunately, he jumped the gun in order to anticipate comments from Black, and presented a paper to the managing director which was not as well argued as it might have been. Black carefully lobbied the MD and convinced him that the proposal was full of holes – he also hinted that this was yet another example of White's inability to understand the wider commercial issues.

The MD accepted this view more or less completely and agreed with Black's suggestion that the whole proposal should be off-loaded on to a board sub-committee – a well-known device to delay if not to stifle new ideas. This was done, and the introduction of new technology was unnecessarily delayed by 18 months. But Black had made his point as the practical man of affairs who would not allow the company to get involved in expensive and unrewarding projects.

39

Problem-solving and decision-making

PROBLEMS AND OPPORTUNITIES

It is often said that 'there are no problems, only opportunities'. This is not universally true, of course, but it does emphasize the point that a problem should lead to positive thinking about what is to be done now, rather than to recriminations. If a mistake has been made, the reasons for it should be analysed, to ensure that it does not happen again. But it is then water under the bridge.

Faced with a continuous flow of problems and decisions you may occasionally feel utterly confused. We all feel like that sometimes.

IMPROVING YOUR SKILLS

How can you improve your ability to solve problems and make decisions? There are a few basic approaches you should use.

Improve your analytical ability

A complicated situation can often be resolved by separating the whole into its component parts. Such an analysis should relate to facts, although, as Peter Drucker points out, when trying to understand the root causes of a problem you may have to start with an opinion. Even if you ask people to search for the facts first, they will probably look for those facts that fit the conclusion they have already reached.

Opinions are a perfectly good starting point as long as they are brought out into the open at once and then tested against reality. Analyse each hypothesis and pick out the parts which need to be studied and tested.

Mary Parker Follett's (20) 'law of the situation' – the logic of facts and events – should rule in the end. And although you may start out with a hypothesis, when testing it, use Rudyard Kipling's six honest serving men:

> I keep six honest serving men
> (They taught me all I knew)
> Their names are What and Why and When
> and How and Where and Who.

Adopt a systematic approach

Use the methods discussed in Chapter 4: analysing the situation, identifying possible courses of action, weighing them up and deciding what to do.

But do not expect the system to produce a black and white solution. Remember that Drucker (17) says:

> A decision is a judgement. It is a choice between alternatives. It is rarely a choice between right and wrong. It is at best a choice between almost right and probably wrong – but much more often a choice between two courses of action neither of which is probably more nearly right than the other.

You should not expect, or even welcome, a bland consensus view. The best decisions emerge from a clash of conflicting points of view. This is Drucker's first law of decision-making – 'one does not make a decision without disagreements'. You need a clash of opinion to prevent people falling into the trap of starting with the conclusion and then looking for the facts that support it.

Alfred P Sloan of General Motors knew this. At a meeting of one of his top committees he said: 'Gentlemen, I take it we are all in complete agreement on the decision here.' Everyone round the table nodded assent. 'Then,' continued Mr Sloan, 'I propose we postpone further discussion of this matter until our next meeting to give ourselves time to develop disagreement and perhaps gain some understanding of what the decision is all about.'

Use your imagination

A strictly logical answer to the problem may not be the best one. Use lateral thinking, analogies and brainstorming to get off your tramlines and dream up an entirely new approach.

Keep it simple

One of the first principles of logic is known as Occam's razor. It states that 'entities are not to be multiplied without necessity'. That is, always believe the simplest of several explanations.

Implementation

A problem has not been solved until the decision has been implemented. Think carefully not only about how a thing is to be done (by whom, with what resources and by when) but also about its impact on the people concerned and the extent to which they will co-operate. You will get less co-operation if you impose a solution. The best method is to arrange things so that everyone arrives jointly at a solution freely agreed to be the one best suited to the situation (the law of the situation again).

PROBLEM-SOLVING AND DECISION-MAKING TECHNIQUES

Effective problem-solving and decision-making require the following steps:

1. *Define the situation.* Establish what has gone wrong or is about to go wrong.

2. *Specify objectives.* Define what you are setting out to achieve now or in the future as you deal with an actual or potential problem or a change in circumstances.

3. *Develop hypotheses.* If you have a problem, develop hypotheses about the cause.

4. *Get the facts.* In order to provide a basis for testing hypotheses and developing possible courses of action, find out what is happening now and/or what is likely to happen in the future. If different people are involved, get both sides of the story and, where possible, check with a third party. Obtain written evidence wherever relevant. Do not rely on hearsay.

   Define what is supposed to be happening in terms of policies, procedures or results and contrast this with what is actually happening. Try to understand the attitudes and motivation of those concerned. Remember that people will see what has happened or is happening, in terms of their own position. Obtain information about internal or external constraints that affect the situation.

5. *Analyse the facts.* Determine what is relevant and what is irrelevant. Establish the cause or causes of the problem. Do not be tempted to concentrate on symptoms rather than causes. Dig into what lies behind the problem. When analysing future events, try to make a realistic assessment in terms of existing trends both within and outside the organization. But be careful not to indulge in crude extrapolations. Consider the various internal and external organizational and environmental factors which may affect future developments.

40

Project management

Project management is the planning, supervision and control of any activity or set of activities which leads to a defined outcome at a predetermined time and in accordance with specified performance or quality standards at a budgeted cost. Project management is concerned with *deliverables* – getting things done as required or promised. While delivering results on time is important, it is equally important to deliver them to meet the specification and within the projected cost.

Project management involves action planning – deciding *what* work is to be done, *why* the work needs to be done, *who* will do the work, *how* much it will cost, *when* the work has to be completed (totally or stage by stage) and *where* the work will be carried out.

The three main project management activities are project planning, setting up the project and project control.

PROJECT PLANNING

Initiation

Project planning starts with a definition of the objectives of the project. A business case has to be made. This means answering two basic questions:

1. Why is this project needed?
2. What benefits are expected from the project?

The answers to these questions should be quantified. The requirement could be spelt out in such terms as new systems or facilities to meet defined business needs, new plant required for new products or to improve productivity or quality. The benefits are expressed as revenues generated, productivity, quality or performance improvements, costs saved and return on investment.

Assessment

Projects involve investing resources – money and people. Investment appraisal techniques are used to ensure that the company's criteria on return on investment are satisfied. Cost–benefit analysis may be used to assess the degree to which the benefits justify the costs, time and number of people required by the project. This may mean identifying opportunity costs which establish whether a greater benefit would be obtained by investing the money or deploying the people on other projects or activities.

Performance specification

This sets out what the outcome of the project is expected to do – how it should perform – and describes the details of the project's configuration or method of operation.

Project plan

The project plan sets out:

- the major operations in sequence – the main stages of the project;

- a breakdown where appropriate of each major operation into a sequence of subsidiary tasks;
- an analysis of the interrelationships and interdependencies of major and subsidiary tasks;
- an estimate of the time required to complete each major operation or stage;
- a procurement plan to obtain the necessary materials, systems and equipment;
- a human resource plan which defines how many people will be allocated to the project with different skills at each stage and who is to be responsible for controlling the project as a whole and each of the major stages or operations.

SETTING UP THE PROJECT

Setting up the project involves:

- obtaining and allocating resources;
- selecting and briefing the project management team;
- finalizing the project programme – defining each stage;
- defining and establishing control systems and reporting procedures (format and timing of progress reports);
- identifying key dates, stage by stage, for the project (milestones) and providing for milestone meetings to review progress and decide on any actions required.

CONTROLLING THE PROJECT

The three most important things to control are:

- time – achievement of project plan as programme;
- quality – achievement of project specifications;
- cost – containment of costs within budget.

Project control is based on progress reports showing what is being achieved against the plan. The planned completion date, actual achievement and forecast completion date for each stage or operation are provided. The likelihood of delays, over-runs or bottlenecks is thus established so that corrective action can be taken in good time. Control can be achieved by the use of Gantt or bar charts and by reference to network plans or critical path analyses.

Progress meetings should be held at predetermined intervals. These can be treated as 'milestone' meetings when they are timed to coincide with the key stages of the project.

STEPS TO EFFECTIVE PROJECT MANAGEMENT

1. Specify objectives and deliverables.
2. Carry out cost–benefit analysis or investment appraisal to justify project.
3. Determine:

   - what should be done;
   - who does what;
   - when it should be done (broken down into stages);
   - how much it should cost.

4. Define resource requirements (people, money, materials, systems, equipment, etc).
5. Prepare programme – identify stages.
6. Define methods of control – charts, network analysis, progress reports, progress (milestone) meetings.
7. Ensure that everyone knows what is expected of them and has the resources required.
8. Monitor progress continuously against the plan as well as at formal meetings.
9. Take corrective action as required; for example, re-allocating resources.
10. Evaluate the end result against the objectives and deliverables.

41

Providing feedback

People need to know how well they are doing in order to carry on doing it to good effect or to understand what they need to do to improve. They take action, they learn through feedback information how effective that action has been and they complete the feedback loop by making any corrections to their behaviour on the basis of the information they have received.

Ideally, feedback should be built into the job. Individuals should be able to keep track of what they are doing so that they can initiate speedy corrective action. But that is not always feasible, and the manager has the responsibility of providing the feedback. This can and should be done regularly, and especially after a particular task has been carried out or a project has been completed. But it can also be provided in more formal performance review meetings.

AIM OF FEEDBACK

The aim of feedback is to provide information to people which will enable them to understand how well they have been doing and how effective their behaviour has been. Feedback should promote this understanding so that appropriate action can be taken. This can be corrective action where the feedback has indicated that something has gone wrong or, more positively, action can be taken to make the best use of the opportunities the feedback has revealed. In the latter case, feedback acts as a reinforcement, and positive feedback can be a powerful motivator because it is a recognition of achievement.

GIVING FEEDBACK

Feedback should be based on fact not subjective judgement. The following are some guidelines on giving feedback:

- *Build feedback into the job.* To be effective, feedback should be built into the job. Individuals or teams should be able to find out easily how they have done from the control information readily available to them. If it cannot be built into the job it should be provided as quickly as possible after the activity has taken place, ideally within a day or two.
- *Provide feedback on actual events.* Feedback should be provided on actual results or observed behaviour, not based on subjective opinion.
- *Describe, don't judge.* The feedback should be presented as a description of what has happened. It should not be accompanied by a judgement.
- *Refer to specific behaviours.* The feedback should be related to specific items of behaviour; it should not transmit general feelings or impressions.
- *Ask questions.* Ask questions rather than make statements: 'Why do you think this happened?' 'On reflection, is there any other way in which you think you could have handled the situation?' 'What are the factors that influenced you to make that decision?'
- *Get people to work things out for themselves.* Encourage people to come to their own conclusions about what they should do or how they should behave. Ask questions such as: 'How do you think you should tackle this sort of problem in the future?' 'How do you feel you could avoid getting into this situation again?'

● *Select key issues.* Select key issues and restrict the feedback to them. There is a limit to how much criticism anyone can take. If it is overdone, the shutters will go up and the discussion will get nowhere.

● *Focus.* Focus on aspects of performance the individual can improve. It is a waste of time to concentrate on areas which the individual can do little or nothing about.

● *Show understanding.* If something has gone wrong, find out if this has happened because of circumstances beyond the individual's control and indicate that this is understood.

42

Quality management

WHAT IS QUALITY AND WHY IS IT IMPORTANT?

Quality can be defined as the degree of excellence achieved by an organization in delivering products or services to its customers. There are three aspects of quality:

● *quality of design* – the degree to which the design achieves its purpose;
● *quality of conformance* – the extent to which the product conforms with the design specification;
● *quality of customer satisfaction* – the level at which value is delivered to customers by satisfying their needs.

A customer-orientated concept

Of these three aspects, the last is by far the most important. Quality of design and quality of conformance serve the sole purpose of satisfying customers. Quality is essentially a customer-orientated concept. Customer satisfaction is obtained by product designs or service programmes which meet their needs, by achieving quality specifications which have been built into the design of the product or service, by attaining high standards of reliability and equally high levels of customer service, and by paying constant attention to customer care.

Measuring quality

The level of quality reached by an organization is measured in terms of the extent to which customer requirements are satisfied. However, the reputation of an organization for quality products or services extends beyond individual customers to the community at large. And this reputation must be protected and enhanced.

Achieving competitive advantage through quality

Competitive advantage is achieved by businesses which provide goods or services to quality levels higher than those offered by competitors. But these competitors will be striving equally hard to match or exceed those levels. This means that policies of continuous improvement have to be implemented to maintain competitive advantage. Quality is a race without a finish. It is a race against tough competitors to achieve and sustain world-class performance. Quality differentiates companies from their competitors.

Quality management

Quality has to be managed. It is not achieved easily – the race is hard. And it cannot be left to chance. Everyone in an organization has to play their part, but what they do must be planned, monitored, measured and controlled. In short, they have to managed.

THE PRINCIPLES OF QUALITY MANAGEMENT

Quality management principles are based on the philosophy of total quality. They can be summed up in the words 'customer satisfaction', 'continuous improvement', 'involving everyone', 'creating commitment to quality' and 'looking at the system as a whole'. This approach provides for the effective management of the dynamic relationship between what organizations need to do to develop and sustain customer satisfaction, and the ever-changing needs of consumers and the continuous pressure of competition. It is a means of ensuring that quality is achieved and improved but does not obviate the need for quality control. Achievements must be measured to ensure that corrective action can be taken; and this action needs to focus on the root causes of the problem, not the symptoms.

The basic principles

The six basic principles of total quality as defined by Ron Collard (11) are:

1. *Top management commitment.* Top management should continuously reinforce a total quality programme by what they do. They have to ensure that everyone knows how important total quality is and appreciates the long-term goals of the organization's total quality processes.
2. *Attitude change.* Total quality requires a complete change in the attitude and culture prevailing in an organization.
3. *Continuous improvement.* The need to create a climate of continuous improvement is linked to attitude change. As Collard states: 'Quality improvement should always be at the forefront of *everything* that is done.'
4. *Supervision.* The successful introduction of total quality gives a key role to supervision in ensuring that the quality message is carried down to grass roots level.
5. *Training.* If the key to success is supervision, then it is important to ensure that the selection, training and motivation of supervision allows for the development of the skills which enable them to become a dynamic force for improving performance.
6. *Recognition.* Performance and achievement in improving quality should be recognized. The recognition of contribution can be made effectively through non-financial means – publicly for individual or team achievement, competitions and prizes for teams.

THE DEVELOPMENT AND IMPLEMENTATION OF QUALITY MANAGEMENT PROCESSES

Quality management is a *process*, a way of doing things. It is not a programme with a finite start and finish. The management of quality is a continuous process which may make use of a number of techniques such as statistical quality control, but ultimately it depends on the attitudes and behaviour of all concerned. Quality management has to be based on a clearly stated policy.

Total quality policy

The policy could include the following points:

- The goal of the organization is to achieve customer satisfaction by meeting the requirements of both external and internal customers.
- The need is to establish customer requirements and respond quickly and effectively to them.
- It is essential to concentrate on prevention rather than cure.
- Everyone is involved – all work done by company employees, suppliers and product outlets is part of a process which creates a product or service for a customer.
- Each employee is a customer for work done by other employees and has the right to expect good work from them and the obligation to contribute work of high calibre to them.
- The standard of quality is 'zero defects' or 'no failures' – everyone has to understand the standards required and the need to do it right first time.
- Sustained quality excellence requires continuous improvement.
- Quality performance and costs should be measured systematically.
- Continuous attention must be paid to satisfying educational and training needs.
- High-quality performance will be recognized and rewarded.
- Quality improvement is best achieved by the joint efforts of all stakeholders.

Planning for total quality

Planning for total quality involves the following:

- Recording the series of events and activities constituting the total process by the use of flow charting and other means of activity analysis.
- Analysing the existing processes and system flows to establish inconsistencies and potential sources of variations and defects.
- Specifying for each activity the necessary quality-related activities, including material and packaging specifications, quality control procedures, process control systems, and sampling and inspection procedures.
- Developing, as appropriate, just-in-time (JIT) systems which provide for the right quantities to be produced or delivered at the right time and ensure that there is no waste.
- Determining how to achieve quality in the purchasing system, with particular reference to the development of long-term relationships with suppliers so that dependable product quality and delivery standards can be defined and maintained.
- Conducting failure mode, effect and criticality studies (FMECA) to determine possible modes of failure and their effects on the performance of the product or service, and to establish which features of product design, production or operation are critical to the various modes of failure.
- Developing planned maintenance systems to reduce the incidence of emergency maintenance.
- Designing quality into the product, making sure that the standards and specifications meet customer needs and can be achieved by existing processes (or, if not, by improving these processes in particular ways).
- Conducting process capability studies to ensure that it will be possible to achieve quality standards through existing processes or, if not, what changes are required.
- Examining quality requirements in manufacturing to ensure that answers can be made to the following questions: Can we make it? Are we making it? Have we made it? Could we make it better?
- Studying storage, distribution and delivery arrangements to ensure that they are capable of meeting customer demands.
- Examining after-sales service procedures and achievements to identify areas for improvement.

MEASURING AND MONITORING QUALITY

The process of managing quality as set out above aims to ensure that everyone is involved and committed to the continuous improvement of quality standards and to 'delighting' customers. But it is necessary to be explicit about the standards of quality required even if these are subject to continuous development, and it is equally important to measure and monitor quality performance against these standards. Only by doing this is it possible to identify where corrective action, aimed at the root causes of the problem, is required. Continuous improvement means doing everything better all the time but it also means learning from problems and mistakes to ensure that they do not happen again. The measurement and monitoring of quality can be carried out by the following means:

- at the most basic level, simply comparing outputs or actions against predetermined standards;
- by inspection – an after-the-event technique which does not address any real quality problems;
- by the various techniques of statistical quality control, namely acceptance sampling, control charts, control by attributes, control by variables;
- by statistical process control;
- by benchmarking;
- by customer and internal surveys.

INVOLVING AND EMPOWERING EMPLOYEES

Total quality will not work unless everyone is involved. This is the main challenge faced by anyone concerned with quality management – 'how can I get people committed to quality?' Clearly, communication and training help, but involvement in the development and application of the principles and practice of total quality achieves a deeper and longer-lasting effect. And empowering people to take control over their own quality practices can be just as important, if not more so.

43

Report writing

The ability to express oneself clearly on paper and to write effective reports is one of a manager's most important skills. As often as not, it is through the medium of reports that you will convey your ideas and recommendations to your superiors and colleagues and inform them of the progress you are making.

WHAT MAKES A GOOD REPORT?

The purpose of a report is to analyse and explain a situation, to propose and gain agreement to a plan. It should be logical, practical, persuasive and succinct.

To be an effective report writer you start by having something worthwhile to say. Clear thinking (Chapter 4), creative thinking (Chapter 13), problem-solving (Chapter 39) and trouble-shooting (Chapter 23) techniques will all help. Your analysis of opinions and facts and your evaluation of options should provide a base for positive conclusions and recommendations.

There are three fundamental rules for report writing:

- Give your report a logical structure.
- Use plain words to convey your meaning.
- Remember the importance of good, clear presentation of material.

STRUCTURE

A report should have a beginning, a middle and an end. If the report is lengthy or complex it will also need a summary of conclusions and recommendations. There may also be appendices containing detailed data and statistics.

Beginning

Your introduction should explain: why the report has been written, its aims, its terms of reference, and why it should be read. It should then state the sources of information upon which the report was based. Finally, if the report is divided into various sections, the arrangement and labelling of these sections should be explained.

Middle

The middle of the report should contain the facts you have assembled and your analysis of those facts. The analysis should lead logically to a diagnosis of the causes of the problem. The conclusions and recommendations included in the final section should flow from the analysis and diagnosis. One of the most common weaknesses in reports is for the facts not to lead on naturally to the conclusions; the other is for the conclusions not to be supported by the facts.

Summarize the facts and your observations. If you have identified alternative courses of action, set out the pros and cons of each one, but make it quite clear which one you favour. Don't leave your readers in mid-air.

A typical trouble-shooting report would start by analysing the present situation; it would then diagnose any problems or weaknesses in that situation, explaining why these have occurred before making proposals on ways of dealing with the problem.

End

The final section of the report should set out your recommendations, stating how each of them will help to achieve the stated aims of the report or overcome any weaknesses revealed by the analytical studies.

The benefits and costs of implementing the recommendations should then be explained. The next stage is to propose a firm plan for implementing the proposals – the programme of work, complete with deadlines and names of people who would carry it out. Finally, tell the recipient(s) of the report what action, such as approval of plans or authorization of expenditure, you would like them to take.

Summary

In a long or complex report it is very helpful to provide an executive summary of conclusions and recommendations. It concentrates the reader's mind and can be used as an agenda in presenting and discussing the report. It is useful to cross-reference the items to the relevant paragraphs or sections of the report.

PLAIN WORDS

'If language is not correct, then what is said is not what is meant; if what is said is not what is meant, then what ought to be done remains undone.' (Confucius)

The heading of this section is taken from Sir Ernest Gowers' *The Complete Plain Words* (21). This book is required reading for anyone interested in report writing. Gowers' recommendations on how best to convey meaning without ambiguity, and without giving unnecessary trouble to the reader, are:

1. Use no more words than are necessary to express your meaning, for if you use more you are likely to obscure it and to tire your reader. In particular do not use superfluous adjectives and adverbs, and do not use roundabout phrases where single words would serve.
2. Use familiar words rather than the far-fetched if they express your meaning equally well; for the familiar are more likely to be understood.

3. Use words with a precise meaning rather than those that are vague, for they will obviously serve better to make your meaning clear; and in particular, prefer concrete words to abstract for they are more likely to have a precise meaning.

You will not go far wrong if you follow these precepts.

PRESENTATION

The way in which you present your report affects its impact and value. The reader should be able to follow your argument easily and not get bogged down in too much detail.

Paragraphs should be short and each one should be restricted to a single topic. If you want to list or highlight a series of points, tabulate them or use bullet points. For example:

Pay reviews
Control should be maintained over increments by issuing guidelines to managers on:

- The maximum percentage increase to their pay roll allowable for increments to individual salaries;
- The maximum percentage increase that should be paid to a member of staff.

Paragraphs may be numbered for ease of reference. Some people prefer the system which numbers main sections 1, 2, etc, sub-sections 1.1, 1.2, etc, and sub-sub-sections 1.1.1, 1.1.2, etc. However, this can be clumsy and distracting. A simpler system, which eases cross-referencing, is to number each paragraph, *not* the headings, 1, 2, 3, etc; sub-paragraphs or tabulations are identified as 1(a), 1(b), 1(c), etc and sub-sub-paragraphs if required as 1(a)(i), (ii), (iii), etc (or use bullet points).

Use headings to guide people on what they are about to read and to help them to find their way about the report. Main headings should be in capitals or bold and sub-headings in lower case or italics.

A long report could have an index listing the main and sub-headings and their paragraph numbers like this:

Your report will make most impact if it is brief and to the point. Read and re-read your draft to cut out any superfluous material or flabby writing. Use bullet points to simplify the presentation and to put your messages across clearly and succinctly.

Do not clutter up the main pages of the report with masses of indigestible figures or other data. Summarize key statistics in compact, easy-to-follow tables with clear headings. Relegate supporting material to an appendix.

44

Risk management

Risk management is concerned with avoiding unacceptable risks and managing existing risks in order to minimize any harmful impact they may make. According to the Economist Intelligence Unit (*Managing Business Risks*, 1995), business risk 'is the threat that an event or action will adversely affect an organization's ability to achieve its business objectives and execute its strategies successfully'. Research carried out among 3,000 executives showed that only 5 per cent of them were absolutely confident that their risk control systems were successfully identifying, evaluating, minimizing and managing all the potential significant risks affecting their business.

Risks may be purely financial – what is the chance of an investment paying off? But the risks which almost destroyed Barings and Daiwa arose because of faults in management control, inadequate systems and staff negligence. An organization may sustain losses by failing to hedge its positions in the futures market. This may be because an inexperienced manager was given responsibility for the task and the company did not exercise reasonable supervision of that manager's activities. Public utilities may face regulatory notices and risks arising from political decisions, and these must be anticipated. Auditors must be aware of the risks they take when, because of their negligence, their audit report does not represent 'a full and fair view'. Overseas sales may be affected by political risks, and a software firm has to be prepared for the risk that a competitor will produce a better product. A company which is a market leader may run the risk of being threatened by competitors – to what extent does the company monitor the competition, regularly assess customer requirements and seek improvements in the product or level of service to maintain competitive edge? A business may rely on one customer for 80 per cent of its sales. What happens if this customer looks elsewhere? How big is this risk? What can be done to lessen it?

These situations and the questions that arise from them are all matters that should be dealt with by a systematic approach to risk management.

CATEGORIES OF RISK

The categories of risk are:

- commercial risk – increased competition, better products or services available elsewhere, price cutting by competition, problems with suppliers, key customers failing or switching their business elsewhere;
- economic risk – recession in the UK or overseas markets, adverse exchange movements, world-wide decline in prices (eg oil);
- political risk – adverse political decisions (eg legislation, tax changes, regulatory changes, Office of Fair Trading investigations);
- technological development – new developments making the company's products or services obsolescent;
- natural disasters – fire, flood, riots, etc.;
- crime – embezzlement, fraud, computer crime, industrial espionage;
- fashion – changes in fashion affecting demand.

MINIMIZING RISK

The main ways to minimize risk are:

1. *Institute financial controls* to prevent fraud.
2. *Set up compliance arrangements* to ensure that regulations are adhered to.
3. *Monitor key transactions* or those above a certain value and the people who make them to ensure that they are carried out in accordance with policies and procedures and do not entail undue risk.
4. *Insure against* such risks as a major customer becoming insolvent, natural disasters, a country to which the company is exporting imposing currency restrictions which prevent payment.
5. *Diversify* into products or services which have a different risk profile; avoid relying too much on one supplier.
6. *Hedge* – take action which will provide compensation if risk occurs. The most typical area where hedging takes place is foreign currency transactions which might involve buying the currency in advance. If the business is vulnerable to a sudden fall in the stock market an option can be bought to provide funds if this happens. If the business is vulnerable to one set of factors it can buy or acquire an interest in a business which would prosper from such factors.

MANAGING RISK

As suggested by the Economist Intelligence Unit, the key approaches to managing risk are as follows:

- recognize that risk assessment is a continuous activity – you cannot take the risk of not assessing risk;
- make risk assessment and management a major concern of the board and top management;
- ensure that everyone in the organization knows that they are in the business of identifying, reporting on and managing risks;
- focus on the avoidance of unacceptable business risks followed by the management of other business risks to reduce them to an acceptable level;

- formulate a business risk controls policy and ensure that everyone knows and understands it;
- anticipate business risk at the source and monitor risk controls continuously.
- remember that the primary sources of business risk are ineffective processes and controls rather than ineffective people.

45

Selection interviewing

THE OVERALL PURPOSE OF A SELECTION INTERVIEW

Selection interviews provide the information required to assess candidates against a person specification. A selection interview should provide you with the answers to three fundamental questions:

1. Can the individual do the job? Is the person capable of doing the work to the standard required?
2. Will the individual do the job? Is the person well motivated?
3. How is the individual likely to fit into the team? Will I be able to work well with this person?

THE NATURE OF A SELECTION INTERVIEW

A selection interview should take the form of a conversation with a purpose. It is a conversation because candidates should be given the opportunity to talk freely about themselves and their careers. But the conversation has to be planned, directed and controlled to achieve your aims in the time available.

Your task as an interviewer is to draw candidates out to ensure that you get the information you want. Candidates should be encouraged to do most of the talking – one of the besetting sins of poor interviewers is that they talk too much. But you have to plan the structure of the interview to achieve its purpose and decide in advance the questions you need to ask – questions which will give you what you need to make an accurate assessment:

- *Content* – the information you want and the questions you ask to get it;
- *Contact* – your ability to make and maintain good contact with candidates; to establish the sort of rapport that will encourage them to talk freely, thus revealing their strengths *and* their weaknesses;
- *Control* – your ability to control the interview so that you get the information you want.

All this requires you to plan the interview thoroughly in terms of content, timing, structure and use of questions. But before doing all this you need to consider who is to conduct the interview and what arrangements need to be made for it.

PREPARING FOR THE INTERVIEW

Initial preparations

Your first step in preparing for an interview should be to familiarize or refamiliarize yourself with the person specification which defines the sort of individual you want in terms of qualifications, experience and personality. It is also advisable at this stage to prepare questions which you can put to all candidates to obtain the information you require. If you ask everyone some identical questions you will be able to compare the answers.

You should then read the candidates' CVs and application forms or letters. This will identify any special questions you should ask about their career or to fill in the gaps – 'what does this gap between jobs C and D signify?' (although you would not put the question as baldly as that; it would be better to say something like this: 'I see there was a gap of six months between when you left your job in C and started in D. Would you mind telling me what you were doing during this time?').

Timing

You should decide at this stage how long you want to spend on each interview. As a rule of thumb, 45 to 60 minutes is usually required for serious, professional or technical appointments. Middle-ranking jobs need about 30 to 45 minutes. The more routine jobs can be covered in 20 to 30 minutes. But the time allowed depends on the job and you do not want to insult a candidate by conducting a superficial interview.

THE CONTENT OF AN INTERVIEW

The content of an interview can be analysed into three sections: the interview's beginning, middle and end.

Beginning

At the start of the interview you should put candidates at their ease. You want them to talk freely in response to your questions. They won't do this if you plunge in too abruptly. At least welcome them and thank them for coming to the interview, expressing genuine pleasure about the meeting. But don't waste too much time talking about their journey or the weather.

Some interviewers start by describing the company and the job. Wherever possible it is best to eliminate this part of the interview by sending candidates a brief job description and something about the organization. If you are not careful you will spend far too much time at this stage, especially if the candidate later turns out to be clearly unsuitable. A brief reference to the job should suffice and this can be elaborated on at the end of the interview.

Middle

The middle part of the interview is where you find out what you need to know about candidates. It should take at least 80 per cent of the time, leaving, say, 5 per cent at the beginning and 15 per cent at the end.

This is when you ask questions designed to provide information on:

- the extent to which the knowledge, skills, capabilities and personal qualities of candidates meet the person specification;
- the career history and ambitions of candidates and, sometimes, on certain aspects of their behaviour at work such as sickness and absenteeism.

End

At the end of the interview you should give candidates the opportunity to ask questions about the job and the company. The quality of these questions can often give you clues about the degree to which applicants are interested and their ability to ask pertinent questions.

You may want to expand a little on the job. If candidates are promising, some interviewers at this stage extol the attractive features of the job. This is fine as long as these are not exaggerated. To give a 'realistic preview' the possible downsides should be mentioned, for example the need to travel, or unsocial working hours. If candidates are clearly unsuitable you can tactfully help them to de-select themselves by referring to aspects of the work which may not appeal to them, or for which they are not really qualified. It is best not to spell out these points too strongly. It is often sufficient simply to put the question: 'This is a key requirement of the job, how do you feel about it?' You can follow up this general question by more specific questions: 'Do you feel you have the right sort of experience?' 'Are you happy about (this aspect of the job)?'

At this stage you should ask final questions about the availability of candidates, as long as they are promising. You can ask when they would be able to start and about any holiday arrangements to which they are committed.

You should also ask their permission to obtain references from their present and previous employers. They might not want you to approach their present employer and in that case you should tell them that if they are made an offer of employment it would be conditional on a satisfactory reference from their employer. It is useful to ensure that you have the names of people you can approach.

Finally, you inform candidates of what happens next. If some time could elapse before they hear from you, they should be told that you will be writing as soon as possible but that there will be some delay (don't make a promise you will be unable to keep). It is not normally good practice to inform candidates of your decision at the end of the interview. You should take time to reflect on their suitability and you don't want to give them the impression that you are making a snap judgement.

PLANNING THE INTERVIEW

When planning interviews you should give some thought to how you are going to sequence your questions, especially in the middle part. There are two basic approaches as described below.

Biographical approach

The biographical approach is probably the most popular because it is simple to use and appears to be logical. The interview can be sequenced chronologically, starting with the first job or even before that at school and, if appropriate, college or university. The succeeding jobs, if any, are then dealt with in turn, ending with the present job, on which most time is spent if the candidate has been in it for a reasonable time. If you are not careful, however, using the chronological method for someone who has had a number of jobs can mean spending too much time on the earlier jobs, leaving insufficient time for the most important, recent experiences.

To overcome this problem, an alternative biographical approach is to start with the present job, which is discussed in some depth. The interviewer then works backwards, job by job, but only concentrating on particularly interesting or relevant experience in earlier jobs.

The problem with the biographical approach is that it is predictable. Experienced candidates are familiar with it and have their story ready, glossing over any weak points. It can also be unreliable. You can easily miss an important piece of information by concentrating on a succession of jobs rather than focusing on key aspects of the candidates' experience which illustrate their capabilities.

Criteria-based or targeted approach

This approach is based on an analysis of the person specification. You can then select the criteria on which you will judge the suitability of the candidate which will put you in a position to 'target' these key criteria during the interview. You can decide on the questions you need to ask to draw out from candidates information about their knowledge, skills, capabilities and personal qualities which can be compared with the criteria to assess the extent to which candidates meet the specification.

This is probably the best way of focusing your interview to ensure that you get all the information you require about candidates for comparison with the person specification.

INTERVIEWING TECHNIQUES

Questioning

The most important interviewing technique you need to acquire and practise is questioning. Asking pertinent questions which elicit informative responses is a skill which people do not necessarily possess, but it is one they can develop. To improve your questioning techniques it is a good idea at the end of an interview to ask yourself: 'Did I ask the right questions?' 'Did I put them to the candidate well?' 'Did I get candidates to respond freely?'

There are a number of different types of questions as described below. By choosing the right ones you can get candidates to open up or you can pin them down to giving you specific information or to extending or clarifying a reply. The other skills you should possess are establishing rapport, and listening, maintaining continuity, keeping contact and note-taking. These are considered later in this section of the chapter.

The main types of questions are described below.

Open questions

Open questions are the best ones to use to get candidates to talk – to draw them out. These are questions which cannot be answered by a yes or no and which encourage a full response. Single-word answers are seldom illuminating. It is a good idea to begin the interview with one or two open questions, thus helping candidates to settle in.

Open-ended questions or phrases inviting a response can be phrased as follows:

- 'I'd like you to tell me about the sort of work you are doing in your present job.'
- 'What do you know about…?'
- 'Could you give me some examples of…?'
- 'In what ways do you think your experience fits you to do the job for which you have applied?'

Probing questions

Probing questions are used to get further details or to ensure that you are getting all the facts. You ask them when answers have been too generalized or when you suspect that there may be some more relevant information which candidates have not disclosed. A candidate may claim to have done something and it may be useful to find out more about exactly what contribution was made. Poor interviewers tend to let general and uninformative answers pass by without probing for further details, simply because they are sticking rigidly to a predetermined list of open questions. Skilled interviewers are able to flex their approach to ensure they get the facts while still keeping control to ensure that the interview is completed on time.

The following are some examples of probing questions:

- 'You've informed me that you have had experience in… Could you tell me more about what you did?'
- 'Could you describe in more detail the equipment you use?'
- 'What training have you had to operate your machine/equipment/computer?'
- 'Why do you think that happened?'

Closed questions

Closed questions aim to clarify a point of fact. The expected reply will be an explicit single word or brief sentence. In a sense, a closed question acts as a probe but produces a succinct factual statement without going into detail. When you ask a closed question you intend to find out:

- what the candidate has or has not done – 'What did you do then?'

- why something took place – 'Why did that happen?'
- when something took place – 'When did that happen?'
- how something happened – 'How did that situation arise?'
- where something happened – 'Where were you at the time?'
- who took part – 'Who else was involved?'

Capability questions

Capability questions aim to establish what candidates know, the skills they possess and use, and what they are capable of doing. They can be open, probing or closed but they will always be focused as precisely as possible on the contents of the person specification referring to knowledge, skills and capabilities.

The sort of capability questions you can ask are:

- 'What do you know about…?'
- 'How did you gain this knowledge?'
- 'What are the key skills you are expected to use in your work?'
- 'How would your present employer rate the level of skill you have reached in…?'
- 'What do you use these skills to do?'
- 'How often do you use these skills?'
- 'What training have you received to develop these skills?'
- 'Could you please tell me exactly what sort and how much experience you have had in…?'
- 'Could you tell me more about what you have actually been doing in this aspect of your work?'
- 'Can you give me any examples of the sort of work you have done which would qualify you to do this job?'
- 'Could you tell me more about the machinery, equipment, processes or systems which you operator/for which you are responsible?' (The information could refer to such aspects as output or throughput, tolerances, use of computers or software, technical problems.)
- 'What are the most typical problems you have to deal with?'
- 'Would you tell me about any instances when you have had to deal with an unexpected problem or a crisis?'

Unhelpful questions

There are two types of questions that are unhelpful:

- *Multiple questions* such as 'What skills do you use most frequently in your job? Are they technical skills, leadership skills, teamworking skills or communicating skills?' will only confuse candidates. You will probably get a partial or misleading reply. Ask only one question at a time.

● *Leading questions* which indicate the reply you expect are also unhelpful. If you ask a question such as: 'That's what you think, isn't it?' you will get the reply: 'Yes, I do.' If you ask a question such as 'I take it that you don't really believe that...?' You will get the reply: 'No, I don't.' Neither of these replies will get you anywhere.

Questions to be avoided
● Avoid any questions that could be construed as being biased on the grounds of sex, race or disability.

Ten useful questions
The following are 10 useful questions from which you can select any that are particularly relevant in an interview you are conducting:

1. 'What are the most important aspects of your present job?'
2. 'What do you think have been your most notable achievements in your career to date?'
3. 'What sort of problems have you successfully solved recently in your job?'
4. 'What have you learnt from your present job?'
5. 'What has been your experience in...?'
6. 'What do you know about...?'
7. 'What is your approach to handling...?'
8. 'What particularly interests you in this job and why?'
9. 'Now you have heard more about the job, would you please tell me which aspects of your experience are most relevant?'
10. 'Is there anything else about your career which hasn't come out yet in this interview but you think I ought to hear?'

ASSESSING THE DATA

If you have carried out a good interview you should have the data to assess the extent to which candidates meet each of the key points in the person specification. You can summarize your assessments by marking candidates against each of the points – 'exceeds specification', 'fully meets specification', 'just meets the minimum specification', 'does not meet the minimum specification'.

You can assess motivation broadly as 'highly motivated', 'reasonably well motivated', 'not very well motivated'.

You should also draw some conclusions from the candidates' career history and the other information you have gained about their behaviour at work. Credit should be given for a career that has progressed steadily, even if there have been several job changes. But a lot of job-hopping for no good reason and without making progress can lead you to suspect that a candidate is not particularly stable. No blame should be attached to a single setback – it can happen to anyone. Redundancy is not a stigma – it is happening all the time. But if the pattern is repeated, you can reasonably be suspicious.

Finally, there is the delicate question of whether you think you will be able to work with the candidate, and whether you think he or she will fit into the team. You have to be very careful about making judgements about how you will get on with someone. But if you are absolutely certain that the chemistry will not work, then you have to take account of that feeling, as long as you ensure that you have reasonable grounds for it on the basis of the behaviour of the candidate at the interview. But be aware of the common mistakes that interviewers can make. These include:

- jumping to conclusions on a single piece of favourable evidence – the 'halo effect';
- jumping to conclusions on a single piece of unfavourable evidence – the 'horns effect';
- not weighing up the balance between the favourable and unfavourable evidence logically and objectively;
- coming to firm conclusions on the basis of inadequate evidence;
- making snap or hurried judgements;
- making prejudiced judgements on the grounds of sex, race, disability, religion, appearance, accent, class, or any aspect of the candidate's life history, circumstances or career which do not fit your preconceptions of what you are looking for.

Coming to a conclusion

Compare your assessment of each of the candidates against one another. If any candidate fails in an area which is critical to success, he or she should be rejected. You can't take a chance. Your choice should be made between the candidates who reach an acceptable standard against each of the criteria. You can then come to an overall judgement by reference to their assessments under each heading and their career history as to which one is most likely to succeed.

In the end, your decision between qualified candidates may well be judgemental. There may be one outstanding candidate but quite often there are two or three. In these circumstances you have to come to a balanced view on which one is more likely to fit the job and the organization *and* have potential for a long-term career, if this is possible. Don't, however, settle for second best in desperation. It is better to try again.

Remember to make and keep notes of the reasons for your choice and why candidates have been rejected. These, together with the applications, should be kept for at least six months just in case your decision is challenged as being discriminatory.

46

Self-development

SELF-MANAGED LEARNING

Self-development takes place through self-managed or self-directed learning. This means that you take responsibility for satisfying your own learning needs to improve performance, to support the achievement of career aspirations, or to enhance your employability, within and beyond your present organization. It can be based on processes which enable you to identify what you need to learn by reflecting on your experience and analysing what you need to know and be able to do so that you can perform better and progress your career.

The case for self-managed learning is that people learn and retain more if they find things out for themselves. But they may still need to be helped to identify what they should look for. Self-managed learning is about self-development, and this will be furthered by self-assessment, which leads to better self-understanding. Pedler *et al* (47) recommend the following four-stage approach:

- *Self-assessment* based on analysis by individuals of their work and life situation.
- *Diagnosis* derived from the analysis of learning needs and priorities.
- *Action planning* to identify objectives, helps and hindrances, resources required (including people) and time-scales.
- *Monitoring and review* to assess progress in achieving action plans.

Mumford (43) suggests that self-managed learning can be carried out as follows:

- identify the individuals' learning styles;
- review how far their learning is encouraged or restricted by their learning style;
- review their core learning skills of observation and reflection, analysis, creativity, decision-making and evaluation, and consider how to use them more effectively;
- review the work and other experiences in which they are involved in terms of the kind of learning opportunity they offer;
- look for potential helpers in the self-development process: managers, colleagues, trainers or mentors (ie individuals other than the manager or a trainer who provide guidance and advice);
- draw up learning objectives and a plan of action – a personal development plan or learning contract;
- set aside some time each day to answer the question: 'What did you learn today?'

HOW TO DEVELOP YOURSELF

The four key approaches to self-development are:

1. identify learning styles;
2. identify learning needs;
3. decide on the means of satisfying those needs;
4. prepare and implement a personal development plan.

These are discussed below.

IDENTIFY LEARNING STYLES

Not everyone learns in the same way. We each have our own learning style and you can learn more effectively if you understand what your learning style is. Honey and Mumford (27) have identified four styles:

1. *Activists*, who involve themselves fully, without bias, in new experiences and revel in new challenges.
2. *Reflectors*, who stand back and observe new experiences from different angles. They collect data, reflect on it and then come to a conclusion.
3. *Theorists*, who adapt and apply their observations in the form of logical theories. They tend to be perfectionists.
4. *Pragmatists*, who are keen to try out new ideas, approaches and concepts to see if they work.

However, none of these four learning styles is exclusive. It is quite possible, for example, that one person could be both a reflector and a theorist and someone else could be an activist/pragmatist, or a reflector/pragmatist. This learning style model is used by companies such as ICL and Littlewoods as a guide for people in preparing their personal development plans.

IDENTIFYING DEVELOPMENT NEEDS

You can use performance management processes as described in Chapter 36 to identify self-development needs on your own or in discussion with your boss. This will include reviewing performance against agreed plans and assessing competence requirements and the capacity of people to achieve them. The analysis is therefore based on an understanding of what you are expected to do, what you have achieved, the knowledge and skills you need to carry out your job effectively, and what knowledge and skills you have. If there are any gaps between the knowledge and skills you need and those you have, then this defines a development need. The analysis is always related to work and your ability to carry it out effectively.

DECIDING THE MEANS OF SATISFYING NEEDS

When deciding how to satisfy the needs you should remember that it is *not* just about selecting suitable training courses. These may form part of your development plan but only a minor part; other learning activities are much more important. As Royal Mail Anglia states in its guidance notes on personal development planning:

> Development needs can be met using a wide variety of activities. Do not assume that a conventional training course is the only option. In many instances, activity more finely tuned to the specific need can be more rewarding and appropriate than a generalised training course.

The examples of development activities listed by Royal Mail Anglia include:

- seeing what other do (best practice)
- project work
- adopting a role model (mentor)
- involvement in other work areas
- planned use of internal training media (interactive video programmes/learning library)
- input to policy formulation
- increased professionalism on the job
- involvement in the community
- coaching others
- training courses.

Other learning activities include guided reading, special assignments, action learning and distance learning.

PERSONAL DEVELOPMENT PLANS

A personal development plan sets out the actions people propose to take to learn and to develop themselves. They take responsibility for formulating and implementing the plan but they may receive support from the organization and their managers in doing so. Personal development planning aims to promote learning and to provide people with the knowledge and portfolio of transferable skills which will help to progress their careers.

Action planning

The action plan sets out what needs to be done and how it will be done under headings such as:

- development needs;
- outcomes expected (learning objectives);
- development activities to meet the needs;
- responsibility for development –what individuals will do and what support they will require from their manager, the HR department or other people;
- timing – when the learning activity is expected to start and be completed;
- outcome – what development activities have taken place and how effective they were.

The outcomes may be set out, as at AA Insurance, as 'SMART' objectives, ie stretching, measurable, agree, realistic/relevant, time related.

Whether or not that formula is used, the aims of the planning process are always to be specific about what is to be achieved and how it is to be achieved, to ensure that the learning needs and actions are relevant, to indicate the time-scale, to identify responsibility and, within reason, to ensure that the learning activities will stretch those concerned.

Approaches to personal development planning

BP Chemicals uses a simple 'personal development review' form which asks for:

- *employee's comments* – 'In order to help you and your team achieve your personal development objectives, what new skills, knowledge and training do you need?';
- *supervisor's comments* on personal development;
- *personal development plan* – agreed between employee and supervisor, including a training plan.

At ICL a *Learning Guide* has been produced, the stated aims of which are to:

help you to increase your personal value through learning by stimulating ideas for developing your own personal capability: skills, knowledge, attitudes and experience. It will help you to achieve better performance in the Company and better employability for you... We learn most of what we know and what we can do from *experience*, both at work and outside of work. Learning is not just about attending training courses. By systematically exploiting our experience in a disciplined way we and the Company will benefit from achieving your full potential. The more we understand about learning, the more we are likely to achieve our ambitions.

The ICL method of completing a personal development plan is summarized as follows:

- identify your learning needs;
- identify your learning style profile;
- review options available;
- note down your learning needs under the headings *knowledge, skill, attitudes* and *experience* (the advice is given – 'Think about what, specifically, you will need to know and do differently');
- against each need, note down the specific action chosen, who is responsible for effecting the action and by what date;
- ensure that your personal learning plan is implemented, reviewed and updated as necessary;
- ensure that a formal review with your manager takes place at least once a year, preferably twice, to establish that all is going according to plan, or to adapt the plan to meet new needs.

TEN SELF-DEVELOPMENT STEPS

As suggested by Fiona Dent ('Taking control', *Professional Manager*, November 1995), the following are 10 steps you can take to develop yourself:

1. *create a development log* – record your plans and action;
2. *state your objectives* – the career path you want to follow and the skills you will need to proceed along that path;
3. *develop a personal profile* – what sort of person you are, your likes and dislikes about work, your aspirations;
4. *list your strengths and weaknesses* – what you are good or not so good at;
5. *list your achievements* – what you have done well so far and why you believe these were worthwhile achievements;

6. *list significant learning experiences* – recall events when you have learned something worthwhile (this can help you to understand your learning style);
7. *ask other people* about your strengths and weaknesses and what you should do to develop yourself;
8. *focus on the present* – what is happening to you now: your job, your current skills, your short-term development needs;
9. *focus on the future* – where you want to be in the longer term and how you are going to get there (including a list of the skills and abilities you need to develop);
10. *plan your self-development strategy* – how you are going to achieve your ambitions.

47

Strategic management

To provide for a successful, long-term future, organizations must have a clearly defined purpose, a sense of direction and an idea of the resources they will need. They do this by managing strategically. This requires managers to understand the nature of strategy, to use strategic management processes and to prepare strategic plans, while recognizing that strategy is constantly evolving and adapting to changing circumstances. It also means understanding the content of strategic capability and what organizations and individuals should do to develop it.

STRATEGY – AIM AND PURPOSE

The overall aim of strategy at corporate level will be to match or fit the organization to its environment in the most advantageous way possible.

Strategy defines where the organization wants to go to fulfil its purpose and achieve its mission. It provides the framework for guiding choices which determine the organization's nature and direction. These choices relate to the organization's products or services, markets, key capabilities, growth, return on capital and allocation of resources. A strategy is therefore a declaration of intent; it defines what the organization wants to become in the longer term.

Strategies form the basis for strategic management and the formulation of strategic plans.

STRATEGIC MANAGEMENT

Strategic management is the process of formulating strategies and managing the organization to achieve them.

Organizations and managers who think and act strategically are looking ahead and defining the direction in which they want to go in the middle and longer term. Although they are aware of the fact that businesses, like managers, must perform well in the present to succeed in the future, they are concerned with the broader issues they face, and the general direction in which they must go to deal with these issues.

Strategic management takes place within the context of the mission of the organization, and a fundamental task of strategic management will be to ensure that the mission is defined and relevant to the basic purpose of the organization within its changing environment. Strategic management is concerned with both ends and means. As an end, it describes a vision of what the organization will look like in a few years' time; as means, it shows how it is expected that the vision will be realized. Strategic management is therefore visionary management, concerned with creating and conceptualizing ideas of where the organization is going. But it must be translatable into empirical management, which decides how, in practice, it is going to get there.

Strategic management creates a perspective which people can share and which guides their decisions and actions. The focus will be on identifying the organization's mission and goals, but attention is also concentrated on the resource base required to make it succeed. It is always necessary to remember that strategy is the means to create value.

Managers who think strategically will have a broad and long-term view of where they are going. But they will also be aware that they are responsible first for planning how to allocate resources to opportunities which contribute to the implementation of strategy and, second, for managing these opportunities in ways which will significantly add value to the results achieved by the organization.

Key concepts in strategic management

The key concepts used in strategic management are:

● *Distinctive competence* – working out what the organization is best at, and what its special or unique capabilities are.
● *Focus* – identifying and concentrating on the key strategic issues.
● *Sustainable competitive advantage* – as formulated by Michael Porter (53), this concept states that to achieve competitive advantage, firms should create value for their customers, select markets where they can excel and present a moving target to their competitors by continually improving their position. Three of the most important factors are innovation, quality and cost reduction.
● *Synergy* – developing a product/market posture with a combined performance which is greater than the sum of its parts.
● *Environmental scanning* – scanning the internal and external environment of the firm to ensure that its management is fully aware of its strengths and weaknesses and the threats and opportunities it faces (SWOT analysis).
● *Resource allocation* – understanding the human, financial and material resource requirements of the strategy, and ensuring that the resources are made available and their use is optimized.

FORMULATING STRATEGIES

As Henry Mintzberg (42) has pointed out, strategy formulation is not necessarily a rational and continuous process. He believes that while most of the time management pursues a given strategic orientation, changes in strategies, when they do occur, happen in brief quantum loops. In practice, 'a realized strategy can emerge in response to an evolving situation'.

Lester Dignam (14) also believes that strategy-making is not always a rational step-by-step process. He suggests that most strategic decisions are event driven, not programmed. They are expressed as preferences rather than as exercises in applied logic. Strategy formulation, according to Dignam, is about correct decision-making, not about the formulation of detailed plans. The most effective strategists are usually creative, intuitive people, employing an adaptive and flexible process.

There is a lot of truth in what Dignam says but there are still strong arguments for adopting a systematic approach to the formulation of strategic plans, as described below.

STRATEGIC PLANNING

Strategic planning is a systematic, analytical approach which reviews the business as a whole in relation to its environment with the object of:

- developing an integrated, co-ordinated and consistent view of the route the organization wishes to follow;
- facilitating the adaptation of the organization to environmental change.

The aim of strategic planning is to create a viable link between the organization's objectives and resources and its environmental opportunities.

FORMULATING STRATEGIC PLANS

A systematic approach to formalizing strategic plans consists of the following steps:

1. *Define the organization's mission* – its overall purpose.
2. *Set objectives* – definitions of what the organization must achieve to fulfil its mission.
3. *Conduct environmental scans* – internal appraisals of the strengths and weaknesses of the organization and external appraisals of the opportunities and threats which face it (a SWOT analysis).
4. *Analyse existing strategies* – determining their relevance in the light of the environmental scan. This may include gap analysis

to establish the extent to which environmental factors might lead to gaps between what is being achieved and what could be achieved if changes in existing strategies were made. In a corporation with a number of distinct businesses, an analysis of the viability of each strategic business unit (portfolio analysis) can take place to establish strategies for the future of each unit.

5. *Define strategic issues* in the light of the environmental scan, the gap analysis and, where appropriate, the portfolio analysis.
6. *Develop new or revised strategies* and amend objectives in the light of the analysis of strategic issues.
7. *Decide on the critical success factors* related to the achievement of objectives and the implementation of strategy.
8. *Prepare operational, resource and project plans* designed to achieve the strategies and meet the critical success factor criteria.
9. *Implement* the plans.
10. *Monitor results* against the plans and feed back information which can be used to modify strategies and plans.

However carefully you plan, remember that strategy is often no more (and no less) than 'just keeping that herd heading broadly west', as the cowboys used to say.

STRATEGIC CAPABILITY

Strategic capability is the ability to think imaginatively about the direction in which you believe the organization or your part of the organization should go. It is concerned with taking a longer-term view of what needs to happen in the future to ensure continued success.

Strategic capability in organizations as defined by Rosemary Harrison (*Employee Development*, IPD, 1997) involves:

● choosing the most appropriate vision, long-run goals and objectives for an enterprise;
● determining and managing the courses of action and the allocation of resources necessary for achieving those goals;
● selecting and ensuring the development of strategic assets that ensure continued profitability of the business.

The strategic capability of an organization depends, of course, on the strategic capability of its managers. People who display high levels of strategic capability know where they are going and how they are going to get there. They recognize that, while they have to be successful now in order to succeed in the future, it is always necessary to think ahead – to create and sustain a sense of purpose and direction. To develop and successfully apply strategic capability it is necessary to:

1. Understand the key strategic issues facing the business – how it will achieve sustained competitive advantage through innovation, product/market development, achieving higher levels of quality and customer service, and cost leadership.
2. Understand the core competences or capabilities of the organization – what it is good at doing.
3. Understand the critical success factors facing the organization – the areas in which it has to succeed.
4. Identify the business priorities of your organization in the medium and longer term.
5. Understand the strengths and weaknesses of the organization, the threats it faces and the opportunities that exist.
6. In the light of this understanding, conduct a strategic review of the longer-term issues facing the business.
7. Analyse each of the main processes/activities you control and the key result areas of your job in order to determine what initiatives are required to improve performance in the longer term.
8. Ensure that your intentions about future developments are aligned to the overall business strategy and the strategies of related functions.
9. Clarify and articulate your own priorities in the longer term.
10. Establish the means of addressing these issues in terms of:

    ● *what* needs to be done;
    ● *why* it is necessary (the business case);
    ● *how* it should be done;
    ● *who* will do it;
    ● *when* it should be done.

48

Team management

One of your most important tasks as a manager is to make the best use of the capacity of your team so that all its members will work well together to deliver superior levels of performance.

This key process of team management means that you have to clarify the team's purpose and goals, ensure that its members work well together, build commitment and self-confidence, strengthen the team's collective skills, and approach, remove externally imposed obstacles, and create opportunities for team members to develop their skills and competences.

To carry out this task effectively you need to understand:

- The significance of teams.
- The use of self-managing teams.
- The factors which contribute to team effectiveness.
- What to do to achieve good teamwork.
- How to conduct team performance reviews.
- How to analyse team performance.

THE SIGNIFICANCE OF TEAMS

As defined by Katzenbach and Smith (34):

> A team is a small number of people with complementary skills who are committed to a common purpose, performance goals and approach for which they hold themselves mutually accountable.

They suggested that some of the main characteristics of teams are as follows:

- Teams are the basic units of performance for most organizations. They meld together the skills, experiences and insights of several people.
- Teamwork applies to the whole organization as well as specific teams. It represents 'a set of values that encourage behaviours such as listening and responding cooperatively to points of view expressed by others, giving others the benefit of the doubt, providing support to those who need it and recognizing the interests and achievements of others'.
- Teams are created and energized by significant and demanding performance challenges.
- Teams outperform individuals acting alone or in large organizational groupings, especially when performance requires multiple skills, judgements and experiences.
- Teams are flexible and responsive to changing events and demands. They can adjust their approach to new information and challenges with greater speed, accuracy and effectiveness than can individuals caught in the web of larger organizational connections.
- High-performance teams invest much time and effort exploring, shaping and agreeing on a purpose that belongs to them, both collectively and individually. They are characterized by a deep sense of commitment to their growth and success.

Richard Walton (63) has commented that in the new commitment-based organization it will often be teams rather than individuals who will be the organizational units accountable for performance.

However, teamwork, as Peter Wickens (67) has said, 'is not dependent on people working in groups but upon everyone working towards the same objectives'. The Nissan concept of teamwork, as quoted by Wickens, is expressed in its General Principles and emphasizes the need to:

- Promote mutual trust and co-operation between the company, its employees and the union.
- Recognize that all employees, at whatever level, have a valued part to play in the success of the company.
- Seek actively the contributions of all employees in furthering these goals.

Waterman (65) has noted that teamwork 'is a tricky business; it requires people to pull together towards a set of shared goals or values. It does not mean that they always agree on the best way to get there. When they don't agree they should discuss, even argue, these differences.'

Richard Pascale (45) underlined this point when he wrote that successful companies can use conflict to stay ahead: 'We are almost always better served when conflict is surfaced and channelled, not suppressed.' The pursuit of teamwork should not lead to a 'bland' climate in the organization in which nothing new or challenging ever happens. It is all very well to be 'one big happy family' but this could be disastrous if it breeds complacency and a cosy feeling that the family spirit comes first, whatever is happening in the outside world.

SELF-MANAGING TEAMS

Tom Peters (50) strongly advocates the use of self-managing teams. He calls it 'the small within big principle' and states that if the organization is built around teams the result will be 'enhanced focus, take orientation, innovativeness and individual commitment'.

A self-managed team typically has the following characteristics:

- The team might be quite large – 12 to 15 members or even more, depending on the work involved, with one team leader.
- Team leaders are accountable for the achievement of schedule, quality, cost and people development goals, as well as being responsible for 'boundary management' for their groups, ie relating to more senior management and support staff and external contacts and working with other groups.
- However, the role of team leaders is primarily to act as co-ordinators and facilitators; their style is expected to be more supportive and participative than directive.

● The team is highly autonomous, responsible to a considerable degree for planning and scheduling work, problem-solving, developing its own performance indicators and setting and monitoring team performance and quality standards.

● Job specialization is minimized, team members operate flexibly within the group, tasks are rotated among them and they are multi-skilled.

● The team meets at least once a week as a group.

● Effectiveness as a team member is a major performance criterion in appraisals.

● Some form of team pay, related to group performance, may be provided.

● The team is encouraged to develop new ideas for improving performance – awards for suggestions are team based.

TEAM EFFECTIVENESS

An effective team is likely to be one in which the structure, leadership and methods of operation are relevant to the requirements of the task. There will be commitment to the whole group task and people will have been grouped together in a way which ensures that they are related to each other by way of the requirements of task performance and task interdependence.

In an effective team its purpose is clear and its members feel the task is important, both to them and to the organization. According to Douglas McGregor (39), the main features of a well-functioning, creative team are as follows:

1. The atmosphere tends to be informal, comfortable and relaxed.
2. There is a lot of discussion in which initially everyone participates, but it remains pertinent to the task of the group.
3. The task or objective of the team is well understood and accepted by the members. There will have been free discussion of the objective at some point until it was formulated in such a way that the members of the team could commit themselves to it.
4. The members listen to each other. Every idea is given a hearing. People do not appear to be afraid of being considered foolish by putting forth a creative thought even if it seems fairly extreme.

5. There is disagreement. Disagreements are not suppressed or overridden by premature team action. The reasons are carefully examined, and the team seeks to resolve them rather than to dominate the dissenter.
6. Most decisions are reached by consensus in which it is clear that everybody is in general agreement and willing to go along. Formal voting is at a minimum; the team does not accept a simple majority as a proper basis for action.
7. Criticism is frequent, frank and relatively comfortable. There is little evidence of personal attack, either openly or in a hidden fashion.
8. People are free in expressing their feelings as well as their ideas both on the problem and on the group's operation.
9. When action is taken, clear assignments are made and accepted.
10. The leader of the team does not dominate it, nor does the team defer unduly to him or her. There is little evidence of a struggle for power as the team operates. The issue is not who controls, but how to get the job done.

WHAT TO DO TO ACHIEVE GOOD TEAMWORK

1. Establish urgency and direction.
2. Select members based on skills and skill potential who are good at working with others but still capable of taking their own line when necessary.
3. Pay particular attention to first meetings and actions.
4. Set immediate performance-orintated tasks and goals.
5 Set overlapping or interlocking objectives for people who have to work together. These will take the form of targets to be achieved or projects to be completed by joint action.
6. Assess people's performance not only on the results they achieve but also on the degree to which they are good team members. Recognize and reward people who have worked well in teams (using team bonus schemes where appropriate) bearing in mind that being part of a high-performance team can be a reward in itself.
7. Encourage people to build networks – results are achieved in organizations, as in the outside world, on the basis of who you know as well as what you know.

8. Set up interdepartmental project teams with a brief to get on with it.
9. Describe and think of the organization as a system of interlocking teams united by a common purpose. Don't emphasize hierarchies. Abolish departmental boundaries if they are getting in the way, but do not be alarmed if there is disagreement – remember the value of *constructive* conflict.
10. Hold special 'off-the-job' meetings for work teams so they can get together and explore issues without the pressures of their day-to-day jobs.
11. Use training programmes to build relationships. This can often be a far more beneficial result of a course than the increase in skills or knowledge which was its ostensible purpose.
12. Use teambuilding and interactive skills training to supplement the other approaches. But do not rely upon them to have any effect unless the messages they convey are in line with the organization's culture and values.

TEAM PERFORMANCE REVIEWS

Team performance review meetings analyse and assess feedback and control information on their joint achievements against objectives and work plans.

The agenda for such a meeting could be as follows:

1. General feedback – review of:

- Progress of the team as a whole.
- General problems encountered by the team which have caused difficulties or delayed progress.
- Overall help and hindrance to the effective operation of the team.

2. Work reviews

- How well the team has functioned (a checklist for analysing team performance is given below).
- Review of the individual contribution made by each team member.
- Discussion of any new problems encountered by team members.

3. Group problem-solving

- Analysis of reasons for any major problems.
- Agreement of steps to be taken to solve them or to avoid their recurrence in the future.

4. Update objectives and work plans

- Review of new requirements, opportunities or threats.
- Amendment and updating of objectives and work plans.

CHECKLIST FOR ANALYSING TEAM PERFORMANCE

- How well do we work together?
- Does everyone contribute?
- How effectively is the team led?
- How good are we at analysing problems?
- How decisive are we?
- How good are we at initiating action?
- Do we concentrate sufficiently on the priority issues?
- Do we waste time on irrelevancies?
- To what extent can people speak their minds without being squashed by other team members?
- If there is any conflict, is it openly expressed and is it about issues rather than personalities?

TEAM WORKING AT DUTTON ENGINEERING

Team working at Dutton Engineering takes the form of groups of about 10 multi-skilled employees who see jobs through from start to finish. This enables members of the team to get much closer to the customer, helping them to improve the product. Over time, the teams have become self-managing. Each team is effectively a self-contained small business. Members have been trained in basic cost accounting so they can set and monitor their own budgets. The quotes are given to customers by the team, and the team is responsible for getting the job done within that budget. Each team gets a monthly report on completed orders, detailing the cost of materials, labour and other overheads, and whether it made money or not. If the job has run over budget, then it is up to the team to devise ways of improving the process so that the job is profitable next time round. Should customers be responsible for cost over-runs, perhaps because they changed the specifications, it again falls to the team to go back and ask for more money.

However, the organization has a 'no blame' culture. This means that employees are not punished if a project runs over budget. As Tina Mason, the company's business manager, points out:

> Control has been swapped for accountability. If you are asking people to make decisions, then it's very important that you support them when things go wrong, otherwise they'll never make one again… when things go pear-shaped, and occasionally they do, we try to treat it as a learning experience. We ask 'What went wrong?' rather than 'Whose fault is it?' We aren't looking for scapegoats. The key thing is to do better next time round so we don't repeat the mistake.

Superiors have been replaced by team leaders, whose role is to act as 'coaches'. As Tina Mason says: 'The job of a team leader should be that of a facilitator, not someone who is going to play Superman, standing there telling everyone what to do.' Team leaders have had to be good communicators who can get the best out of employees and encourage a 'bring your brains to work' philosophy among workers who had previously been trained to leave them at home. Team leaders were given training to help them get the best out of their team members.

49

Time management

I wasted time, now doth time waste me (*Richard II*).

If you were told by your chairman that you were needed for a special assignment which would mean working directly under him, give you the opportunity to deal with strategic issues, broaden your experience and provide you with excellent promotion prospects, would you take it? The answer would, of course, be yes. If, however, you were told that you would spend one day a week on this assignment and carry out your present duties in the remaining four days, would you still accept the job? Of course you would. But you would be admitting that you could, if you organized yourself better, do your existing work in four-fifths of the time you spend at the moment.

To recover that one-fifth or more, you need to think systematically about how you use your time. You can then take steps to organize yourself better and to get other people to help or at least not to hinder you.

ANALYSIS

The first thing to do is to find out where there is scope for improving your use of time.

Your job

Start with your job – the tasks you have to carry out and the objectives you are there to achieve. Try to establish an order of priority between your tasks and among your objectives.

It is more difficult to do this if you have a number of potentially conflicting areas of responsibility. A good example of this was a director of administration who had a ragbag of responsibilities including property, office services and staff. He had perpetual problems with conflicting priorities and, all too frequently, at the end of the day he would say to himself: 'I have wasted my time, I have achieved next to nothing.'

He took a day off to think things through and realized that he had to take a broad view before getting into detail. He felt that if he could sort out the relative importance of his objectives he would be in a better position to attach priorities to his tasks. He quickly realized that, as an administrator, his first objective was to set up and maintain systems which would run smoothly. Having done this, he could rely on preventive maintenance to reduce problems. But when a crisis did occur – which was inevitable in his area – he could concentrate on fire-fighting in one place without having to worry about what was going on elsewhere.

His second objective, therefore, was to give himself sufficient free time to concentrate on major problems so that he could react swiftly to them. He then classified the sort of issues that could arise and decided which could safely be delegated to others and which he should deal with himself. He was thus prepared to allocate priorities as the problems landed on his desk and to select the serious ones to deal with himself, knowing that the administrative system would go on without interruption.

How you spend your time

Having sorted out your main priorities you should analyse in more detail how you spend your time. This will identify time-consuming activities and indicate where there are problems as well as possible solutions to them.

The best way to analyse time is to keep a diary. Do this for a week, or preferably two or three, as one week may not provide a typical picture. Divide the day into 15-minute sections and note down what you did in each period. Against each space, summarize how effectively you spent your time by writing V for valuable, D for doubtful and U for useless. If you want to make more refined judgements give your ratings pluses or minuses. For example:

Time	Task	Rating
9.00– 9.15	Dealt with incoming mail	V
9.15– 9.30	Dealt with incoming mail	V
9.30– 9.45	Discussed admin problem	D
9.45–10.00	Discussed admin problem	D
10.00–10.15	Deputized at meeting	U
10.15–10.30	Deputized at meeting	U
10.30–10.45	Deputized at meeting	U
10.45–11.00	Deputized at meeting	U

At the end of the week analyse your time under the following headings:

- Reading
- Writing
- Dictating
- Telephoning
- Dealing with people (individuals or groups)
- Attending meetings
- Travelling
- Other (specify).

Analyse also the VDU ratings of the worth of each activity under each heading.

This analysis will provide you with the information you need to spot any weaknesses in the way in which you manage time. Use the time-consumer's checklist at the end of this chapter to identify problems and possible remedies.

ORGANIZING YOURSELF

Such an analysis will usually throw up weaknesses in the way you plan your work and establish your priorities. You have to fit the tasks you must complete into the time available to complete them, and get them done in order of importance.

Some people find it difficult, if not impossible, to plan their work ahead. They find that they work best if they have to achieve almost impossible deadlines. Working under pressure concentrates the mind wonderfully, they say. Journalists are a case in point.

But ordinary mortals, who work under a variety of conflicting pressures, cannot rely upon crisis action to get them out of log-jams of work. For most of us it is better to try to minimize the need for working under exceptional pressure by a little attention to the organization of our week or day. At the very least you should use your diary for long-range planning, organize your weekly activities in broad outline and plan each day in some detail.

Use the diary

Attempt to leave at least one day a week free of meetings and avoid filling any day with appointments. In other words leave blocks of unallocated time for planning, thinking, reading, writing and dealing with the unexpected.

Weekly organizer

Sit down at the beginning of each week with your diary and plan how you are going to spend your time. Assess each of your projects or tasks and work out priorities. Leave blocks of time for dealing with correspondence and seeing people. Try to preserve one free day, or at least half a day, if it is at all possible.

If it helps you to put everything down on paper, draw up a simple weekly organizer form and record what you intend to do each morning, afternoon and, if it's work, evening.

Daily organizer

At the beginning of each day, consult your diary to check on your plans and commitments. Refer to the previous day's organizer to find out what is outstanding. Inspect your pending tray and in-tray to check on what remains and what has just arrived.

Then write down the things to do:

1. Meetings or interviews.

2. Telephone calls.
3. Tasks in order of priority:

    A – must be done today;
    B – ideally should be done today but could be left till tomorrow.
    C – can be dealt with later.

Plan broadly when you are going to fit your A and B priority tasks into the day. Tick off your tasks as they have been completed. Retain the list to consult next day.

You do not need an elaborate form for this purpose. Many successful time managers use a blank sheet of paper, but a simple form which you can use is shown below.

DAILY ORGANIZER   Date ....

Meetings and appointments

Committee/person	Where	When

To telephone

Person	About what	When

To do

Tasks *(in order of priority)*	Priority rating* A, B or C	Approximate timing

*A = must be done today. B = ideally done today. C = later.

Figure 49.1   *Example of a daily organizer*

ORGANIZING OTHER PEOPLE

Your first task is to organize yourself, but other people can help, if you can guide and encourage them. They include your secretary, boss, colleagues, subordinates and outside contacts.

Your secretary

A secretary can be a great help: sorting incoming mail into what needs immediate attention and what can be looked at later; managing appointments within your guidelines; keeping unwanted callers at bay; intercepting telephone calls; dealing with routine or even semi-routine correspondence; sorting and arranging your papers and the filing system for easy accessibility; getting people on the telephone for you, and so on. The list is almost endless. Every efficient boss will recognize that he or she depends a lot on an efficient secretary.

Your boss

Your boss can waste your time with over-long meetings, needless interruptions, trivial requests and general nitpicking. Maybe there is nothing you can do about this. But you can learn how to avoid doing the same to your own staff.

On your own behalf you can cultivate the polite art of cutting short tedious discussions. Such formulas as 'I hope you feel we have cleared up this problem – I'll get out of your hair now and get things moving' are useful. And you might be able, subtly, to indicate that your boss is going to get better performance from you if he or she leaves you alone. It's difficult but it's worth trying.

Your colleagues

Try to educate them to avoid unnecessary interruptions. Don't anger them by shutting them out when they have something urgent to discuss. But if it can wait, get them to agree to meet you later at a fixed time. Try to avoid indulging in too many pleasantries over the telephone. Be brisk but not brusque.

Your subordinates

You will save a lot of time with your subordinates if you systematically decide what work you can delegate to them. You save even more time if you delegate clearly and spell out how and when you want them to report back.

An 'open door' policy is fine in theory but time wasting in practice. Learn to say no to subordinates who want to see you when you are engaged on more important business. But always give them a time when they can see you and stick to it.

Talking generally to your staff about their job and outside interests can be time well spent if it helps to increase mutual understanding and respect. Allow for this in your schedule and be prepared to extend business discussions into broader matters when the opportunity arises. But don't overdo it.

Outside contacts

The same rules apply to outside contacts. Prevent them from seeing you without an appointment. Ask your secretary to block unwanted telephone calls. Brief your contacts on what you expect from them and when meetings should be arranged.

TIME-CONSUMER'S CHECKLIST

Problem	*Possible remedies*
TASKS 1. Work piling up	● Set priorities ● Set deadlines ● Make realistic time estimates – most people underestimate – add 20 per cent to your first guess.
2. Trying to do too much at once	● Set priorities ● Do one thing at a time ● Learn to say no to yourself as well as other people.
3. Getting involved in too much detail	● Delegate more.

335

Problem	Possible remedies

4. Postponing unpleasant tasks
- Set a timetable and stick to it
- Get unpleasant tasks over with quickly – you will feel better afterwards.

5. Insufficient time to think
- Reserve blocks of time – part of a day or week – for thinking. No paperwork, no interruptions.

PEOPLE
6. Constant interruptions from people calling into your office
- Use secretary to keep unwanted visitors out
- Make appointments and see that people stick to them
- Reserve block times when you are not to be interrupted.

7. Constant telephone interruptions
- Get your secretary to intercept and, where appropriate, divert calls
- State firmly that you will call back when convenient.

8. Too much time spent in conversation
- Decide in advance what you want to achieve when you meet someone, and keep pleasantries to a minimum at the beginning and end
- Concentrate on keeping yourself and the other person to the point – it is too easy to divert or be diverted
- Learn how to end meetings quickly but not too brusquely.

PAPERWORK
9. Flooded with incoming paper
- Get your secretary to sort it into three folders: action now, action later, information
- Take yourself off the circulation list of useless information
- Only ask for written memos and reports when you really need them

Problem	*Possible remedies*
	● Encourage people to present information and reports clearly and succinctly
	● Ask for summaries rather than the whole report
	● Take a course in rapid reading.
10. Too many letters/memos to write or dictate	● Use the telephone more
	● Avoid individually typed acknowledgements
	● Practise writing a succinct 'yes/no/let's talk' on the memos you receive and return them to the sender.
11. Paperwork piling up	● Do it now
	● Set aside the first half hour or so in the day to deal with urgent correspondence
	● Leave a period at the end of the day for less urgent reading
	● Aim to clear at least 90 per cent of the paper on your desk every day.
12. Lost or mislaid papers	● Arrange, or get your secretary to organize, papers on current projects in separate, easily accessible folders
	● Don't hang on to papers in your pending tray – clear it daily
	● Set up a filing and retrieval system which will enable you to get at papers easily
	● Ensure that your secretary keeps a day book of correspondence as a last resort method of turning up papers
	● Keep a tidy desk.

Problem	Possible remedies

MEETINGS

13. Too much time spent in meetings

- If you set up the meeting: avoid regular meetings when there is nothing that needs saying regularly, review all the meetings you hold and eliminate as many as you can
- Get yourself taken off committees if your presence is not essential or it someone else is more appropriate
- As chairman: set limits for the duration of meetings and keep to them, cut out waffle and repetition, allow discussion but insist on making progress, have a logical agenda and stick to it
- As a member: don't waffle, don't talk for the sake of talking, don't waste time scoring points or boosting your ego.

TRAVELLING

14. Too much time spent on travelling

- Use the phone or post
- Send someone else
- Ask yourself, every time you plan to go anywhere, 'is my journey really necessary?'
- Plan the quickest way – air, rail or car.

50

Valuing people

People will contribute more and co-operate more wholeheartedly if they feel that they are valued. This happens when they are recognized for what they are and what they do, and are rewarded according to their contribution. Rewards are provided by both financial and non-financial means.

FINANCIAL REWARDS

Financial rewards need to be provided fairly, equitably and consistently for people to believe that they are valued appropriately. In accordance with expectancy theory, they also have to expect that their efforts will lead to a worthwhile reward – there must be a 'line of sight' between what they do and what they get, between the effort and the reward. They will also respond more to financial rewards if the system is transparent – they know how it works, the basis upon which they are rewarded.

Fairness

People will react positively to financial rewards if they feel that they are fair – this is the 'felt fair' principle. Perceptions on fairness are based on the extent to which people believe that the procedure followed in making the reward is fair (procedural justice) and their feelings about the fairness with which the payments have been distributed – that they are rewarded according to their deserts (distributive justice). If there is a performance-related pay system they will want to feel that the method of assessing their performance was based on what they had actually achieved and was not affected by bias, prejudice or ignorance. They will also want to feel that their rewards are commensurate with their performance compared with that of other people, ie equitable, as discussed below.

Equity

Equity is achieved when people are rewarded appropriately in relation to others within the organization and in accordance with their worth and the value of their contribution. An equitable reward system ensures that relative worth is measured as objectively as possible, that the measurement processes are analytical and that they provide a framework for making defensible judgements about job values and grading.

Consistency

The system should allow consistent decisions to be made about reward levels and individual rates of pay. Policy guidelines should be available to line managers to ensure that they avoid making decisions which deviate irrationally from what would be generally regarded as fair and equitable.

NON-FINANCIAL REWARDS

Non-financial rewards can provide a better basis for valuing people because they are more under your control. Financial rewards are restricted by financial budgets and company procedures. You are in the best position to value people through non-financial rewards. The main ways of valuing people, as described more fully in Chapter 32, are:

- providing them with the opportunity to achieve;
- recognizing their contribution by praise and by 'applause' (letting others know how well you value an individual);
- giving people more responsibility (empowering them);
- providing them with the opportunity to grow – offering learning opportunities, encouraging and supporting the preparation and implementation of personal development plans, and broadening their experience (job enlargement).

HOW TO VALUE PEOPLE

People will not feel that they are valued just because there is a passing reference in the Annual Report by the chairman that 'people are our most important asset' (according to Dilbert, one of the 10 great lies of management). Valuing people is primarily a matter of recognition and reward as described above. But people will also feel valued if a positive 'organization climate' (the atmosphere in the organization as indicated by how people feel about it and its management) is maintained. This will include feelings about:

- *responsibility* – being trusted to carry out important work;
- *feedback* – giving recognition for work well done;
- *reward* – ensuring that people are rewarded fairly according to their contribution, using both financial and non-financial rewards;
- *identity* – being recognized as a valued member of a cohesive working team;
- *support* – the helpfulness of managers and co-workers;
- *listening* – managers, team leaders and co-workers as for opinions, listen to what people have to say, take note and either act on what they have heard or at least give a reasoned explanation why action along the lines suggested is not possible or is only partly possible.

Managers and team leaders are in a position to make the difference in all these areas. But remember that if you want people to be more committed because they feel more valued, it is deeds, not words, that count. Inconsistency between what is said and done is the best way to undermine trust and generate employee cynicism, lack of interest or even open hostility.

General bibliography

1 Adair, J (1984) *Action Centred Leadership*, McGraw-Hill, London.
2 Anderson, B (1993) The visionary leader, *Management Theory and Practice*, September, pp 3–7.
3 Back, K and K (1982) *Assertiveness at Work*, McGraw-Hill, Maidenhead.
4 Bandura, A (1986) *Social Boundaries of Thought and Action*, Prentice-Hall, Englewood Cliffs, NJ.
5 Beckhard, R (1969) *Organizational Development: Strategy and Models*, Addison-Wesley, Reading, MA.
6 Beer, M (1984) Reward systems, in *Managing Human Assets*, M Beer *et al* (eds), The Free Press, New York.
7 Beer, M, Eisenstat, R and Spector, B (1990) Why change programs don't produce change, *Harvard Business Review*, November–December.
8 Bell, C (1971) *The Conventions of Crisis*, Oxford University Press, Oxford.
9 Bennis, W and Nanus, B (1985) *Leaders*, Harper & Row, New York.
10 Burns, J (1978) *Leadership*, Harper & Row, New York.
11 Collard, R (1993) *Total Quality: Success through People*, 2nd edn, Institute of Personnel and Development, London.
12 De Bono, E (1971) *Lateral Thinking for Managers*, McGraw-Hill, London.

13 Deming, W E (1986) *Out of the Crisis*, MIT Center for Advanced Engineering Study, Boston, Mass.
14 Dignam, L (1990) *Strategic Management: Concepts, Decisions, Cases*, Irwin, New York.
15 Dixon, N (1979) *On the Psychology of Military Incompetence*, Futura, London.
16 Drucker, P (1955) *The Practice of Management*, Heinemann, London.
17 Drucker, P (1967) *The Effective Executive*, Heinemann, London.
18 Drucker, P (1988) The coming of the new organization, *Harvard Business Review*, January–February.
19 Egan, G (1990) *The Skilled Helper: A Systematic Approach to Effective Helping*, Brooks Cole, London.
20 Follett, M P (1924) *Creative Experience*, Longmans Green, New York.
21 Gowers, Sir Ernest (1987) *The Complete Plain Words*, Penguin, London.
22 Hall, W (1976) Survival strategies in a hostile environment, *Harvard Business Review*, March–April.
23 Handy, C (1989) *The Age of Unreason*, Business Books, London.
24 Handy, C (1994) *The Empty Raincoat*, Hutchinson, London.
25 Harvey-Jones, J (1988) *Making it Happen*, Collins, Glasgow.
26 Heller, R (1982) *The Business of Success*, Sidgwick & Jackson, London.
27 Honey, P and Mumford, A (1986) *The Manual of Learning Styles*, Peter Honey, Maidenhead.
28 Industrial Society (1997) Leadership – steering a new course, *Briefing Plus*, October, pp 4–5.
29 Institute of Personnel Management (1992) *Statement on Counselling in the Workplace*, IPM, London.
30 Jay, A (1967) *Management and Machiavelli*, Hodder & Stoughton, London.
31 Kakabadse, A (1983) *The Politics of Management*, Gower, Aldershot.
32 Kanter, R M (1984) *The Change Masters*, Allen & Unwin, London.
33 Kanter, R M (1989) *When Giants Learn to Dance*, Simon & Schuster, London.
34 Katzenbach, J and Smith, D (1993) *The Wisdom of Teams*, Harvard Business School Press, Boston, Mass.
35 Koestler, A (1984) *The Act of Creation*, Hutchinson, London.
36 Kotter, J (1980) What leaders really do, *Harvard Business Review*, May–June.
37 Maslow, A (1954) *Motivation and Personality*, Harper & Row, New York.
38 McClelland, D (1975) *Power, The Inner Experience*, Irvington, New York.
39 McGregor, D (1960) *The Human Side of Enterprise*, McGraw-Hill, New York.
40 Mintzberg, H (1973) *The Nature of Managerial Work*, Harper & Row, New York.
41 Mintzberg, H (1981) Organization design: fashion or fit, *Harvard Business Review*, January–February.

42 Mintzberg, H (1987) Crafting strategy, *Harvard Business Review*, July–August.
43 Mumford, A (1989) *Management Development: Strategies for Action*, Institute of Personnel Management, London.
44 Pascale, R and Athos, A (1981) *The Art of Japanese Management*, Simon & Schuster, New York.
45 Pascale, R (1990) *Managing on the Edge*, Viking, London.
46 Pasuram, A, Zeithami, W and Berry, I (1985) A conceptual model of service quality and its implications for future research, *Journal of Retailing*, **44**, pp 12–40.
47 Pedler, M, Burgoyne, J and Boydell, T (1986) *A Manager's Guide to Self-Development*, McGraw-Hill, Maidenhead.
48 Peter, L (1972) *The Peter Principle*, Allen & Unwin, London.
49 Peters, T and Waterman, R (1982) *In Search of Excellence*, Harper & Row, New York.
50 Peters, T (1988) *Thriving on Chaos*, Macmillan, London.
51 Pettigrew, A and Whipp, R (1991) *Managing Change for Competitive Success*, Blackwell, Oxford.
52 Pickard, J (1993) The real meaning of empowerment, *Personnel Management*, November.
53 Porter, M (1985) *Competitive Advantage: Creating and Sustaining Superior Performance*, Free Press, New York.
54 Richardson, W (1993) The visionary leader, *Administrator*, September.
55 Schelling, T (1960) *Strategy of Conflict*, Harvard University Press, Boston, Mass.
56 Schumacher, C (1976–77) Structuring work, *Industrial Participation*, Winter.
57 Stebbing, S (1959) *Thinking to Some Purpose*, Penguin Books, Harmondsworth.
58 Steibel, D (1997) *When Talking Makes It Worse*, Whitehall and Norton, New York.
59 Stewart, R (1967) *Managers and Their Jobs*, Macmillan, London.
60 Stewart, V and Stewart, A (1982) *Managing the Poor Performer*, Gower, Aldershot.
61 Taylor, F (1911) *Principles of Scientific Management*, Harper & Row, New York.
62 Townsend, R (1970) *Up the Organization*, Michael Joseph, London.
63 Walton, R (1985) From control to commitment, *Harvard Business Review*, March–April.
64 Ware, J and Barnes, L (1991) Managing interpersonal conflict, in *Managing People and Organizations*, J Gabarro (ed), Harvard Business School Publications, Boston, Mass.
65 Waterman, R (1988) *The Renewal Factor*, Bantam, New York.
66 Welch, J (1991) quoted in *Managing People and Organizations*, J Gabarro (ed), Harvard Business School Publications, Boston, Mass.
67 Wickens, P (1987) *The Road to Nissan*, Macmillan, London.

Further reading from Kogan Page

Armstrong, M (1993) *A Handbook of Management Techniques*, 2nd edn
Carter, S (1999) *Renaissance Management: The rebirth of learning through people and organizations*
Charney, C (1995) *The Instant Manager: The 100 most important tasks facing managers today*
Corrigan, P (1999) *Shakespeare on Management: Leadership lessons for today's managers*
Kamp, D (1999) *The 21st Century Manager: Future focused skills for the next millennium*
Morris, M J (1994) *The First Time Manager: The first steps to a brilliant management career*, 2nd edn
Thompson, P (1999) *Persuading Aristotle: A masterclass in the timeless art of persuasion*
Wellman, D A (1997) *The Making of a Manager: How to launch your career on the fast track*
Whatmore, J (1999) *Releasing Creativity: How leaders can develop creative potential in their teams*

A complete list is available from the publishers: Kogan Page, 120 Pentonville Road, London N1 9JN (tel: 020 7278 0433; fax: 020 7837 6348).

345

Index